ROUTLEDGE LIBRARY EDITIONS: HISTORY OF THE MIDDLE EAST

Volume 10

REVOLUTION IN IRAN

REVOLUTION IN IRAN
The Roots of Turmoil

MEHRAN KAMRAVA

Routledge
Taylor & Francis Group
LONDON AND NEW YORK

First published in 1990 by Routledge

This edition first published in 2017
by Routledge
2 Park Square, Milton Park, Abingdon, Oxon OX14 4RN

and by Routledge
711 Third Avenue, New York, NY 10017

Routledge is an imprint of the Taylor & Francis Group, an informa business

© 1990 M. Kamrava

All rights reserved. No part of this book may be reprinted or reproduced or utilised in any form or by any electronic, mechanical, or other means, now known or hereafter invented, including photocopying and recording, or in any information storage or retrieval system, without permission in writing from the publishers.

Trademark notice: Product or corporate names may be trademarks or registered trademarks, and are used only for identification and explanation without intent to infringe.

British Library Cataloguing in Publication Data
A catalogue record for this book is available from the British Library

ISBN: 978-1-138-22002-7 (Set)
ISBN: 978-1-315-39118-2 (Set) (ebk)
ISBN: 978-1-138-22351-6 (Volume 10) (hbk)
ISBN: 978-1-138-22360-8 (Volume 10) (pbk)
ISBN: 978-1-315-40454-7 (Volume 10) (ebk)

Publisher's Note
The publisher has gone to great lengths to ensure the quality of this reprint but points out that some imperfections in the original copies may be apparent.

Disclaimer
The publisher has made every effort to trace copyright holders and would welcome correspondence from those they have been unable to trace.

Revolution in Iran
The Roots of Turmoil

Mehran Kamrava

Routledge
London and New York

First published 1990
by Routledge
11 New Fetter Lane, London EC4P 4EE

Simultaneously published in the USA and Canada
by Routledge
a division of Routledge, Chapman and Hall, Inc.
29 West 35th Street, New York, NY 10001

© 1990 M. Kamrava

Typeset by LaserScript Limited, Mitcham, Surrey
Printed and bound in Great Britain by Mackays of Chatham

All rights reserved. No part of this book may be reprinted
or reproduced or utilized in any form or by any electronic,
mechanical, or other means, now known or hereafter
invented, including photocopying and recording, or in any
information storage or retrieval system, without permission
in writing from the publishers.

British Library Cataloguing in Publication Data
Kamrava, Mehran
  Revolution in Iran: The roots of turmoil.
  1. Iran political events, 1941
  I. Title
  955'.053

ISBN 0-415-03562-7

Library of Congress Cataloging in Publication Data
Kamrava, Mehran, 1964–
  Revolution in Iran: the roots of turmoil/Mehran Kamrava.
    p.   cm.
  Bibliography: p.
  Includes index.
  ISBN 0-415-03562-7
  1. Iran—History—Mohammed Reza Pahlavi, 1941–1979. I. Title.
DS318.K27 1990
955.05'3—dc20

89-10392
CIP

Contents

List of tables	vii
Preface	ix
1 Causes of revolution	1
Theories of revolution	1
Conclusion	12
2 The Pahlavi state	14
The imperial Iranian government	15
The collapse of the regime	32
3 Opposition to the regime	51
Political parties	52
The intellectuals	65
The ulema	78
Opposition activities	86
4 Social change	95
The process of social change	95
Social change in Iran	97
Classes in Iran	102
Social change and the revolution	115
5 Revolutionary mass mobilization	118
Economic grievances	119
Political demands	122
Socio-cultural grievances	126
Khomeini's leadership	128
6 Conclusion	131
Appendix	135

Contents

Notes	138
Bibliography	154
Index	167

List of tables

Table 3.1	Fedaiyan activities before the revolution	63
Table 3.2	Comparison of the two types of Shi'ism	75
Table 4.1	Sectoral distribution of percentage of gross national product, 1963–78	105
Table 4.2	Estimated total fixed investment in the Fifth Plan	106
Table 4.3	The Iranian labour force, 1956–77	108

Preface

This book examines the causes of Iran's 1978–1979 revolution. Many scholarly works have appeared in recent years which in different ways examine the economic, social, and historical conditions that led to the Iranian revolution. My aim here has been to introduce two new perspectives into the study of the revolution: first, I have tried to gather and analyse, in as much detail as possible, all of the factual data relevant to the revolution, especially those pertaining to the structure of the Pahlavi state, the organizations and the activities of groups opposing the regime, and the social and economic changes that occurred in Iran prior to the revolution. Second, my interpretation of the causes of the revolution differs from those of the existing literature.

Writing on the Iranian revolution has been both a personal and an academic endeavour for me, and I have made an attempt through this book, however meagre, towards reaching a better understanding of that historically important movement.

I am greatly indebted to a number of people who in different ways assisted me in completing this work. I am grateful to John Dunn and Ernest Gellner for reading and commenting on earlier versions of different chapters. John Barber, Geoffrey Hawthorn, and Edward Mortimer also read the entire manuscript and gave invaluable advice on its content and format. Peter Avery deserves special thanks. As my supervisor and teacher at King's College, Cambridge, he followed my work with enthusiasm and patience, and I feel greatly privileged to have been his student. Mrs. Afkhami of the Foundation for Iranian Studies and Dr. Qassemi of Kanoun Iran kindly furnished contacts with a number of civilian and military veterans of the Pahlavi regime, and I am grateful for their trust and encouragement. I also wish to thank all of the individuals who agreed to be interviewed for this project, and I hope to have adequately presented their views and assessments here. I am also indebted to Valerie Heydar for her editorial assistance and diligent word processing. Last but not least I thank my parents and the many friends

Preface

who supported and encouraged me through the task of writing this book. I accept full responsibility for any mistakes and shortcomings from which this work may suffer.

Chapter one

Causes of revolution

Social scientists have long been engaged in an ongoing debate over the concept of revolution, its causes, and its consequences. The Iranian revolution has added great stimuli to this debate by challenging some of the main premises on which most theories of revolution are based. At the same time, it has validated some other premises of the existing theories, although in all instances this validation has been limited and has not been inclusive of an entire theoretical framework. The Iranian revolution has, in essence, called forward the necessity of re-evaluating existing explanations for why revolutions take place. Such a re-evaluation has yet to occur in a systematic and in-depth manner. Nevertheless, the Iranian revolution has prompted at least one expert on the study of revolutions to alter some of her original arguments.[1] This chapter will examine the applicability of some of the prominent theories of revolution to the Iranian example. Based primarily on the Iranian model, an effort will also be made to try to identify the main areas where future scholarship on revolutions needs to place greater emphasis.

Theories of revolution

One of the main theoretical frameworks for the study of revolution has come to be known as the value-systems approach. According to this paradigm, revolutions are likely to occur when discrepancies develop between a society's values and the realities of its social life. This line of argument, elaborated by Chalmers Johnson, identifies the rapid displacement of social values and norms as the underlying cause of mass opposition to a regime. Johnson argues that revolutions need to be studied in the context of the social systems in which they occur. 'The analysis of revolution', he writes, 'intermeshes with the analysis of viable, functioning societies, and any attempt to separate the two concepts impairs the usefulness of both.'[2] Johnson argues that social systems are homeostatic, (i.e. self-regulating) and can thus adapt to changes and influences that act on them in their environment.[3] When a

1

society loses its capability to adapt to environmental changes, it becomes 'disequilibrated', a condition that arises out of 'dissynchronization' between a society's values and its division of labour.[4] The disequilibration of a system does not automatically lead to revolution. There still need to be appropriate 'accelerators' as well as 'elite intransigence' in a disequilibrated system for revolutions to occur.[5] Johnson identifies three types of accelerators: military weakness or disarray within the incumbent forces; the confidence of the revolutionaries in overpowering the elite; and the military and strategic actions that the revolutionaries initiate against the elite's armed forces.[6] The regime, losing its legitimacy because of the displacement of values, relies increasingly on its coercive forces in order to stay in power. Once the regime's values are no longer considered to be legitimate, the success of the revolution depends primarily on the revolutionaries' military victory over the intransigent elite.[7]

A second group of scholars examine causes of revolution by relying on an 'aggregate psychological' approach. The proponents of this approach argue that the stability or the instability of a political system 'is ultimately dependent on a state of mind, a mood, in a society'.[8] A mass of people frustrated with a regime and in close contact with one another form a 'critical mass', one that is capable of mobilizing itself in opposition to a regime.[9] Ted Gurr and James Davies have relied on this approach extensively in explaining the reasons that underlie various forms of political unrest. Davies argues that revolutions are likely to erupt when people perceive, rather than actually experience, a reduction in their social and economic opportunities.[10] In a statement that has come to symbolize his theory, Davies claims: 'Revolutions are likely to occur when a prolonged period of objective economic and social development is followed by a short period of sharp reversal.'[11] An abrupt termination of economic growth and opportunities for social and economic advancement will lead to the frustration of hopes and expectations, leading in turn to political opposition. Identifying psychological frustration as the main factor in causing revolutions, Davies contends that revolutions will not occur in a society 'where there is the continued, unimpeded opportunity to satisfy new needs, new hopes, new expectations'.[12] Similarly, revolutions will not take place where there is 'no hope, no period in which expectations have risen'.[13]

Gurr adopts an approach similar to that of Davies, although his theoretical framework is considerably more comprehensive and stronger than Davies'. Similar to Davies, Gurr sees psychological frustration as the principal cause of revolutions. Frustration arises when the expectations that are commonly perceived to be attainable are not realized. Gurr calls this condition 'relative deprivation'.[14] He outlines three patterns of relative deprivation, namely aspirational, decremental, and progressive deprivation. Decremental deprivation occurs when value expectations remain relatively constant but value capabilities are thought to decline – deprivation is experienced in relation to one's own past. Traditional societies and transitional societies are most likely to be affected by decremental deprivation.[15] A more common form of deprivation occurs when rising expectations are not fulfilled and the desire to gain is frustrated. Gurr calls this aspirational deprivation, which occurs when capabilities remain static but expectations rise.[16] There is also progressive deprivation, occurring when expectations increase but at the same time capabilities decrease. This form of deprivation is most prevalent in modernizing societies, where newly emerging social classes frequently find their social and economic opportunities restricted by the limited capabilities of their society.[17] Relative deprivation, according to Gurr, prepares the society for the occurrence of revolution. 'Discontent', he writes, 'leads men to political violence when their attitudes and beliefs focus it on political objects, and when institutional frameworks are weak enough, or opposition organizations strong enough, to give the discontented a sense of potency.'[18] In order to gain dominance over one another, both the contenders and the incumbents must maintain 'enduring social support by providing patterns of action that have predictably rewarding consequences for their followers'.[19] The success of a regime or that of dissident organizations depends on such characteristics as their scope, cohesiveness, and complexity, and on the dissidents' ability to provide their supporters with 'value opportunities, satisfactions and means for expressive protest'.[20]

Johnson, Davies, and Gurr all agree that revolutions start non-voluntarily and without the cognitive initiatives of would-be agitators. Charles Tilly, on the other hand, holds that revolutions are brought about by the wilful efforts of contending political actors. Tilly explains causes of revolution in basically political terms. Arguing that 'multiple sovereignty' is the identifying feature of revolutionary situations,[21] Tilly claims that revolutionary movements arise when 'previously acquiescent members of the population find themselves confronted with strictly incompatible demands from the government and from an alternative body claiming control over the government, and those previously acquiescent people obey the alternative body'.[22] The important preconditions for the occurrence of revolutions, according to Tilly, are not social or social-psychological developments but rather 'interests, mobilization, strategy, repression, and power positions'.[23] Three sets of circumstances, he argues, lead to revolutions: the appearance of contenders making exclusive claims to power; commitment to those claims by a significant segment of the population; and the unwillingness or the incapacity of the government to suppress the alternative coalition.²⁴ Revolution, therefore, necessitates that significant segments of the population recognize as legitimate the political authority of a body independent of the government. How such an alternative and revolutionary body is formed, according to Tilly, 'remains one of the mysteries of our time'.²⁵

Besides Tilly, a number of other scholars have also sought to explain the causes of revolutions by examining the political dynamics of the pre-revolutionary states. Theda Skocpol, Samuel Huntington, and more recently Jerrold Green are some of the more notable representatives of this group of social scientists.²⁶ Huntington and Green focus on the social ramifications of the process of state building undertaken by the pre-revolutionary regime. Skocpol, however, concentrates mainly on the structural collapse of the pre-revolutionary polity.

Huntington sees revolutions as a side-effect of modernization.²⁷ He argues that modernization leads to the emergence of new social classes who, among other things, demand the right to participate in the political process.²⁸ The greatest demands for political participation come from the middle class, which constitutes the 'true revolutionary class' in most modernizing societies.²⁹ This revolutionary class emerges in societies that have experienced some social and economic development, especially in places where the process of political development lags behind the process of social and economic change.³⁰ More specifically, revolutions are likely to occur when (1) political institutions are capable of providing new channels for the participation of new social forces into politics, and (2) when the social classes that are currently excluded from politics wish to take active part in the political process.³¹

Jerrold Green agrees with this general approach, although he divides the process of political participation into the 'mobilization' and the 'countermobilization' stages. Modernization, Green argues, implicitly politicizes a population. 'The denial of political participation to such politicized sectors can lead to popular unrest. This in its most extreme form may spell revolution.'³² Demands for political participation lead to political mobilization. If the government is incapable of controlling this mobilization (through political parties, voting systems, or other mechanisms for political input), then 'countermobilization' occurs, which, Green claims, is itself a form of revolution. The conditions that lead to 'countermobilization' are: a decline in the coercive powers of the state; a simplification of politics; the politicization of traditionally non-political groups; crisis-initiating events; and exacerbating responses by the regime.³³ As an 'antecedent to full-scale countermobilization', a simplification of politics divides the pre-revolutionary society into two crude groupings: those who oppose the regime and those who support it.³⁴ As the opposition to a regime widens, 'the oppositional pole exercises an undiscerning, almost magnetic pull, passively *attracting* supporters rather than actively recruiting them' (original emphasis).[35] This passive attraction to opposition groups or at least to their causes and ideals by large segments of society results in the politicization of groups who would otherwise remain aloof of politics. Finally, a series of crises or government initiatives occur and result in the final pre-condition for 'countermobilization', namely the transition from reformism to revolution.[36] The revolution feeds itself, Green argues, 'with each triumph leading to greater heights of unity and cohesion'.[37]

The last theoretical explanation for the occurrence of revolutions considered here is that put forward by Theda Skocpol. Instead of pointing to the appearance of 'multiple sovereignty' or a 'participation crisis' as the underlying cause of revolutions, Skocpol originally focused on the political collapse of states and on class-based antagonisms. She argued that revolutionary crises develop when the state becomes unable to meet the challenges of evolving international situations. Such challenges often arise out of military conflicts between competing states. Skocpol based her arguments on the examples of the French, Russian, and Chinese revolutions. 'Caught in the cross-pressure between domestic class structures and international exigencies', she wrote, 'the (pre-revolutionary) autocracies and their centralized administrations and armies broke apart, opening the way for social revolutionary transformations spearheaded by revolts from below.'[38] Relying on a 'structural perspective',[39] Skocpol argued that once the old regime states were broken apart, political and class conflicts were set in motion, not to be resolved until the establishment of new administrative and military organizations.[40] Her emphasis on structural dynamics led her to conclude that revolutions start non-voluntarily and non-purposively, emphasizing 'objective relationships and conflicts among variously situated groups and nations, rather than the interests, outlooks, or ideologies of particular actors in revolutions'.[41] Despite the role often ascribed to 'vanguard' parties, Skocpol argued that revolutions 'come about only through inter- and intranational structural contradictions and conjunctural occurrences beyond the deliberate control of avowed revolutionaries'.[42]

At first glance, it would seem that all of the theories discussed here apply to the example of the Iranian revolution. Johnson's systems-value theory is validated by its contention that the rapid social and cultural changes that occurred in Iran in the 1960s and the 1970s led to the 'disequilibrium' of Iranian society and ultimately resulted in a revolutionary eruption in 1978–79. The 'accelerators' that propelled Iran's disequilibrated society into revolutionary circumstances, according to this frame of reference, included among other things the abrupt reduction of oil prices after 1973 and President Carter's human rights policies. The theories of Davies and Gurr are also both validated by the sudden reversal of the generally positive economic conditions of the early 1970s after 1975 and a subsequent rise in the level of unemployment among aspiring groups and classes.

Political explanations for the causes of revolution appear to be equally applicable to the case of Iran. The gathering in Paris of a coalition of Iranian revolutionaries and their claim that the government in Tehran was 'illegal' corresponds with Tilly's identification of 'multiple sovereignty' as the leading pre-condition for revolutionary episodes. Huntington's arguments find similar applicability, particularly in presenting an accurate description of the groups who spearheaded the revolution and the reasons why they did so. The Pahlavi state was indeed overthrown by the social classes that were brought about as a result of social and economic modernization. These classes became revolutionary when the state was unable to absorb them. For his part, Green bases his entire theoretical framework on the Iranian revolution.[43] He argues that the failure of the state-run Rastakhiz party to mobilize the politically aware lower and middle classes in support of the regime led to their 'countermobilization' and ultimately resulted in their victory over the incumbent regime. Finally, Skocpol's structural-class analysis also appears to apply to the Iranian revolution. The international pressures that the Iranian government faced in the late 1970s, coming especially from Washington, and the concurrent discomfort (if not necessarily the agitation) of Bazaari merchants and rural immigrants were important developments leading to the Iranian revolution.

The applicability of these theories to the Iranian revolution, however, does not extend beyond these superficial observations. To begin with, most of these theories have been challenged on a number of significant conceptual points and their very validity as theories of revolution has been questioned.[44] The theories that fail to consider the undermining of political authority as a main pre-condition for revolutionary causation have been subject to the strongest criticism.[45] In order for revolutions to occur, the state must first be made susceptible to being overthrown by its citizens. The significant curtailment of the state's powers and its ability effectively to govern the society has been a recurrent feature of all historical examples of revolutions.[46] Skocpol argues forcefully that revolutions begin when the state's power is weakened by international developments such as economic competition or military conflicts.[47] Conceptually at least, these is no reason to suggest that indigenous political crises, such as the sudden death of an authoritarian political figure in a personalized system, cannot have the same weakening effect on the state.

Whereas the non-political theories of revolution give little consideration to the occurrence of political developments in pre-revolutionary states, most politically oriented theories ignore the equally significant social and cultural setting in which revolutions occur. The arguments of both Skocpol and Huntington suffer from a striking analytical paucity of the socio-cultural context of revolutionary episodes. Since the Iranian revolution Skocpol has in fact modified her strictly political (and non-voluntary) interpretation of revolutions and has argued that cultural factors can indeed play a determining role in the start and the outcome of revolutions.[48] Equally significant is the re-evaluation of her original claims regarding the non-voluntary and non-purposive nature of revolutions.[49] By abandoning her unremitting insistence on the non-voluntary character of revolutionary episodes, Skocpol has answered perhaps the most important objection other scholars had raised against her theory: that human agency, beliefs, and actions are also fundamental attributes of each revolutionary episode.[50] Despite Skocpol's important and highly impressive re-evaluation of her original arguments, her discussion of the role of cultural dynamics in revolutions neither goes far enough nor does it even point in the right direction.[51] Contrary to what she seems to imply, the pervasiveness of a particular value system over a society is not by itself sufficient to determine the ideological character or the outcome of a revolution.[52] It is the positions of the different oppositionally inclined groups in society, the means that they have at their disposal to disseminate their propaganda throughout the society, and the degree to which people can understand and relate to this propaganda that determine which opposition groups and ideologies dominate the revolutionary movement. Leaders of revolutions emerge not necessarily because of their ideologies but because of a coalescence of verbal and organizational skills, doctrinal and practical preparedness, and because of their position in relation to other groups in society.[53]

Despite his heavy reliance on the analysis of pre-revolutionary 'systems', Huntington also ignores the relevance of social and cultural conditions in the occurrence of revolutions. The breadth of his social analysis is limited to identifying the middle classes and especially the intellectuals as the main class of revolutionaries.[54] He does not explain how and why the protesting masses are prompted to rally behind one group of revolutionary leaders rather than other groups. Does social organization not have a determining role in the domination of one particular revolutionary cadre and their ideology within the revolutionary movement? Huntington vaguely alludes to this question when he argues that 'the patterns of social organisation in the slums may ... discourage political radicalism' among slumdwellers and other members of the 'lumpenproletariat'.[55] He does not extend his argument to analyse the types of social institutions and relations that can inject 'political radicalism' into the groups and classes (such as the lumpenproletariat) with potential for revolutionary mobilization.

Green bases his theory solely on the Iranian example. Unlike Huntington and Skocpol, Green does examine the social characteristics of (Iranian) society and considers those characteristics to be instrumental in determining the leadership of the revolution.[56] By pointing to the strength of the religious classes and institutions in Iran, Green argues that the mosques carried forward the process of 'countermobilization' when the state failed to 'mobilize' its citizens.[57] He correctly suggests that religious institutions were capable of providing the appropriate facilities for the public's general desire for political participation. How 'countermobilization' itself actually occurred, however, is left unclear. The pre-conditions Green lists for 'countermobilization' imply that revolts occur largely spontaneously and do not come about as a result of efforts of a revolutionary leadership cadre.[58] He thus minimizes the role and significance of the revolution's leaders and does not pay enough attention to the importance of their actions and manoeuvres in mobilizing the masses.

The recent example of the Iranian revolution affords us the opportunity to modify and improve on the existing theories of revolution. While none of the existing theories have been falsified because of the Iranian case, they have been shown to be unable to explain all of the factors that are necessary to bring about a revolution. Those theories that examine revolutions within the rigid frameworks of only one discipline – such as psychology (the theories of Gurr and Davies), sociology (Johnson), or politics (Skocpol's original theory) – are particularly limited in their explanatory abilities. Clearly, an examination of causes of revolution requires a multidisciplinary approach, particularly one that considers in detail the pre-revolutionary politics (the state) and the socio-cultural setting (society) of the country in question. Overlooked by most theorists, the conceptual separation of state and society and the examination of developments in both areas are fundamental to an accurate and complete understanding of causes of revolution. Within this broad division of state and society, a revolution can be defined as a movement by various groups that are strategically located throughout society, when the state is weak and vulnerable, to acquire the powers and authority of the governing élite.[59] Although groups that oppose a regime may exist at all times, the intensity and the extent of their efforts to acquire political power, and their success or failure, depend upon the existence of a number of social and political conditions. In order to understand what these conditions are, the pre-revolutionary state *and* society need to be analysed in detail.

The state

For revolutions to occur, the state needs to have lost a substantial degree of its coercive abilities and to have become vulnerable to being overthrown. Regardless of the existence of other conditions conducive to revolutionary occurrences, the ability of the regime to subdue its opponents will prevent the development of revolutionary circumstances. The recurrent example of South Africa, and more recently South Korea, demonstrate the importance of the vulnerability of the state as the most central cause of revolutions. Despite the noticeable internal and international pressures the two regimes face, both the South African and the South Korean republics have so far resisted revolutions due to the strength of their governing elites and the intact nature of their state structures.[60] As mentioned earlier, all revolutions that have succeeded have begun only after a significant reduction occurred in the state's ability to govern effectively.

How the state's governing abilities are suddenly reduced varies from one case to the next. In most instances, states are weakened because of the development of internal or international crises. Skocpol had originally suggested that the political crises that lead to revolutions are possible only in an international context. In modifying her arguments later on, she has argued that indigenous political crises (as in the case of Iran and, arguably, in France), can also bring about revolutionary circumstances.[61] Economic bankruptcy and military conflicts are two of the more common developments that can lead to political crises and, ultimately, to revolution. In recent times, largely because of the phenomenal growth in the complexity of international relations, political crises can occur in one state as a result of diplomatic pressures exerted on it by another, often more powerful state. US diplomatic pressure on the Shah of Iran and on President Marcos of the Philippines represents two recent instances when states have faced crises not because of wars or bankruptcy but because of strained or conditional diplomatic relations with other countries.[62]

The weakening of the state is not by itself sufficient to produce the political crises necessary for a revolution. While crises may occur at any time, revolutions will not develop unless the state's political exigencies are exploited by groups who specifically aim to overthrow the ruling elite. The political actions and manoeuvres of the revolution's leadership cadre assume paramount importance in propelling a weakened or collapsing state towards full-scale revolution. Unless directly challenged by political contenders, even those states that have become substantially weak will not be engulfed in revolutions by themselves. The importance of political challenges to a weakened state is underscored by the previously mentioned consensus among theorists that revolutions are to a large extent products of human initiative.[63] In all revolutions, there have always existed opposition groups that have used the opportunities they acquired as a result of the state's loss of power to overthrow the governing élite.[64] Adversely, the absence of such a contending group in contemporary Iraq, for instance, is one of the main reasons why an apparently weak state (engaged in war for many years) has not been overthrown in a revolution.[65]

Society

In considering the role that society plays in the occurrence of revolutions, attention needs to be paid to the characteristics of each of the classes and groups that comprise a society's strata, the various groups that seek to overthrow the existing state by mobilizing popular support, and the connections that are forged or which already exist between the social classes on the one hand and the opposition groups on the other. These variables determine which one of the opposition groups (and consequently which revolutionary ideology) dominate the revolutionary movement and emerge as the revolution's leaders. Before even having acquired the sympathy or support of the population, the revolution's leaders are determined by the virtue of their dominant position within society and by the strength of the social organizations at their disposal. Clearly, the subsequent actions that the revolutionary groups initiate can greatly augment or curtail their legitimacy and support among the population. The popularity and appeal of a certain ideology is also important in increasing the popular support of a revolutionary group. However, as long as revolutionary parties and groups are not situated in society in a way that would enable them to have access to the popular classes (both in terms of communication and organization), they will not be able effectively to propogate their ideals or to publicize their revolutionary actions among the population at large. The social positions and organizations of the various revolutionary groups, therefore, are important social determinants in shaping the character and the nature of revolutions. Very few social scientists pay enough attention to the social links that bind revolutionary groups to the general population, and the instrumentality of these links in determining a revolution's leaders have so far been generally ignored.[66]

In certain instances the necessary links between the revolutionary groups and the popular classes are facilitated through the existing social institutions and arrangements (e.g. the *ulema* and their mosques in Iran). In most other successful revolutions, however, such bonds have been forged through the deliberate creation of certain institutions and organizations. These organizations have provided the link between the revolutionary groups and those social classes that were perceived to have the most potential for revolutionary mobilization. The Soviets and Cuu Quocs served precisely such a role in the Russian and the Vietnamese revolutions respectively, where both facilitated the links between one of the revolutionary groups (the Bolsheviks in Russia and the Vietminh in Vietnam) and the main revolutionary classes.[67]

It would be misleading to suggest that the general social and social-psychological dispositions of a population at large have no effect on the occurrence of revolutions. While mass outbreaks of social and psychological anguish do not by themselves lead to revolutions, certain socio-cultural and psychological conditions can and often do provide the necessary ingredients needed to achieve the revolutionary mobilization of previously passive masses. People will not revolt against a regime unless there is a compelling reason for them to do so.[68] There must exist a certain readiness among people in order for them to follow the groups that seek to overthrow the political establishment. This readiness may be caused by a number of developments. They include, most notably, the disorientation of values and doubts about the legitimacy of the political establishment,[69] the society-wide emergence of psychological conditions such as frustration or rising expectations,[70] or as the case may be, a combination of both (as in Iran).

The existence of oppositional tendencies among the population, albeit often latent and difficult to discern, at times becomes instrumental in determining the leaders of revolution. Addressing or capitalizing on the social or psychological sources that trouble the public strengthens the links between revolutionary leaders and the people. In order for the opposition groups to understand the moods and dispositions that prevail throughout society, social positions and organizations are instrumental. The fewer contacts a revolutionary group has with a population, the less likely it is to appreciate the sentiments and the entrenched values that prevail throughout society. Social organization is, therefore, instrumental not only in the dissemination of revolutionary propaganda throughout society, but also in enabling contenders for political power to detect and gauge (and thereby exploit) the socio-cultural or psychological sources that may increase the public's willingness to participate in revolution. In certain instances the conditions that attract the popular classes to a revolutionary group may be readily available in a society. Therefore, all a revolutionary group needs to do in order to attract popular support is to say the right things and to make the right moves at the right time. This was the case in Iran, where the *ulema*'s revolutionary propaganda and their ideology (Shi'ism) were not only easily understandable but also appeared to many to offer the best remedy for Iran's social and cultural ills (see Chapters 4 and 5). In other historical instances, the revolutionary groups themselves may need to provide the social and cultural conditions under which they can augment their mass following. China and Cuba offer the best examples of successful revolutions in which the revolutionaries themselves forged the socio-cultural or psychological conditions that were needed to attract a mass following. Mao was keenly aware of the importance of the appeal of the revolutionaries among the different classes. After analysing Chinese society, he concluded that the peasantry – 'the blank masses', as he called them – were 'uncorrupted' by bourgeois ideas and were the only class capable of spearheading the Chinese revolution.[71] The Fidelista guerrillas in Cuba also recognized that by branding themselves as *los Humildes* (men of people), and through good behaviour and conduct, they could attract the support of the Cuban peasantry.[72]

Conclusion

To briefly sum up the main points of the foregoing argument, the occurrence of a successful revolution requires the development of a necessary set of political as well as social conditions. Politically, it is necessary that the powers and the authority of the ruling élite be significantly weakened by internal or international developments. The ensuing weaknesses and exigencies then need to be exploited by specific groups that seek to overthrow the existing élite. The society as a whole needs to embody some degree of receptivity to revolutionary change. For opposition groups to acquire popular legitimacy and to attract the support necessary to overthrow the regime, two social factors are important. First, the opposition groups themselves need to have the appropriate social means to disseminate their propaganda and to establish the necessary links with the popular classes. Such means may include a culturally enriched ideology (as in Iran) or social institutions created specifically in order to expand the contacts between the revolutionaries and the people (the Soviets in Russia and the Cuu Quocs in Vietnam). Second, the popular classes must be dissatisfied with the existing conditions and therefore be inclined to support the opposition groups. The specific reasons for general dissatisfaction vary from case to case and from time to time. Nevertheless, the most common (as well as significant) condition that increases the inclinations of a population towards revolutionary change is the frustration of aspirations, whether they be aspirations for political participation, social assimilation, or economic advancement. Together, the appearance of appropriate social conditions and the necessary political developments cause revolutions.

Within such a framework, the causes of the Iranian revolution of 1978–79 can be identified as

1. drastic reductions in the state's powers and authority due to internal and international developments;

2. the activities of opposition groups amid the political weaknesses of the state;
3. the appearance of social conditions conducive to the dissemination of revolutionary sentiments throughout society; and
4. the effective development of links between the various opposition groups and those classes whose support they sought.

The deceptively strong Pahlavi state began to fall apart when it faced diplomatic pressures from its main ally, the United States, and when its ambitious economic programmes needed to be sharply curtailed after the decline of oil prices in 1974. Finding new life in the increasingly relaxed political atmosphere of the late 1970s, the various opposition groups began to act against the regime and at the same time increased their support among the general population. Most social classes, meanwhile, were frustrated by the systemic limitations that surrounded them and had become disillusioned by the regime's policies. The revolutionary group with the best organization and with the most easily understandable and widely shared ideology, the *ulema*, dominated the emerging revolutionary movement and spearheaded it. The revolutionaries, with the mass support they gradually acquired, brought about the collapse of the dying state and replaced it with a political system of their own.

Chapter two

The Pahlavi state

The Iranian state in several important ways contributed to the occurrence of the 1978–79 revolution, both because of the historical trajectory in which it had led Iran by the late 1970s and because of the manner in which it had developed over the years. Despite its image as 'an island of stability in one of the more troubled areas of the world',[1] the Pahlavi state had long suffered from a number of fundamental systemic difficulties. Following a series of highly damaging internal and international developments in the 1970s, the deceptively strong state soon started to crumble. It was within the context of a collapsing state, and largely because of it, that the Iranian revolution developed and eventually succeeded.

The Pahlavi era marked the establishment of a highly differentiated and structurally strong political system in Iran. Under the Pahlavis, Iran became a transitional society, socially and economically as well as politically. Both Pahlavi monarchs actively engaged in the construction of a solid and comparatively modern state and embarked on a rapid and intense course of modernization. This process was achieved by reinforcing national unification and by establishing modern armed forces. Both shahs succeeded not only in tearing down the old order and in establishing a new one in its place, but also in enabling the country to launch primary capitalist production and accumulation, and later acquiring something of an industrial infrastructure, which was previously non-existent. Nation-building occurred in two historically distinct phases. Initially, during Reza Shah's reign between 1921 and 1941, most of the basic institutions needed for the elementary needs of society were created. Reza Shah did not so much establish these institutions but rather secularized them by transferring their control from the *ulema* over to the state, a task in which he often used brutal tactics. Such newly secularized institutions included the educational, administrative, health, and judicial systems, most of which were often modelled after those in Europe. Some other institutions, notably the military and the state bureaucracy, were rebuilt almost entirely and created anew.[2] Nation-building entered into its second phase during the reign of Reza Shah's son, Mohammad Reza, when most existing political institutions were made more efficient and modern and when the foundations of the regime were strengthened. However, at the same time as it was reaching the height of power, the Pahlavi state underwent atrophy. After 1975 the state structure began to fall apart from within, and whatever the Shah did in order to save his regime met with disapproval and condemnation from abroad. Soon afterward the regime died a speedy death, a bereavement expedited internationally by President Jimmy Carter's human rights policies and domestically by the attacks of the revolutionaries. In 1978 the Pahlavi state collapsed like a house of cards.

The imperial Iranian government

The Pahlavis came to power in Iran in 1921 through a military *coup* by the commander of the only effective military unit available, named Reza Khan. The Qajar dynasty had never fully recovered from the 1905–1911 revolution, which had temporarily instituted a constitutional monarchy. The court of the last Qajar monarch, Ahmad Shah, was already in a state of collapse when Reza Khan undertook his march towards Tehran from Qazvin, a city to the west. The ineffectual Qajar Shah capitulated immediately as he probably suspected that a power he could not contend with, that of the British, was behind the *coup*. Reza Khan and his civilian colleague, Seyyed Zia al-Din-Tabataba'i, took over the government as the commander of the army and the prime minister respectively. Reza Khan soon removed the latter and named himself prime minister in 1923. He also retained the War Ministry and started to build up an effective army. He later assumed the name Pahlavi and in 1925, with a semblance of constitutional procedures, declared himself Shah. In 1931 he insisted that Persia's name should be known internationally as Iran and continued to rule over the country until 1941, when his pro-German sympathies led the British and the Soviets to remove him from power and to install his 22-year-old son as the new king. The young Mohammed Reza Pahlavi wielded little real authority at first as Iran was occupied by the Allied Forces throughout the Second World War. After Reza Shah's departure, the parliament (Majlis), which he had effectively emasculated although never suppressed, found new life and the office of the prime minister once again became dominant over an inexperienced ruler. Since the 1906 Constitutional Revolution, political power had alternated between the Court and the office of the prime minister. With Reza Khan's assumption of authoritarian rule this division had ceased. In 1941, when his son Mohammed Reza came to power, the system of constitutional monarchy was revitalized and continued to function until 1953. In fact, the growth of the power of the prime minister and parliament reached such proportions that in 1951 Prime Minister Mussadiq nearly overthrew the Shah (see Chapter 3). Even after Mussadiq was himself overthrown by the US Central Intelligence Agency in 1953,[3] the prime minister's office was still responsible for the political and the administrative running of the country. The Shah's personal leadership over the government was solidified only after 1965, when he chose Amir Abbas Hoveida as his prime minister. Nevertheless, while the 1953 *coup* reinstated the power of the monarchy, it did not immediately consolidate the Shah's personal rule and in fact it heightened his unpopularity. Mussadiq had enjoyed widespread public support and was seen to have been removed by a combination of foreign intervention by forces inimical to the aspirations of the majority of the people. From 1953 to 1965 a succession of prime ministers followed, each enjoying some individual political leverage, although this depended more on the throne than on a timorous and corruptly elected parliament.

After the 1953 *coup* the conditions that emerged inside the country and in the international arena afforded the Shah the opportunity to concentrate on building a strong state and on solidifying his personal rule. Internally, the *coup* seemed to have removed the last vestiges of opposition to political absolutism, namely liberal nationalists loyal to the 1906 Constitution.[4] In fact, a co-ordinated campaign to oppose the regime and its policies was not to occur until a decade had passed, when in 1962-63 the *ulema* opposed the government's proposal to institute universal suffrage and the 'White Revolution'. Internationally, the Shah's efforts to solidify his rule benefited greatly from the rivalry of the superpowers during the Cold War, because of which the United States gave Iran lucrative economic and military assistance in order to strengthen its 'anti-communist' monarch.[5] With the absence of domestic opposition and with foreign support, the Shah energetically began to establish new state institutions and modernized the existing ones. In the process, the state became increasingly more centralized as it acquired more and more political power, grew less tolerant of opposition activities, and employed harsher measures to subdue its opponents, and at the same time became diplomatically, militarily, and psychologically dependent on the support it received from the United States.

The state that subsequently emerged had three principal foundations.[6] First, there was the person of the Shah. By installing himself at its apex and by making all other institutions dependent on his Court, the Shah became an integral part of the state. The second source of power for the state was its administrative network, comprised of the cabinet, the Rastakhiz party, the Majlis, and the bureaucracy. Lastly, the state relied on a number of military and para-military institutions, the most notable of which were the armed forces and SAVAK.

Shah Mohammad Reza Pahlavi

The Shah was himself the most important element of the state, surpassing the power and significance of all other state institutions.[7] After 1953 a series of prime ministers were appointed. Although not entirely subservient to the monarch, none of them were by any means able to enjoy the independence and the political power that had been Mussadiq's. The Shah himself believed that he could sustain the Pahlavi dynasty only if he directly intervened in the country's political process. Accordingly, the personal power of the Shah increased after 1953, while virtually all other institutions lost effective authority and political relevance. All affairs of the ministry of war came under the direct control of the Shah and he personally devised the military budget without the prime ministers having any control over military affairs.[8] The Shah's personal dominance over the political process was completed in 1965, when he appointed Hoveida as his new premier. A former finance minister, Hoveida's prime-ministership lasted for some thirteen years, and it was only due to an economic crisis and growing apprehension that the system was not working that the Shah felt obliged to appoint a new prime minister in 1977. Under Hoveida an elaborate political system evolved, resembling a pyramid with the Shah at the apex, and supported by a cabinet under a prime minister who was the impresario of the system, as well as an expanding bureaucracy. In 1975 the Shah capitalized his system by the formation of a single legal political party, the Rastakhiz (Resurgence) Party. After experimenting with two parties, one a government and the other intended to be a 'loyal' opposition party, he then made Iran into a one-party state. This action took Iran a step nearer to eventual revolution.

The Shah personally assumed onerous duties and consumed himself in the daily running of the country. His primary preoccupation was with issues pertaining to foreign affairs, the economy, and the military. Most cabinet members had weekly audiences with the Shah, during which they reported on the activities of their ministries or discussed particular issues. Influential ministers and some wealthy industrialists were able to gain private audiences with the Shah when they wished to bypass the bureaucracy and take advantage of favouritism, often leading to tensions and personal animosity within the cabinet and among industrialists.[9] A number of individuals, including the prime minister and the Ministers of Foreign Affairs and War were in constant contact with the monarch. Junior ministers were not permitted to have royal audiences, except at official ceremonies or if their senior colleagues were away on official business.[10] The Shah personally made all ministerial, military, and ambassadorial appointments, and none of the appointees were consulted or informed prior to their selection.[11] All military commanders were answerable directly and strictly to the Shah. He also chaired the weekly meetings of the High Council of Economics, which comprised the Ministers of mines and industries, commerce, labour, economics and financial affairs, the prime minister, and the heads of the central bank and the Budget Plan Organization. There was also the Shah's Special Bureau, which fulfilled the monarch's secretarial needs, such as summoning ministers or arranging for audiences. The Shah also consulted with a group of twenty to thirty experienced and trusted political veterans,[12] but their advice appears to have been of little significance in influencing his decisions. Within the Court, the Shah was undeniably the strongest figure, although his twin sister, Princess Ashraf, wielded considerable influence over him.[13] This influence was often in the form of getting the Princess's favourites appointed to higher positions, such as ambassador to Britain.[14] His Empress, Farah, also wished to see some of her political choices elevated to higher offices, but she did not have nearly as much influence over the Shah as did Princess Ashraf.[15] The Court was not without intrigue, and high-ranking officials were aware of intense competition and rivalry between Ashraf and Farah.[16] It is not precisely ascertainable how such intrigues affected the court's political life.

The personal character of the Shah and his attitude towards political power underwent changes during his thirty-five-year reign. By all accounts, he was shrewd, intelligent, and an indefatigable worker. Having ascended to the throne at a young age, the monarch always remained mistrustful of more experienced politicians and felt intimidated by them.[17] He did not like the expression of opinions contrary to his own, preferring sycophants, and it was for this reason that Hoveida was able to remain prime minister for thirteen years. An official who served the government under Hoveida later admitted that the prime minister's political longevity was due to the fact that he 'effectively perpetuated and covered over the contradictions of a political system which was isolated from reality and with which he in turn conveyed an inaccurate picture of the Iranian social and political climate to the Shah'.[18] Another observer has called Hoveida's premiership a 'quipocracy', because the prime minister 'constantly deflected questions with clever quips and one-liners'.[19] Hoveida minimized the access of all but a selected number of cabinet ministers to the Shah, and those who could see him gave the Shah only the news he wished to hear. When the Court suffered its first revolutionary shocks in early 1978, Empress Farah was said to have complained that the Court

The Pahlavi state

had previously been prevented from receiving adequate and accurate information about the state of the country and the feelings of the people.[20] The Shah himself admitted that despite having had 'eyes and ears among the population', he had been furnished with 'little in the way of conclusive information' regarding the ramifications of the policies he had fervently pursued.[21] By 1977 both the Shah and Hoveida felt that the prime minister had been in office 'too long', and a new prime minister, Jamshid Amuzegar, was appointed.[22]

The cabinet

The pattern and the nature of the cabinet's functions remained basically unaltered when prime minister Amuzegar took office in August 1977. Under Hoveida, the cabinet had for the most part become the ultimate caretaker of the state bureaucracy while the Shah maintained his personnel control over a number of key ministries. The ministries of war, foreign affairs, the Court, and finance (whose minister represented Iran at OPEC) were in constant contact with the Shah. The Shah also gave top priority to those ministries that were responsible for the economic development of the country. Representative of this group were the ministries that comprised the High Council of Economics. All other ministries served mere administrative functions. They included the ministries of culture and arts; health; housing and town planning; transportation; post, telephone, and telegraph; energy; information and tourism; justice; and the ministry of state for executive affairs. Administrative co-operation within the cabinet was common among junior ministers, as they were often joint members of several commissions. It was not until Amuzegar's resignation in August 1978 and the subsequent appointment of Ja'far Sharif-Emami, the speaker of the Senate and a former prime minister, that the cabinet's functions changed from being purely administrative and the ministers were given the power to make actual decisions.

The Rastakhiz

As noted above, it was during Hoveida's tenure that the Shah dissolved the country's only two legal parties in March 1975 and formed a single, 'all-embracing' party called Rastakhiz (Resurgence). 'The old system', the Shah argued, 'was no longer efficient, since whichever party was in power would claim all of the benefits of progress and minority parties were one hundred percent the losers despite the fact that they were totally loyal.'[23]

> I thought that through eliminating an opposition party, I could solicit the aid of all capable political personalities without concern

for party politics. For the future I saw [Rastakhiz] as a great political and ideological school, able to engender the civic spirit necessary for administrative reform.[24]

Organizationally the party comprised two wings, the Progressive and the Constructive, both of which considered themselves to be liberal. The Progressive wing tended to lean towards greater social welfare and equality, encouraged bureaucratic decentralization, and argued for broader political participation. The Constructive wing, headed by the minister of economy, Hooshang Ansari, emphasized rapid economic growth and industrialization. Majlis deputies and cabinet ministers were obliged to participate in either of the party's wings, but the ministers neither explained nor discussed any of the policies of their ministries at the party's meetings. The party was organized according to a rigid vertical hierarchy, descending from the highest to the lowest. The secretary general, elected by party congress, was in charge of the overall supervision of the party. Representatives of the party's regional and local cells, called *kanuns*, formed the party's highest organ, the executive committee. Hoveida served as the party's first secretary general from 1975 to 1977, during which time the party's constitution, organization, and membership were to be developed and after which new officers were to be elected.[25]

The formation of a single, grand political party was intended to create an active base of support for the regime in the cities similar to the one that had been developed in the countryside as a result of the 1962 Land Reform Programme.[26] Rastakhiz was supposed to be an official 'guiding body for the political maturation of the country', 'an all-embracing party which would embody all social and political forces'.[27] It was designed to give a 'firm and serious direction to the country's political process', and to 'accomplish the political mobilisation which the two previous parties had failed to achieve'.[28] It has been suggested that the formation of Rastakhiz was partly inspired by a superficial understanding of Samuel Huntington's *Political Order in Changing Societies* (by Iranian political science Ph.Ds returning home from the United States), and partly by ex-Tudeh party sympathizers who saw a Leninist-style party organization as an ideal means of integrating the masses into the political process.[29] A combination of all such motives appears to be a more plausible explanation for the creation of the Rastakhiz. The organizational set-up and the party's functions after it was formed signified the Shah's attempt to further legitimize his regime and to strengthen his traditional political authority in the face of the social and economic modernization of the country. After his overthrow the Shah admitted that he had hoped the party 'would foster the convergence of many essential goals which we were then pursuing through government channels'.[30] Nevertheless, the party's formation was not intended to rectify as yet undetected flaws within the system or radically alter the very components of the state. In 1975, when the Rastakhiz was formed, the government did not face any internal or external pressures to change or to reform itself. What seems instead to have prompted the Shah to form an 'all-embracing' political party was not so much any conceivable threat but rather sheer greed for greater power. He felt confident enough to dissolve the two existing parties – Iran Novin and Mardum – appoint his trusted prime minister, Hoveida, as the new party's secretary general, and to declare that his long promised Great Civilization was at hand.[31] In the process he employed a group of highly educated political recruits who viewed Rastakhiz as an attractive alternative to the established oligarchy. These recruits did not comprise any selected category of political activists and came from diverse social and economic backgrounds. Their only shared characteristic was that they were mostly highly educated and were very much concerned with social and economic mobility.

It is difficult to determine how much popular support the Rastakhiz really had. The ironic complementarity between the ambitions of the Shah and those of some of the professional groups initially generated some degree of enthusiasm for the Rastakhiz among the middle classes. Furthermore, the concept of an all-encompassing party that would provide organizational cohesion and direction to the country's political set-up was at first appealing to a number of educated and professional groups, especially those with some type of vested interest in the political establishment. Most notable among this category were government administrators, university professors, journalists, and officials of the National Radio and Television Organization. These professional classes themselves comprised or were in relatively close contact with the higher ranks of the governing elite but did not necessarily approve of the method in which the country was being governed. This disapproval was often caused by a frustration of their political ideals and aspirations due to monarchical absolutism. The close convergence of the social and economic interests of such professionals with those of the establishment often prevented them from openly criticizing the regime or forming opposition parties. Rastakhiz appeared to them to be a plausible organization specifically designed to cater to the political exigencies of the system.[32] It was seen as a safe and effective device through which the political order could be gradually reformed while the general status quo was maintained. But many of the silent dissidents, whose numbers were growing (as was their resolve as a result of this party's formation), believed that the formation of Rastakhiz spelt undisguised regimentation as in a dictatorship and, above all, in its emphasis on 'guidance', an attempt to mould people's minds and shape their aspirations towards goals in which they did not believe; for many, it was fascism. Even the hopes the more docile or complacent entertained were soon to fade, and disenchantment with Rastakhiz soon set in as the party was bureaucratized and became another component of the state administration. In 1976 the party launched a widely publicized price control campaign aimed at preventing profiteering and curbing inflation. The public viewed the campaign as a further demonstration of the fallacy of Rastakhiz as an institution dedicated to political mobilization. The party was seen to be attempting to redirect the public's attention towards non-political issues and to be interfering in private business. Additionally, the manner in which the campaign was carried out aroused even greater resentment towards the party and heightened its unpopularity. Rastakhiz had recruited university students to inspect shops and businesses and to impose fines on those found guilty of overpricing. Some recruits, however, were overly zealous and damaged merchants' wares. Other allegedly guilty merchants were subjected to public humiliation. Their stores were shut down and covered with large banners that notified the public of the store owners' guilt and of the penalties imposed on them.

It did not take long for the negative ramifications of such a campaign to entangle both the Rastakhiz and in fact the entire regime. Rastakhiz, far from its promises of political mobilization and reform, appeared to be the repressive organ of the regime many had feared it would be.[33] Middle- and upper-class urban dwellers had generally acquiesced in absorbing inflationary prices as the cost of rapid and upward economic mobility and did not consider inflation to be a pressing concern. The party was perceived to be using the merchants as a scapegoat in order to direct attention away from the debilitating shortages of water and electricity during the summer of 1975. The political cost that the regime itself incurred as a result of Rastakhiz's price-control campaign was thus significant in expediting the collapse of the state, as will be further discussed below. Within two years after it was formed, Rastakhiz had lost any ideological appeal it had once had among some of the non-oppositional but politically concerned middle classes – it had come to symbolize the cumbrous and popularly despised structure of political power. There were two levels of public reaction to the Rastakhiz. First, a limited number of intellectuals initially saw some hope in the party but were soon disillusioned with it as it failed to fulfill any of their aspirations and political ideals. On a more general level, the middle and the upper middle classes generally viewed the party as only a laughing stock and as another one of the regime's deceitful gimmicks. Within this latter group the *ulema* and the Bazaaris saw themselves particularly threatened by the new party.[34] When the first violent demonstrations against the regime broke out in Qom in January 1978, the demonstrators attacked and looted Rastakhiz's local headquarters. Party officials later conceded that Rastakhiz 'never enjoyed any support among the various classes of society', since people were 'suspicious of the party's founders from the very beginning'.[35] While in exile the Shah himself admitted that 'experience was to show that the creation of [Rastakhiz] was an error'.[36]

Majlis

The government was constitutionally responsible to the parliament, a bicameral body comprised of a lower house, Majlis, and an upper house, the Senate (Sena). The 1906 Constitution set the term of the Majlis at four years and the number of its deputies at 200, allowing for the addition of one member for every 100,000 new eligible voters added to the population in a ten-year span (Articles 4 and 5). In the 1975 elections, 268 members were elected to the lower chamber. The Senate had sixty deputies, half of whom were popularly elected while the other half were appointed by royal decree. Of all appointed and elected senators, half represented the capital city and half the provinces (Articles 43 and 45).

Despite its legal complexities, the parliament had steadily lost political power since the overthrow of Mussadiq, and by the time Prime Minister Hoveida departed from office in 1977 the Majlis resembled anything but a parliament. Neither of the chambers wielded any meaningful degree of influence and the activities of their deputies were almost exclusively limited to voicing non-political and regionally confined concerns of some of their constituents. Occasionally the deputies worked directly with cabinet ministers on various local development projects, such as the building of a new factory or vaccination of schoolchildren in a certain city, but the level of such interactions often did not extend beyond the exchange of information and/or the provision of appropriate methodological guidelines.

The bureaucracy

In closer proximity to the decision-making process and the power structure was the overwhelming state bureaucracy. Virtually all government programmes and initiatives were specifically designed to accelerate and give direction to the country's social and economic modernization. An extensive bureaucratic network was needed, therefore, to develop and implement such programmes and, additionally, to publicize the intentions of the government and the Crown. As such, each government ministry maintained bureaus and agencies even in the most remote cities and towns.

The importance of the bureaucracy to the Pahlavi state was paramount. The Court, totalitarian and absolutist in nature, was bent on modernizing Iran socially and economically, but not politically. In attempting to preserve his traditional centre of political authority in a rapidly changing transitional society,[37] and in order to counter the image of despotism and oligarchy that surrounded his court, the Shah tended to put greater emphasis and reliance on the bureaucracy rather than the military. The state bureaucracy also served as a channel through which new members were recruited into the power elite. The regime, through several agencies and programmes, made extensive efforts to assimilate intellectuals, especially those who had previously demonstrated apathy to opposition parties and to specific political doctrines. Such efforts were often crystallized by the formation of think tanks that were in one way or another related to the Court, or by the appointment of certain intellectuals to high-level bureaucratic posts.[38] Overall, however, the regime's intellectual recruits were very few in number and were largely ineffectual in giving the regime a political direction or in reducing its vulnerability to revolution.

As in most other modernizing states, Iran's extensive bureaucracy suffered from a number of acute inadequacies and shortcomings. While indigenous cultural, geopolitical, and economic variables are not without influence, bureaucracies in most modernizing states tend to suffer from certain similar deficiencies. Corruption is one such characteristic that is common to most modernizing bureaucracies. As the established means of access to higher office are generally limited and procedural methods are often overly inert and inefficient in modernizing countries, there is a general tendency to circumvent bureaucratic practices and to 'beat the system'. Furthermore, the inefficiency and wastefulness that mark most bureaucracies in modernizing states often arise out of factors such as the practice of nepotism and the recruitment and promotion of unqualified personnel within the bureaucracy; the civil servant's lack of incentive to achieve higher levels of productivity, and the fear of negative reports to higher authorities.[39] Reflecting on his personal experience, the Shah's ambassador to London observed that 'fear, rather than rationality, fear rather than commonsense, fear rather than patriotism, seem the governing forces in the life of an Iranian public servant'.[40] Whatever their actual causes, corruption and inefficiency had become marked attributes of the Pahlavi state bureaucracy. After the revolution President Banisadr estimated that within the bureaucracy left over from the Pahlavi era each civil servant performed only one hour and eleven minutes of productive duty per working day.[41] Additionally, corruption was so rampant throughout the regime that it astonished and angered even the most senior members of the government.[42] One of the more conspicuous developments that signified the beginning of the end of the Pahlavis in Iran was the Shah's creation of an imperial commission in

November 1976, intended to investigate the failure of the different ministries in meeting their development schedules. The commission, however, tried to represent the Shah as separate and beyond the government's faltering bureaucracy and began to clamp down on high-level bureaucrats.[43] Most ministers and civil servants justifiably saw themselves as being used as scapegoats in an effort to distance the throne from perpetual corruption and inefficiency.[44]

The armed forces

The Iranian military establishment was another significant and integral part of the Pahlavi state. The Pahlavis owed their very genesis to a military *coup* in 1921, and, again, it was the armed forces which in 1953 ousted prime minister Mussadiq at the behest of the CIA and restored Mohammed Reza Pahlavi to his throne. By the mid-1970s, when the Shah's thirty-five year reign was nearing an end, the institutions of the monarchy and the military were completely intertwined, and as the course of events during the revolution demonstrated, the strength and the survival of one directly depended on that of the other. From 1953 to the very last days of his reign, the Shah embarked on an intense programme to expand the Iranian armed forces and attempted to build Iran into a regional military superpower, a process accelerated after 1971, when Britain withdrew from the Persian Gulf. The armed forces were given a free hand in purchasing whatever equipment they deemed necessary, although most of the purchased weaponry was personally selected by the Shah himself. Often the only restriction in buying arms was to find a country willing and capable of providing the needed hardware.[45] Iran's military establishment comprised the Imperial ground forces, the Imperial Navy, the Imperial Iranian air force, the gendarmerie, the national police (Shahrbani), and the 'Eternal Guard'. The gendarmerie originally served as the country's rural police when it was established by Reza Shah, but in more recent times its functions had grown to include general city policing as well. The secretive and elusive Eternal Guard was supposed to be composed of elite commando units whose duty it was to protect the person of the Shah and other members of the royal family. By 1978 the army, the navy, and the air force were reported to embody a total of 342,000 soldiers on active duty and more than 300,000 on reserve, while an additional 70,000 belonged to the Eternal Guard, the national police, and the gendarmerie, thus making the Iranian armed forces one of the world's largest military establishments.[46] Military officers enjoyed special privileges and prerogatives that were not commonly given to other employees of the state. Such measures included special housing, the provision of free domestic help (the servants were usually selected from among conscripts who did not have high school diplomas), exclusive social and sports clubs, and special discount stores. Consequently, a great deal of social prestige was accorded to military officers, both as a result of the regime's direct tutelage and also because of the officers' enjoyment of comfortable and affluent life styles. Accordingly, the Shah was hardly troubled by the possibility of a military *coup* that would depose him. During the revolution he was in fact opposed to suggestions that the military once again reinstate his monarchical absolutism and instructed the chairman of the joint chiefs of staff to make sure that 'no one does anything crazy'.[47]

All military commanders reported to the Shah separately, and the monarch held regular weekly audiences with his commanding generals. While no documents exist that could outline the exact line of command within the military, the Shah is known to have been the ultimate source of authority and to have frequently given orders regarding the day-to-day running of the various branches. The Shah required his personal authorization for the transfer of all officers above the rank of second lieutenant from one branch of the military to another. And the promotion of all commissioned officers was possible only after royal approval was granted, which in the case of colonels and generals was by individual royal decrees (*firmans*). All promotions to higher ranks were made in an arbitrary manner and were based on the recommendations of a committee that the Shah personally oversaw. At the Shah's whim, any officer could be demoted as rapidly as he could be promoted.[48] The Shah also required the issuance of his personal permission to every military plane to land at or take off from an airport. The permission was granted only for a specific itinerary and excluded any rerouting. Overall military strategy was devised by the Shah, while the details for its execution were left to the individual forces. There was also a National Security Council (*Shoraye Amniyate Melli*), which comprised the prime minister, the foreign minister, the heads of SAVAK and the national police, the directors of the military intelligence and the military personnel bureaus, the minister of the interior, and the chairman of the joint chiefs of staff.[49] There is no evidence to suggest, however, that the Council met on a regular basis or that its function was of any significance to the life of the Iranian military or the state. It was only immediately prior to the collapse of the Pahlavi regime that the Security Council played a determining role in the unfolding of events. It was later revealed that many top commanders had felt intense personal animosity towards one another and that the Shah knowingly placed them in contending positions in order to minimize the risk of a collaborated *coup* by his generals.[50] Representative of such antagonistic men were the commander of the ground forces, General Oveisi, and the commander of the gendarmerie, General Gharabaghi.

SAVAK

In 1957 the Shah established a security apparatus specifically designed to provide intelligence information on 'anti-state' activists operating both inside and outside Iran. The State Intelligence and Security Organization, SAVAK, had by 1978 acquired an infamous reputation for efficiency and omnipresence, and was accused by international human rights organizations of brutally torturing its victims.[51] Contrary to this widespread perception, former members of the regime have themselves accused SAVAK of incompetence and inefficiency.[52] It is not fully known to what extent SAVAK was successful in gathering intelligence or in identifying and arresting political activists, or how much the regime actually benefited from such operations. The primary activities of the organization appear to have been divided into three categories: counter-intelligence operations directed against the allegedly extensive Soviet spy network in Iran; the identification and often the arrest of 'anti-state elements', especially members of the two guerrilla organizations, the Mujahadeen and the Fedaiyan; and the placement of operatives within the bureaucracy to prevent the state's infiltration by those not loyal to the Crown. From the early 1960s onward, when the two guerrilla organizations were formed and became active, SAVAK concentrated most of its efforts on the identification and arrest of guerrilla activists and actually reduced its interference in the affairs of the bureaucracy. In fact, immediately prior to the extravagant celebrations marking the anniversary of 2,500 years of monarchy in Iran in 1971, SAVAK uncovered and imprisoned almost the entire leadership cadre of the Mujahadeen. The Mujahadeen themselves later admitted to having underestimated SAVAK's capabilities and its determination to foil sabotage activities.[53] SAVAK effectively reduced the abilities of the Mujahadeen and the Fedaiyan to carry out attacks against the establishment throughout the 1970s.[54] Within the bureaucracy, SAVAK maintained an operative in each ministry whose duties involved running security background checks on all employees and overlooking the classification of confidential documents. Each ministry also maintained contact with a SAVAK liaison who was in charge of overall security within the ministry building.[55]

Amuzegar's cabinet

The system of government that had evolved largely during Prime Minister Hoveida's thirteen-year tenure was dismantled rapidly after he resigned from office in August 1977. Jamshid Amuzegar, Hoveida's finance minister and Iran's representative at OPEC, was appointed as the new prime minister and Hoveida, whose council the Shah 'valued', was retained as the Court minister. While the Shah's appointment of Hoveida to the Court ministry was intended to ensure the monarch of the former prime minister's 'continued advice on a close, personal basis',[56] other members of the government believed that the move turned the Court into a 'centre of conspiracy' against the office of the new prime minister.[57] Little is known about the exact nature and the extent of the friction between the two institutions. During his brief tenure, however, Amuzegar pursued policies that were radically different from those of the previous administration. While Hoveida tended to cover up the system's internal contradictions and prevented problems from becoming openly manifest, Amuzegar directly confronted most of the issues within the range of his authority. The new prime minister curbed government expenditure, lowered inflation, and initiated moves to reduce administrative inefficiency. Thus government expenditure rose by only 7 per cent during 1977–78 as opposed to a 23.4 per cent rise in the previous years. Government investments in the construction industry, the main area of employment for rural immigrants, decreased by 50 per cent as opposed to an increase of 69 per cent during the preceding years.[58] As inflation was reduced, unemployment rose. Amuzegar is also said to have sharply reduced the size of the government's 'secret budget'. If true, this assertion explains the friction between the Court and Amuzegar's administration, since the secret budget was rumoured to contain unaccounted stipends to most courtiers. Of more significance was Amuzegar's alleged termination of salaries and bribes given to a number of opposition politicians and clerics who were allegedly also paid out of the government's secret budget to keep quiet. Almost all members of the Pahlavi establishment, including the Shah himself, claim that such a salary did exist but that it was discontinued by Amuzegar due to 'economic exigencies the country was facing at the time'.[59] However, no documents have so far been produced that would substantiate such claims or which directly link any of the opposition figures to payments from the government.[60] Amuzegar himself refutes having ever discontinued the clergy's government-paid allowances. The Religious Endowments Organization (Sazman-e Owaqaf), originally established in 1934 as an organ of the government intended to take over most of the clergy's financial obligations and to undermine their authority, did pay stipends to seminary students and financially supported religious schools (*madrasahs*). Such stipends, however, were considerably lower than those paid to the students by high-ranking ayatollahs themselves.[61]

Amuzegar and his entire cabinet resigned on 28 August 1978 amid increasingly threatening discontent and street demonstrations. During his prime ministership, Amuzegar had tried to separate the bureaucracy from the prevailing political currents and had concentrated on reducing corruption and inefficiency within the government. A distinguished technocrat, Amuzegar believed that the government's problems were primarily administrative and could be easily solved through technical solutions.[62] He therefore did little to tackle the incipient opposition that was beginning to mount against the regime, and his only political programme was limited to pursuing a quasi-official policy aimed at promoting 'an open political atmosphere'.[63] Theoretically, the policy was intended to ease censorship restrictions on the press and to give greater liberties to members of the Majlis in criticizing the government. In practice, however, the political atmosphere was never 'opened' and the policy was observed by literally none of the regime's own members. Amuzegar's departure from office was a direct result of the growing incongruity between his style of government and the increasingly volatile political climate. Amuzegar's resignation signified the imminent collapse of the regime. The state that the Shah had gradually engineered during Hoveida's premiership suddenly found itself unable adequately to deal with the pressures it faced from both inside Iran and abroad. In the course of the year that was to follow, the Shah tried to do whatever he could in order to preserve his dying system; yet the trend was not to be reversed. Within only five months after Amuzegar's resignation, the monarchical system had reached a point of irreversible disintegration and the only option open to the Shah was to escape from the country. Within those final five months, the Shah's despondency led him to change his prime minister three times, all, however, to no avail. Each time he tried a new tactic, he unwittingly deepened his own demise. The regime, with the Shah at its apex, had lost all the mythical resilience and survivability for which it had become famous. Combined pressures from the society at large and those that resulted from the inauguration of a new administration in Washington were overwhelming for the Shah and his system. This structural breakdown of the state was caused by two significant political developments. Internally, the regime's breakdown was facilitated by systemic flaws, which were compounded and exploited by the activities of the various opposition groups. Externally the regime was greatly damaged by the abandonment in the United States of the 'Nixon Doctrine' following the election of President Jimmy Carter in 1976. While these developments were not entirely related, their combined force had fatal ramifications for the Iranian regime.

Despite its apparent strength, the very nature of the Pahlavi state's institutions and the manner in which it had evolved rendered the state weak and highly vulnerable. This weakness was rooted in the shallow foundations of power on which the state was based. Revolving around the personality of the monarch, the state was particularly dependent on the Shah's continued presence, on his state of mind, and on royal decrees (firmans). The state's administrative apparatus was also in disarray, embodying an uncoordinated cabinet, a farcical political party, a symbolic parliament, and an inept and overgrown bureaucracy. The military institutions were also of little value in strengthening the state's political power, for the armed forces were designed primarily to counter foreign aggression, and SAVAK to foil foreign espionage. The state's weaknesses were further accentuated by its dependence on the United States, a dependence fostered over the years by Iran's access to special privileges in procuring the arms it needed and by Washington's increasing support for the Shah and his policies (see next section). The political crises in which the state was entangled at first and which ultimately resulted in the revolution were exacerbated by these very weaknesses. The economic slowdown after 1974 and the termination of unconditional US support brought about acute political crises which the state could not effectively deal with. Exploited by the various opposition groups, these crises ultimately resulted in the 1978–79 revolution.

US–Iranian relations

The indigenous breakdown of the bureaucracy was expedited by a number of international developments. Since the earliest days of its establishment, the Iranian government was dependent on the superpowers, particularly Britain and later the United States. Until the early 1950s this dependence often took the form of direct intervention in the internal affairs of the country by either Britain or the Soviet Union.[64] The Shah himself complained that in the 1940s the Soviet and British ambassadors to Tehran presented him with lists of candidates whom both superpowers wanted to see elected to the Majlis.[65]

The 1953 *coup* ended the overt intervention of the Soviet Union and Britain in Iranian affairs and instead made Tehran heavily dependent on the United States. The geopolitical and strategic position of Iran *vis-à-vis* the Soviet Union and the Persian Gulf made it a valuable asset for the United States in terms of the latter's foreign policy objectives, particularly in the light of intense US–Soviet rivalry during the cold war in the 1950s and 1960s. Thus Iran received generous US financial support and technical assistance under Presidents Eisenhower and Kennedy.[66] US *carte blanche* to the Shah was considerably augmented and was given doctrinal cohesion and consistency under the Nixon-Kissinger Doctrine. Based on the principle of 'multipolarity', the Nixon-Kissinger Doctrine aimed at developing regional middle powers under US auspices. Brazil, Indonesia, Zaire, and Iran were chosen for this purpose.[67] These countries were to provide stable regional conditions that would facilitate an orderly devolution of US power, thereby creating a 'linkage policy' in which superpower *détente* would take place.[68] In the case of Iran, the large extent to which the aims of the Nixon-Kissinger Doctrine and the interests of the Shah concurred in specific relation to the Soviet Union singled out US–Iranian relations as the paradigmatic application of Washington's foreign policy approach. Obsessed with the 'Soviet threat' and with the omnipresence of communist-inspired intrigue and conspiracy against his reign,[69] the Shah was more than eager to serve as the United States' 'middle power' in the region. Iran thus became the largest single recipient of US military hardware, loans, and other forms of assistance. Until 1978 US trade with the whole of Latin America and Africa together totalled $3.2 billion and $8.8 billion with South Korea. US trade with Iran, however, was more than $10 billion, most of which took place after 1972.[70] In 1973 the Shah proudly declared that 'we can get anything non-atomic that the U.S. has'.[71]

The natural ramification of all this was the growing structural and psychological dependence of the Iranian state and its leaders on the US government and its pursuit of the Nixon-Kissinger Doctrine in particular. With Jimmy Carter's election in 1976, however, the Nixon-Kissinger Doctrine was ostensibly abandoned and replaced by a new and supposedly more far-seeing approach to foreign policy. Hoping to 'remove reasons for revolutions that often erupt among people who suffer from persecution', the newly elected president declared that he was 'determined to combine support for our more authoritarian allies and friends with the effective promotion of human rights within their countries'.[72] In specific relation to Iran, the Carter administration's objective was to compel the Shah to be more observant of human rights without destabilizing Iran or jeopardizing the close ties between the two countries.[73] There was, consequently, great pressure on the Iranian government to reform itself if it wished to maintain its privileged relations with Washington. In early 1977 a high-ranking official of the Carter administration reportedly remarked that 'this is a new administration. If the Shah thinks he will get anything he wants in the arms field, he is in for a big surprise.'[74] In 1978, for the first time in many years, the United States refused to sell Iran electronically enhanced F-4 aircraft.[75] Similarly, there was a considerable row in the United States over the ill-fated proposal to sell advanced warning airborne control system (AWACS) planes to Iran. The Shah, who was always searching for signs in the American diplomatic language for his security or demise and who was paranoid about US–Soviet masterplans to partition Iran, was greatly disillusioned by his diplomatic setbacks in Washington and reluctantly started to initiate some reforms. In the absence of the major structural readjustments needed in order to maintain the system, such short-sighted and hastily implemented reforms only expedited the state's collapse.

Before analysing how the regime's reforms deepened the crisis it was in, it is necessary to see exactly what factors prompted the Shah to institute these reforms. He decided to reform his reign because of certain domestic developments and considerations. They included the realization that excessive repression could heighten the popularity of his opponents, his growing concern for the future reign of his son, and his employment of younger and more pragmatic advisors.[76] There had been speculations that the Shah wanted to transfer his throne to his son sometime in the early 1990s and he therefore wished to inaugurate a less autocratic and more institutionalized political system before then.[77] Furthermore, the same class of young intellectuals who had successfully persuaded the Shah to create the Rastakhiz Party subtly pointed out to him the potential negative ramifications that the regime's conformist policies might have. Added to these domestic considerations were pressures from abroad, resulting from both the policies of the Carter administration and the growing attention the international media and organizations were beginning to focus on Iran.

Despite the public statements of its leaders and policy-makers, the Carter administration did not pressure the Shah as bluntly as it may appear. Convinced of Iran's exceptional importance for the United States, the new administration was much more concerned about Iran's military and economic needs than about its violation of human rights.[78] President Carter in fact continued the existing arms policy toward Iran and endorsed the Shah's multimillion-dollar proposal for further purchases.[79] The U.S. Congress fiercely debated over the proposed sales and put substantial limitations on them.[80] Combined with the pronouncements made by some members of the administration, the Shah saw the prevailing mood in the US Congress both as a serious blow to his international prestige and as a signal to him to reform his regime. It was this psychological pressure that led to the reforms that followed.[81] The opposition groups, who were mostly as paranoid about foreign involvement in Iranian affairs as the Shah was, were also encouraged by what they perceived as US efforts to force the Shah to democratize his state and saw that as license to wage war against the regime.[82] Thus the reforms only served to push the state closer to collapse.

The collapse of the regime

There were two fundamental reasons why the regime's reforms furthered its own demise. First, those reforms that were initiated under Amuzegar before 1978 were largely cosmetic and were primarily aimed at appeasing Washington. Consequently, while doing little to rectify the structural inadequacies of the system and especially of the bureaucracy, the reforms permitted some marginal oppositional activity by intellectual groups. Equating 'reforms' with an easing of pressure on political activists, Amuzegar's cabinet merely facilitated the polarization of anti-regime sentiments throughout the country. In fact, the series of measures that the new cabinet did take towards reforming the regime, such as its economic austerity programme and bureaucratic 'house-cleaning', all had negative consequences of one sort or another. By trying to lower inflation, Amuzegar inadvertently increased the level of unemployment. His 'house-cleaning', meanwhile, meant that many high-ranking bureaucrats were made redundant or were demoted, thus depriving the regime of a potentially significant base of support.

Second, a more important reason for the failure of the regime's reforms was their inconsistency with the very nature of the state structure. Because of the way the regime was set up – its authoritarian conformism, organizational rigidity, and its monopoly over all forms of political activity – any moves to make it more receptive to input from the public at large or from previously unauthorized groups meant the dismantling of some significant state institutions. Reforming the Iranian state in such a fashion meant abolishing SAVAK, re-electing all members of the Majlis through new and free elections, and de-politicizing the monarchy and transforming it into a symbolic institution. Long before calling for the total overthrow of the regime, these were indeed the demands of the revolutionaries. They were also the main premises on which Bakhtiar promised to base his government. However, in actual practice these reforms were too radical for the Shah to accept and to the bitter end he refused to acknowledge the necessity of their implementation. These reforms meant in effect that the Shah would reign as a constitutional monarch rather than govern the country as an authoritarian despot. This involved a rechannelling of all civilian and military lines of command away from the Court and into the newly elected and politically independent Majlis or the prime minister's office. Neither the Shah nor the liberal administration in Washington was willing to go so far in altering the nature of the Iranian regime. There was no guarantee that such reforms could have saved the regime even if they had actually been implemented. Yet these were the only concessions that most revolutionaries were demanding prior to 1978. By January 1979 when Bakhtiar finally proclaimed their implementation to be his cabinet's top priority, the public had long abandoned such relatively moderate demands and settled for nothing less than the total abolition of the Pahlavi dynasty. The regime's reforms did not go far enough at first, and when they did it was already too late. Disillusioned and limited in the options he was willing to take, the Shah decided not to reform his regime structurally but instead to modify its response to opposition activities. What resulted was a procrastinating political system and a revolutionary movement gaining increasing momentum and hegemony. The regime's subsequent reforms and its attempts to appease the revolutionaries only served to further the cause of the revolution.

Prior to the beginning of summer 1978, anti-government demonstrations had been held in as many as thirty cities, including Tehran, Isfahan, Tabriz, Mashhad, and virtually all other major cities.[83] The first major demonstrations had taken place in Qom on 7 January and in Tabriz on 18 February 1978. The Qom demonstrations on 7 and 8 January were of particular significance as it was after their occurrence that Ayatollah Khomeini emerged as one of the central players in the events that were to follow. The January demonstrations, precipitated after the publication of a newspaper article that attacked Khomeini by name, led to the death of a handful of demonstrators.[84] During the traditional mourning ceremonies that were held on the fortieth day after the death of the Qom demonstrators, street marches again took place in Tabriz, and again in the clashes that followed with government troops a number of demonstrators were injured or killed. Anti-government demonstrations were held throughout the summer, spreading to more cities and becoming increasingly violent.[85] On 5 August, which in 1978 marked the beginning of the Moslem holy month of Ramadan, violent demonstrations took place in Tabriz, Mashhad, Abadan, Shiraz, and Isfahan. Two weeks later, on 19 August, a cinema in Abadan was set on fire and 377 people reportedly died.[86] Massive demonstrations took place in all major cities the following day. While no proof was found to substantiate the regime's complicity in the fire, the public at large saw the government as having been directly responsible for the tragedy. Amuzegar's cabinet resigned on 28 August, thus heightening the public's suspicions of the government's alleged role in the cinema fire.

As late as the summer of 1978, the regime had miscalculated the nature and the strength of the opposition. The government did not consider the *ulema*'s opposition to be significant or popular and thought that in 1978 the religious establishment could be as easily defeated as it had been in 1963. The guerrillas, especially those the Shah had himself labelled as 'Islamic Marxists', were instead perceived to be the most potent enemies of the regime. Khomeini was seen by the Shah as no more than a 'frail and crazy old man'.[87] The monarch, even after his overthrow, saw the universities and not the mosques as the main institutions that had fomented agitation against his throne.[88] The 'modernized' Iranian society was thought to be more susceptible to the appeals of the communist intelligentsia than those of the traditional clergy. By late summer of 1978, however, it had become clear, even for the regime, that it was the *ulema* who were in fact the main centre of opposition and that it was Islam and not communism that the government had to contend with. Administrative and bureaucratic house-cleaning, as proposed by Amuzegar's administration, was seen as irrelevant and no longer of any practical utility in quieting the opposition. The Shah decided to shift his strategy. He appointed a new prime minister with a supposedly religious background and ordered him to head a 'government of national reconciliation'. Recognizing the immense powers of the clerical opposition, the government of Prime Minister Ja'far Sharif-Emami soon began to appease the religious establishment and surrendered major concessions to the clergy.

The initial appointment and the subsequent performance of Sharif-Emami's cabinet signified a major shift in the overall policy of the government in relation to the prevailing political atmosphere. Sharif-Emami gave major concessions to the religious opposition. Nevertheless, in October 1978 the Iranian government compelled Iraq to expel Khomeini. The Ayatollah's attempts to gain asylum in another Arab country were unsuccessful.[89] He then travelled to France, seemingly because most of the activists he knew (e.g. Banisadr and Qotbzadeh) had already gathered there. The Shah had hoped that by being further away from Iran Khomeini would alienate himself from the growing opposition movement inside the country. The Shah also believed that the inevitable attention of the international media on Khomeini would expose the Ayatollah's backward mentality and would thus discredit the extremist faction of religious opposition.[90] Inside Iran, meanwhile, the more moderate opposition elements were appeased as the government continued its campaign to grant them major concessions. The commander of the gendarmerie, General Gharabaghi, was personally ordered by both the Shah and by the Empress to make certain that all demands made by the more moderate Ayatollah Shariatmadari were met.[91] Sharif-Emami, who had been the deputy director of the Pahlavi Foundation charity organization prior to his appointment as prime minister, dissolved the allegedly corrupt body and shut down several of its gambling casinos and night-clubs. He also reintroduced Iran's traditional Islamic calendar, which had previously been replaced by a royal calendar that began with the establishment of Iran's first recorded imperial dynasty. The time zone, which had been altered to maximize daylight saving time, was also reversed to its original setting since it offended many Moslems because it distorted their prayer time. More significantly, there was a sudden and noticeable change in the style of government, with the Shah deliberately abstaining from active participation in the political process and relegating more authority to the cabinet. Heated debates against the government were also voiced in the Majlis and were for the first time nationally televised. Having earlier informed his military commanders that 'the prevailing circumstances necessitate changes in the style of leadership', the Shah allowed more military decisions to be formulated within the higher ranks of the armed forces.[92] In the meantime, the monarch had surrounded himself with a group of consultants and advisors that was made up primarily of elderly political veterans and senior civil servants.

Sharif-Emami's performance and programmes were, however, greatly detrimental to the regime. To begin with, the prime minister himself was believed to be a grand master in the popularly despised Freemasonry.[93] To the public he appeared as an integral part of the corrupt political system. His seemingly impressive credentials were his biggest handicap. He had been an unpopular prime minister for nine months in 1960. A notable courtier ever since, he had served as the president of the Senate and had been the deputy director of the Pahlavi Foundation. The new cabinet, meanwhile, which enjoyed relatively higher authority than its predecessors, was besieged with internal divisions and disagreements among the ministers. Similar to previous cabinets, none of the ministers were consulted or even informed of their ministerial posts prior to their appointments. As the cabinet lacked cohesion and unity, it was unable to meet most of the objectives it had set for itself.

It was also during Sharif-Emami's tenure when 'Black Friday' occurred in Tehran on 7 September 1978, and when most major cities became subject to martial law. Having been unable to prevent or even to contain the spread of large-scale disturbances throughout the country, the government had for some time planned to declare martial law in cities where clashes between the demonstrators and government troops had been most intense. The decision to declare a curfew was made in an extraordinary session of the National Security Council, which lasted through the early hours of Friday, 7 September. In an attempt to prevent the demonstrations that had been planned for the next day in Tehran, the Council decided to put martial law regulations into immediate effect and to inform the public of its provisions through frequent radio broadcasts throughout the night.[94] The next day, however, many demonstrators gathered at the planned location as most people were unaware of the overnight imposition of martial law. Bloody clashes soon ensued between the troops and the demonstrators. Some reports put the number of dead at 2,000.[95] The military governor of Tehran, however, reported that only 86 demonstrators were killed and 205 were wounded.[96] News of Black Friday soon spread throughout the country when the government-controlled television station surprised the nation and broadcast brief footage of the massacre in its evening news programme. The imposition of martial law, however, temporarily halted further mass demonstrations. Nevertheless, within only six weeks after the appointment of Sharif-Emami, the Shah once again decided to name a new prime minister and to employ alternative tactics to regain the initiative.

On 6 November 1978 the monarch appeared before national television and announced Sharif-Emami's resignation and the appointment of a military government. He also informed the people of having heard their 'revolutionary message', promised to 'end repression and to prevent past mistakes', and appealed for public calm and the restoration of law and order (see Appendix). The chairman of the joint chiefs of staff, General Gholam Reza Azhari, was appointed prime minister and entrusted with the formation of a military cabinet. Within hours after the speech was televised, twelve high-ranking officials and former cabinet ministers, including Hoveida, were arrested and imprisoned, soon to be joined by three more ministers of Sharif-Emami's cabinet.[97] Those who were arrested included six former cabinet ministers, the director of SAVAK for fourteen years, and the mayor of Tehran.[98] According to General Gharebaghi, the Shah was also persuaded by some of his advisors to have Hoveida and a number of his former cabinet ministers executed, but was later dissuaded by the justice minister on grounds of not having sufficient evidence against the accused.[99] Many other high-ranking civil servants were either forced to resign or were relieved of their duties. The televised speech, the subsequent arrests, and the Shah's apparent willingness to have Hoveida executed epitomized the monarch's adoption of an entirely new set of tactics, if not his desperation. The Shah's speech explicitly endorsed the revolutionary movement, albeit under his personal leadership, and his appointment of a military cabinet at the same time demonstrated his resolve at all costs to retain control over the country. By cynically arresting former ministers and officials, he hoped to place the blame for the country's problems on former administrations and to distance the monarchy and the Court from an establishment that had admitted to being corrupt. Sharif-Emami's resignation came immediately after the Shah's speech was nationally broadcast. Within two hours, at about ten o'clock at night, General Azhari introduced nine members of his cabinet to the Shah in an audience in the royal palace.[100] The speed with which the new cabinet was inaugurated demonstrated the Shah's intention to attain quick results from his new tactics. Azhari was at first unable to persuade many personalities to serve in what was seen as his military government, but he eventually formed a regular cabinet.[101] Once in power, he continued Sharif-Emami's policy of reducing the Shah's role in the daily affairs of the government. Military commanders were told to make their own decisions instead of awaiting orders from the Shah.[102] Within the cabinet, a seven-member 'crisis committee' was formed in order to expedite decision-making regarding emergency issues. The committee, however, met only once.[103]

Initially the appointment of General Azhari's military cabinet proved effective in quieting the disturbances. The active engagement of the military in the political process as such was a rare development in the history of modern Iran, and the public was fearful of a military government and the manner and the extent to which it would react to the opposition movement. The armed forces and the degree of their vigilance during the unrest was also a major preoccupation of Ayatollah Khomeini and most opposition leaders associated with him.[104] The resulting fear and uncertainty temporarily normalized the situation throughout the country as demonstrations subsided and many striking workers returned to their jobs. The National Iranian Oil Company had for some time been producing as little as 1 million barrels of petroleum a day due to a crippling strike by its workers. But its level of production rose by 4 million barrels a day within one week after the military government was appointed.[105] The Shah himself claimed that 'during the first few days of the Azhari government, we still had hope'.[106] But the trend towards stability was soon to be reversed as General Azhari proved both incapable and unwilling to use his military machinery to quell the disturbances. The prime minister's lack of firmness and his conciliatory posture became evident only within a week after his appointment, when, in order to appease the revolutionaries, he started his inaugural speech to the parliament by reciting a Koranic verse. Furthermore, the military was unable fully to enforce martial law regulations since it had faced continued desertions and a lowering of morale and discipline among its personnel ever since Black Friday.[107] Azhari was himself seriously ill and within a month after his appointment he could no longer preside over cabinet meetings. Scattered riots occurred throughout the country in November. The 2nd of December, which in 1978 coincided with the beginning of the month of Moharram in the Moslem year, was marked by massive street demonstrations. Three subsequent days of violence left hundreds dead and injured. With prior government permission, spectacular demonstrations were held on the days of Tas'ua and Ashura, the ninth and tenth of Moharram, which mark the anniversary of Imam Hossein's martyrdom. By December 1978 the military government had visibly failed in its attempt to solidify and prevent the collapse of the Pahlavi regime. The prime minister had suffered a heart attack and was confined to his bed at home;[108] the armed forces had all but withered away; the opposition had acquired the overwhelming support of international public opinion and that of almost the entire Iranian population; and the Shah was desperately searching for a compromise solution that would be acceptable to the opposition. On 30 December, as a last move to save his dynasty, the Shah appointed as prime minister former opposition figure Dr Shapour Bakhtiar.

The spectacular Ta'saua and Ashura demonstrations in Tehran and throughout the country had vividly demonstrated the inevitability of the collapse of the Pahlavi state. Over 500,000 people marched in Tehran and thousands more demonstrated in other cities.[109] The demands of the Paris-based opposition, by now the most powerful authority inside Iran, had long included the abdication of the Shah, abrogation of the imperial constitution, and the establishment of an Islamic republic.[110] The military government had largely failed in its attempts to prevent the outbreak of demonstrations, and numerous industrial strikes had crippled the economic life of the country. By November some 30,000 workers employed at the country's oil refineries as well as half of the country's public employees had gone on strike, demanding higher wages and declaring their allegiance to Ayatollah Khomeini. The military was able to provide for its needed petroleum only when tankers from the US Navy rushed fuel to Iran's southern ports.[111] The Shah, meanwhile, was engaged in the provision and execution of several contingency plans. He had devised two hypothetical alternatives by which he hoped to save his collapsing dynasty: the possibility of a military *coup*, or greater liberalization and appeasement of the opposition. His stream of latter-day advisors were also broadly distinguished by those who urged greater liberalization (notably Dr Amini) and those who argued for tougher military action, headed especially by the commander of the ground forces, who was also the military governor of Tehran. A compromise between these two possibilities had crystallized in the appointment of General Azhari's cabinet. Amini had urged, from the beginning of the unrest, the Shah to publicly blame and punish members of the establishment who were generally known to be corrupt and to appoint a prime minister who would demand some degree of popular respect. Despite the Shah's repeated requests, and an assurance by Mehdi Bazargan, a prominent figure in the opposition movement, that the revolutionaries would support him if he were to be appointed prime minister, Amini consistently refused to accept the Shah's offer and to name a cabinet.[112] Before the resignation of General Azhari, the Shah is also said to have considered plans to have his top generals stage a military *coup*. With only one or two exceptions, the entire line of the military command was eager and saw itself capable of launching a takeover.[113] After the revolution some plans for a military *coup* were partially uncovered that revealed detailed provisions for the arrest of literally all opposition figures residing inside Iran and their imprisonment in naval camps on Iranian islands in the Persian Gulf.[114] However, even if such plans had been adopted, they were unlikely to produce the intended results since the armed forces were in a state of virtual disintegration: absences and desertions within the army were high; most injured military personnel were denied treatment at many hospitals; the opposition's propaganda tactics had been effective in gaining the sympathy of many conscript soldiers; and the morale of those troops who had remained loyal to the Shah was very low.[115]

The Shah was at first reluctant to acknowledge the rapid deterioration of his once powerful armed forces.[116] As the massive anti-government marches of early December had demonstrated, a military solution would not bring lasting stability for the regime. A further point that was epitomized by the huge processions was that the Shah and other members of the royal family were popularly despised, to such an extent that large numbers of people were willing to risk their lives in order to express their antipathy. After the marches Empress Farah was rumoured to have argued that 'if [the people] don't want us, we should go'.[117] The Shah himself had apparently lost all hope of retaining his Crown but was also unwilling to undertake measures that could cause further bloodshed.[118] His refusal to use excessive force in order to regain full control was largely due to Empress Farah's wishes. She did not want the future reign of her son, Crown Prince Reza, to be attained after the bloody suppression of a popular uprising. Having been turned down by Amini, the Shah then offered the premiership to two other notable moderate figures within the opposition: Dr. Karim Sanjabi, the *ad hoc* leader of the National Front Party, and Gholam Reza Sadiqi, a professor at Tehran University, also associated with the Front. Sanjabi, in a meeting he had had with Khomeini in Paris in November, had been advised by the Ayatollah not to accept the Shah's offer of prime ministership if such an offer were ever made. For his part, Sadiqi tried to form a cabinet, but was eventually dissuaded after he was publicly warned by the National Front of the adverse consequences of collaborating with the Shah. It was then that the Shah appointed Shapour Bakhtiar, another member of the National Front, who had once served as the deputy labour minister in Mussadiq's cabinet.

US foreign policy

At this juncture, a further axiom of the Iranian revolution began to manifest itself. As already mentioned, the Pahlavi regime was structurally and psychologically dependent on the support it received from the United States. Despite this heavy dependence, at this critical moment when the Iranian state was breaking apart, the United States, quite inadvertently, did nothing but accelerate the collapse of the Pahlavis. The Carter administration viewed the Shah as a strong and important ally whose continued leadership was instrumental in maintaining stability and security in Iran, in the Middle East, and in fact around the globe.[119] With the possible exception of a few low-ranking officials in the State Department, who saw the Shah's fall from power as a major victory for human rights, no one in the US government wanted to see a total discontinuation of the Pahlavi regime as such. All key US policy-makers – including President Carter, his national security advisor Zbigniew Brzezinski, Secretary of State Cyrus Vance, and the US ambassador to Tehran, William Sullivan – almost all of whom had their own opinion regarding the Iranian crisis, agreed on the fundamental point that the Shah's regime or at least the Pahlavi dynasty in one form or another needed to be preserved. Nevertheless, the Carter administration contributed to the advance of the Iranian revolution by its failure to come to the timely rescue of the Shah. US policy-makers were at first caught totally by surprise when they discovered that the Shah was faced with serious challenges that threatened the very foundations of his regime. The Shah's invincible image abroad had long overwhelmed any suspicions regarding domestic resentment or opposition to his rule. When there was finally the realization in Washington that the Shah was in fact faced with a revolutionary situation, the administration's officials disagreed over how best to handle the crisis. There soon developed a 'bitter and collegial contest' among President Carter's key advisors over the Iranian crisis.[120] State Department officials mostly saw the events in Iran as an ample opportunity to pressure the Shah to expedite the liberalization of his authoritarian regime. The Defense Department, headed by Secretary Harold Brown, and the National Security Council (NSC), under Brzezinski, were less enthusiastic about liberalization and were more concerned with the adverse strategic and international consequences of losing the Shah. They thus argued that any incipient revolutionary movement in Iran must not be permitted to take root, and if necessary the Iranian military should take over the government to prevent the regime's collapse. President Carter himself wavered between these two conflicting options. What resulted was the administration's failure to develop a coherent and unanimous policy towards the faltering Pahlavi regime. At a time when the Shah most needed it, US support was often fragmentary and inconsistent and its advice to the psychologically dependent Shah was often contradictory and indecisive.

Throughout the first half of 1978 Washington was convinced that the Shah was fully capable of putting down the brewing disturbances without much difficulty. Viewing the Shah's regime as invulnerable to internal threats, the Nixon and Ford administrations had done little to explore the nature of the domestic opposition to the Shah. The Carter administration's knowledge of groups working to overthrow the Shah was thus very 'sketchy'.[121] The US embassy in Tehran had also had very little information on groups opposing the Shah prior to 1977, presumably because it did not see any need for such intelligence data.[122] There had been certain indications of resentment among Iranian intellectuals against the Shah's authoritarian rule.[123] However, all intelligence reports reaching Washington invariably discarded fears of serious opposition to the Iranian regime. In August 1978 a CIA report concluded that Iran 'is not in a revolutionary or even a pre-revolutionary situation'.[124] In the following September the Defense Intelligence Agency (DIA) projected that the Shah would remain actively in power for at least another decade.[125] Ambassador Sullivan was equally optimistic about the Shah's prospects as late as July 1978.[126] The miscalculation of the Shah's fortunes was not exclusive to the US government. Practically no other foreign power, including the Soviet Union, had been able to detect that the Shah was facing serious trouble. The CIA's director at the time, Admiral Stansfield Turner, claimed that he knew of no other intelligence service which had predicted that the Shah was faced with an incipient revolution.[127]

By autumn the Shah's acute problems had become visibly apparent to outside observers, and US policy-makers needed to hurriedly devise ways and means to deal with the crisis in Iran. To explore the nature of the unrest, Secretary Vance instructed the US embassy in Tehran to initiate contacts with the lower echelons of the Iranian opposition in order to assess their demands, power base, and other relevant data.[128] The embassy obliged, initiating contacts with those it considered to be moderate clerics (e.g. Ayatollah Beheshti), members of the National Front (e.g. Bakhtiar, among others), the Liberation Movement (e.g. Bazargan), and to a lesser extent with members of the Mujahadeen guerrillas (e.g. Rajavi). The embassy tried to assess the extent and the nature of the Shah's problems, and it concentrated on expanding its contacts with the liberation movement when it realized that they had closer ties with important elements of the clerical opposition.[129] The embassy in Tehran, with its contacts with the opposition, turned into one of the State Department's main sources of information for formulating policy toward Iran. This channel of information was consistent with the humanitarian and liberal values that at the time dominated the moral dispositions of most State Department officials. Zbigniew Brzezinski, supported by Secretary Brown and later by Energy Secretary James Schlesinger, viewed contacts of any sort with the Iranian opposition as having the potential of undermining US support for the Shah and of being misconstrued by both the Shah and the opposition. All three took an avowedly hard line, trying to redirect US policy towards encouraging the Shah to use whatever means necessary, including the armed forces, to quell the disturbances.[130] Brzezinski's principal contact and source of information was Ardeshir Zahedi, Iran's flamboyant ambassador to the United States.[131] Zahedi shared Brzezinski's commitment to maintaining the Shah's authoritarian rule intact. Sharp frictions inevitably ensued between the State Department and the National Security Council over the Iranian crisis. As the Iranian revolution progressed, thus increasing the need for decisive action by the United States to save its dependent ally, so did the friction heighten in Washington regarding the appropriate policy to adopt.[132]

The United States drifted through the crucial months of October, November and early December with no particular, coherent policy toward Iran. U.S. policy was generally based on the assumption that the Shah's political survival was of primary importance. To this end, the United States supported whatever action the Shah deemed appropriate, including the appointment of a military government.[133] A similar hands-off approach was adopted by Britain's Labour government of the time and relayed to its ambassador to Tehran, Sir Anthony Parsons. Ambassador Parsons viewed the unrest as a 'peculiarly Iranian crisis' in which foreign interference would do 'nothing but harm'.[134] Such an approach by both the British and the US governments was hardly gratifying to the Shah, whose psychological dependence on support from abroad grew with the revolution.[135] Policy-makers in Washington saw the Shah as trying to stave off responsibility and to let the United States make the necessary but unpopular decisions for him.[136] The Shah had begun having 'long, discursive audiences' with Ambassadors Parsons and Sullivan on an almost daily basis after the appointment of Sharif Emami's cabinet.[137] Sullivan found the Shah to have become 'a totally ravaged man' who had lost all of his self-confidence.[138] Washington sent a number of high-ranking emissaries to Tehran to convey the administration's support for the Shah and to assess the situation. They included various CIA officials, Treasury Secretary Mike Blumenthal, and Senate Majority Leader Robert Byrd.[139] Yet no coherent policy was formulated by the administration. The unending contention between officials at the NSC and the State Department undermined the administration's ability to fully and accurately realize the gravity of the crisis in Iran and to devise clear-cut policy objectives to deal with the situation. Until December the United States refused to encourage the Shah to adopt 'any particular solutions'. Ambassador Sullivan's instructions from Washington were indicative of an absence of any clear policy objectives. 'We are not advising you or urging you', he was told, 'to go in any particular direction.'[140] It was not until early December, by which time the failure of General Azhari's military government had become a reality, that the United States began a series of concerted efforts to save the Iranian regime.

The Carter administration's first serious attempt to deal with the incipient revolution in Iran came in late November 1978, when it commissioned former Undersecretary of State George Ball to study the Iranian crisis and to propose possible solutions. Ball was brought in largely because of an almost complete breakdown of consensus and understanding between Ambassador Sullivan and the White House.

Sullivan had concluded as early as November that the Shah's loss of authority and his subsequent departure from the country were inevitable.[141] He therefore continuously recommended that Washington expand its ties with the moderate elements of the opposition, including even Khomeini. Sullivan hoped that such contacts would reduce the possibility of an extremist and xenophobic post-revolutionary regime in Iran.[142] While the ambassador's assessments found much appeal among State Department officials, they were forcefully rejected by both Brzezinski and the president. Brzezinski argued that 'a military solution in Iran was the only way to avoid a complete collapse'.[143] If the Shah's departure was an absolute necessity, then a military government would be the 'only viable option' open to the United States.[144] He thus advocated the establishment of a military government in Iran that could eventually become 'increasingly civilianized', as had been the case in Brazil and Turkey.[145] While not sharing Brzezinski's enthusiasm for a *coup*, President Carter also disagreed with Sullivan's assertion that the Shah's forced abdication was imminent. Carter, concerned with protecting his image as a patron of human rights, endorsed the idea of a *coup* in Iran only implicitly and as a last resort.[146] He proclaimed that the United States would do 'everything possible' to strengthen the Shah.[147]

Ball was given only two weeks to study the nature of the crisis in Iran and to propose policy options for the administration's approach to the situation. In his report Ball concluded that the Shah's only hope for survival was to cede authority to a civilian government. He proposed that such a government be chosen by a Council of Notables, itself made up of a broad coalition of politicians from varying backgrounds and persuasions. The Shah would remain in Iran, but his power and authority would be reduced considerably.[148]

Despite the initial significance that was attached to it, George Ball's report and his proposals were readily rejected by both Ambassador Sullivan and Brzezinski. The Carter administration once again began approaching the Iranian revolution without a clear policy. The seemingly decisive set of instructions Washington relayed to Sullivan on 28 December fell short of providing the Shah with a much-needed conclusive plan of action. On 26 December the Shah had asked Sullivan 'point-blank' what the United States wanted him to do.[149] After relaying the Shah's appeal to Washington, Sullivan received a four-point message in reply: first, continued instability and uncertainty can potentially undermine the morale of the army; second, if possible, the preferred alternative would be to form a moderate civilian government; if it were impossible to form such a civilian government, then a firm, military government that would effectively end bloodshed and violence would be the third desirable option; finally, if the Shah were forced to leave the country, then a Regency Council should preside over a military government.[150] Within less than a week after Washington's reply, the Shah appointed Shapour Bakhtiar as prime minister.

Bakhtiar's Appointment

Bakhtiar's premiership marked a crucial point of departure for the Iranian revolution. The appointment of Bakhtiar was the Shah's last desperate attempt to save his collapsing state. It is difficult to imagine what the Shah and Bakhtiar hoped to achieve through the latter's appointment. Bakhtiar's biggest handicap was that he took himself seriously. He hoped to reshape the monarchical oligarchy and to make it fully accountable to the 1906 Constitution, bring the military under his own firm control, and then use the armed forces to suppress the revolution. However, the regime that Bakhtiar hoped to preserve had by now collapsed in all but name. The armed forces, which were being deserted by an increasing number of soldiers every day, were reluctant to whole-heartedly support Bakhtiar after nearly thirty-five years of unquestioning obedience to the Shah. The revolutionary movement, whose forcefulness was demonstrated by a daily stream of marches and rallies, had also proven to be undeterred by the regime's military might. The Shah was himself aware of such facts and doubted whether Bakhtiar would succeed, even before the new prime minister took office.[151] Ambassadors Parsons and Sullivan were equally pessimistic about Bakhtiar's chances.[152]

Bakhtiar claims to have accepted the Shah's offer to become prime minister because he was 'resolutely determined to prevent bloodshed and to try to save the monarchial constitution'.

> Accommodation with Khomeini meant surrender to an anti-Iranian element who was also against freedom and civility. In the struggle for the life or death of a nation, one must sacrifice and bear heavy costs.... I am not someone who would be easily frightened off.[153]

The Shah's intent in appointing Bakhtiar was perhaps somewhat different. First, the Shah might have appointed Bakhtiar because Washington had advised him to appoint a civilian government. Bakhtiar's appointment could have also served as a face-saving way for the Shah to accede to the revolutionaries' most crucial demand of leaving the country. Finally, the Shah might have appointed Bakhtiar with the intent to shortly sweep him aside from power. The Shah would leave Iran and then Bakhtiar would command the military to crush the revolution. Thus Bakhtiar and the armed forces, not the Shah, would be held accountable for suppressing a popular movement. The Shah could then return to Iran triumphantly as he had done in 1953.[154] For his part, the Shah later complained that he appointed Bakhtiar 'with some reluctance and under foreign pressure'.[155] There is a measure of truth in this assertion. Ambassador Sullivan and his colleagues in the State Department had been forcefully arguing since November that the Shah and even the United States should find ways to accommodate moderate members of the Iranian opposition.[156] The appointment of Prime Minister Sharif-Emami had been a half-hearted attempt in this direction. When both Sharif-Emami and the subsequent military government of General Azhari failed, the Shah might have reluctantly come to accept Ambassador Sullivan's suggestion by naming Bakhtiar as the new prime minister. However, by the time of Bakhtiar's appointment in January 1979, neither the British nor the US ambassador thought that the new prime minister could realistically survive the revolutionary movement. In Washington, meanwhile, Brzezinski was arguing that the Shah needed to go in the opposite direction and to name a firm military government in order once again to regain full power. By the time he appointed Bakhtiar there was thus little foreign pressure on the Shah to do so. While having encouraged a policy of accommodation with the opposition earlier, Ambassador Sullivan saw Bakhtiar's appointment as too little effort that came too late.

By January 1978, when Bakhtiar became prime minister, the Shah's departure from Iran had come to be the main demand of the opposition. Having been 'appointed' by Khomeini, Mehdi Bazargan negotiated with the striking oil workers and was able to arrange for a partial production rise to meet the domestic needs of the country. The opposition thus acquired popular legitimacy. Yet the nation's economy was still in a state of collapse: the bureaucratic network had practically stopped functioning; marches and demonstrations often turned into violent lootings and attacks against banks, cinemas, cultural centres of Western countries, and airline offices and travel agencies; and most businesses were either on strike or remained closed for fear of being attacked by the demonstrators if they opened. The armed forces, meanwhile, were procrastinating. All that remained of the military were high ranking officers and a fraction of the conscript personnel, whose morale was at an all-time low. General Oveisi, the commander of the Imperial ground forces and the military governor of Tehran, had resigned from his post and left the country, adding strength to the public's impression of hopelessness within the military. Despite all the contingency plans in Tehran and Washington for a military *coup*,[157] the Shah had repeatedly asked the chairman of the joint chiefs of staff to make sure 'none of the commanders does anything crazy'.[158] His aversion to widespread bloodshed has already been alluded to and may have been related to his awareness that in any event the troops would probably have refused orders to mow down compatriots. Among themselves, the commanders had previously decided that the solution to the country's problems was 'basically political and not military'.[159] There was also communication, through a liaison, between Khomeini's group in Paris and some military leaders in Tehran.[160] Yet once it became clear that the Shah was in fact going to leave Iran, his commanders 'begged him' to stay, even if it necessitated a military *coup*.[161]

Bakhtiar's official appointment came on 6 January 1979. With great difficulty, he was able to persuade eleven men to serve in his cabinet, but the justice minister resigned within twenty-four hours after receiving the Majlis's vote of confidence. A four-star general had agreed to serve as the War Minister only after the Shah had personally ordered him to do so.[162] In repeated newspaper interviews, the new prime minister promised the quick departure of the Shah, the release of all political prisoners, the abolition of SAVAK, and a return to democratic constitutional monarchy.[163] On the Shah's directive, the chairman of the joint chiefs of staff publicly reiterated the military's support for Bakhtiar and discredited rumours of an impending *coup*.[164] An eight-member regency council, a body constitutionally empowered to act as the country's sovereign during the monarch's absence, was formed on 14 January. In a brief interview given in Tehran's Mehrabad airport on 16 January, the Shah announced that he was leaving the country for 'a vacation' and that the length of his stay would depend on his 'health condition'.[165] The country erupted in joyful celebrations and festivities. Bakhtiar had meanwhile initiated moves to meet with Khomeini in Paris, all allegedly designed as 'political manoeuvres' to win time and gain the initiative.[166] When the secret negotiations failed, Khomeini denounced Bakhtiar and accused his government of being 'illegal'. Many cabinet ministers were prevented from entering ministry buildings by striking civil servants, and the army was being deserted by an estimated 1,000 to 1,200 soldiers a day.[167] The *ad hoc* head of the regency council, Jalal Tehrani, had meanwhile flown to Paris and had personally offered his resignation to Khomeini. Bakhtiar had ordered the closure of Tehran's airport to prevent Khomeini's return to Iran, but was forced to order it open after bloody demonstrations took place in protest over his action. On 1 February 1979, Khomeini and his group of associates, by now the single most dominant centre of opposition to the monarchical regime, returned to Iran.

Although the Carter administration fully supported Bakhtiar, many in the State Department, including Ambassador Sullivan, did not think he could survive through January. President Carter, Brzezinski, and Secretaries Brown and Schlesinger disagreed. In order to ensure that Bakhtiar would in fact survive, Washington decided to dispatch a high-ranking military officer to Iran to rally the Iranian armed forces behind the new prime minister. General Robert Huyser, deputy commander of NATO forces in Europe, was chosen for this mission. Huyser had travelled to Iran on several occasions and personally knew most of the Iranian military leaders.[168] He was instructed to leave for Iran immediately, and to convey the president's concern and assurances to military leaders in Tehran. He was to urge them to 'remain cohesive and to work closely together' and not to leave the country.[169] Huyser's proposed mission was strongly opposed by his immediate superior, supreme commander of NATO forces General Alexander Haig, and by Ambassador Sullivan.[170] Huyser was equally apprehensive about the feasibility of his task. 'I did not see what I could achieve', he wrote later.[171] Furthermore, there were disagreements in Washington over the exact purpose of the general's trip to Iran and the meaning of the instructions that were given to him. Carter saw the instructions as endorsing a *coup* only as a last resort. Brzezinski, however, viewed Huyser's mission and his accompanying instructions as the green light for a *coup*. 'The purpose of the Huyser mission', he later wrote, 'was to lay the ground work for a military takeover, if it should become necessary, and in the process to develop the requisite leadership.'[172] By this time, Brzezinski had 'reluctantly' come to the conclusion that a military government without the Shah was the 'only viable option'.[173]

Huyser arrived in Tehran on 4 January and moved quickly to meet with all key military leaders. After extensive meetings with the commander of each military branch and with other top officers, Huyser found them to be in a 'totally helpless state'.[174] They were all concerned about their personal safety and wanted to leave with the Shah if he ever left the country. Most of them were also furious at Ambassadors Parsons and Sullivan for pressuring the Shah to leave the country. They also wanted the United States to use its influence to silence Khomeini and the British Broadcasting Corporation's candid coverage of the unrest in Iran.[175] They all argued that Bakhtiar could achieve very little, calling him 'just a man with a desk and a chair'.[176] Huyser also discovered that the military was faced with serious shortages of petroleum because of the oil strike, but, in his estimation, it was still capable of staging a *coup* if necessary.[177]

Huyser was largely successful in his efforts to keep the Iranian armed forces intact, especially after the Shah's departure on 16 January. During his extensive meetings with military leaders, there was never any explicit planning for a military takeover, although it was implicitly assumed by those involved that as a last resort the military option should not be ruled out. There were, nevertheless, some figures in the military command, such as the commander of the elite Eternal Guard, General Khosrowdad, who wanted to stage a *coup* on the day of the Shah's departure. But they were soon dissuaded after Huyser asked them a few practical questions about the logistics of such an operation. The commanders had earlier complained to Huyser that they were unable to devise plans for a *coup* in only a few weeks and wanted the US government to do the planning for them. Through Huyser, Brzezinski assured them that while the United States could not devise plans for a *coup* in Iran, it would alleviate any external threats the country might face, so that the armed forces could concentrate on internal problems.[178] Despite such assurances Bakhtiar, the armed forces, and even General Huyser himself were encountering mounting pressures every day. Bakhtiar's cabinet was only nominally functioning. The army was also faced with continued desertions by conscript soldiers and there had been signs of dissension in the air force.[179]

Huyser's presence in Tehran had meanwhile been discovered and subsequently reported by the press. His picture was soon put on placards and carried by street demonstrators, who added 'Death to Huyser' to an array of revolutionary slogans.[180] From then on, Huyser's continued presence in Iran not only threatened his own safety but also had the potential of arousing local resentment against Americans living in Iran. Ambassador Sullivan and those in Washington all agreed that Huyser's continued stay in Iran would be counter-productive. He had achieved the basic goals of his mission. The military had not collapsed following the Shah's departure, and none of its leaders had fled from the country as they had threatened to do. Instead, Huyser had succeeded in persuading the commanders to lend their full support to Bakhtiar and not to stage a premature *coup*. Given these considerations, General Huyser was instructed to leave Iran on 3 February.

The progressive withering of the Bakhtiar administration was concurrent with the rapid establishment of a rival political apparatus by the revolutionaries. Only three days after his arrival, on 4 February, Khomeini asked Bazargan to form a provisional government and to become the country's legitimate prime minister. The secretive Council of Revolution, which was set up to co-ordinate the activities of the revolutionary cadre in Paris and in Tehran, swiftly assumed wide-ranging functions in running the daily affairs of the country and in preparing the ground for the foundation of a new political system. Prior to his departure the Shah had refrained from making the usual arrangements for his military commanders to be in direct contact with him while he was abroad.[181] The armed forces were left entirely on their own and had only been instructed to obey Bakhtiar. For the first time in the Shah's reign, all decisions were to be made within the military ranks and were subject only to the prime minister's approval.[182] The military commanders, however, were unwilling to fully obey Bakhtiar's instructions instead of those of the Shah. When on 11 February Bakhtiar ordered the bombardment of an air base in Tehran that had been taken over by mutinous air force technicians, the military command decided to discard his orders and to declare its 'neutrality' in the 'political conflict'.[183] The mutiny had started on 10 February, when a clash had occurred inside the air base between loyal troops and a group of special air force technicians, called the Homafaran, whose members had in recent weeks demonstrated growing sympathy towards the revolution at air bases in Isfahan and Shiraz. News of the fighting in the air base quickly spread throughout Tehran and a flood of people rushed to the aid of the technicians. In the bloody armed confrontation that ensued, many were killed and wounded. The military command executed several plans to regain control of the base, but they were all aborted.[184] Fighting lasted throughout the night and into the next day, when several more police and army facilities were attacked and occupied by the people. Refusing Bakhtiar's orders, on the morning of 11 February 1979, twenty-seven commanders and high-ranking officers of the military met in an extraordinary session and decided to declare their neutrality. In their communiqué, released and broadcast from the radio immediately afterward, they announced that 'in order to prevent further bloodshed and destruction, it has been decided to declare neutrality in the current political conflict, and orders have been issued to all Forces to return to their barracks'.[185] Within minutes after the broadcast, Bakhtiar went into hiding.[186] Many of the military commanders who had issued the communiqué and who could be found were soon arrested by the people, while others escaped and became fugitives. On 14 February, five generals, including the longtime head of SAVAK and the martial law administrator of Tehran, were executed. Bazargan, the prime minister of the provisional government, appointed a new chairman of the joint chiefs of staff and promoted most second- and third-ranking officers to commanding posts. In March elections were held to elect new deputies to the parliament, soon to be followed by a national referendum on whether to establish an Islamic republic. The new system of government was approved by 98.2 per cent of the votes cast. The collapse of the Pahlavi regime was thus completed, and its successor was popularly legitimized. The Islamic Republic of Iran was officially established on 11 April 1979.

Chapter three

Opposition to the regime

Revolutions are brought about by the structural collapse of the political machinery on one hand and by the activities of groups and organizations exploiting such political exigencies on the other. A revolution will not occur unless these two developments overlap, whereby revolutionary groups can present a political alternative to the dying regime. When political institutions are weakened but there are no groups with popular support to initiate measures for the regime's overthrow, internal power struggles or palace *coups* may take place. But revolutions entail the actual replacement of political systems. Political instability is not a sufficient prerequisite for revolutionary development. It needs to be complemented with the activities of opposition groups that can mobilize people towards specifically revolutionary goals. This chapter examines the nature and activities of groups opposing the Iranian regime prior to the revolution and outlines their manoeuvres and initiatives during the revolutionary crisis. Added to the structural collapse of the regime, discussed in the previous chapter, the actions of opposition groups provided the politically determinant causes of the Iranian revolution.

Enthusiastic and active support for the Pahlavi state never extended beyond the confines of the countryside. The premises of the White Revolution, especially the Land Reform Programme, had increased the regime's popularity among the peasantry. Urban dwellers, however, had almost always been forced to acquiesce in the Shah's rule. The Shah was never able to gain any meaningful degree of support in the cities, except among members of the military establishment, factory owners, and other industrialists who were closely linked with the power élite. The regime, nevertheless, strove hard to maintain a populist image and to convince the public that they loved the Shah and his family. On almost every national holiday, especially on the birthdays of the members of the royal family, the regime sponsored grand celebrations and street marches to commemorate the event. On most occasions the Shah would not even show up himself, and the marches would parade to salute his portrait. Gradually his public appearances became even more rare and he eventually moved, even from one palace to another, exclusively by helicopter. Classes in most primary and secondary schools were usually cancelled on such days and students were led by their teachers to participate in the festivities. Flags were waved, photographs of the Shah and of his family were abundantly displayed, the royal anthem was played (as opposed to the national anthem), and patriotism appeared to mean the glorification of the Shah. To the public such pompous celebrations only represented breaks in the everyday routine, not genuine displays of affection. These shows might have been impressive in form, but they were void of substance. Their extravagance and farcical nature aroused the anger and the antagonism of a people always more ready to criticize than to revere a government that they certainly could not regard as their own.

Throughout his reign, the Shah faced three centres of opposition: the *ulema* (i.e. scholars learned in the Islamic sciences), guerrilla organizations and political parties, and members of the intelligentsia. Although one group might have been more active than the others in particular periods, all three remained actively oppositional throughout the Shah's thirty-five-year reign. The groups were not exclusive of one another, although they formed separately identifiable blocks of opposition to the regime.

Political parties

The Tudeh Party

One of the most important of the political parties was the Tudeh Party. At the height of its active period, the Tudeh, which for a long time remained Iran's only communist party, reached an unprecedented degree of popularity and significance. But from the start the party owed its popularity less to its ideological or political appeal among Iranians than to international and geopolitical influences. Ever since its formation in 1941, it followed an overtly pro-Soviet line of communism, and, without making serious attempts at concealing it, served as an instrument of Soviet foreign policy in Iran. In the 1940s and the early 1950s, Anglophobia provided the language in which Iranian nationalism was expressed.[1] The Tudeh Party and its Soviet connection, therefore, found wide-ranging appeal among the public. Beginning in the 1960s, however, the Iranian and Soviet governments embarked on a *rapprochement* and the Tudeh Party's popularity and significance diminished as a result. Even when the party radically changed its tactics in 1961 and chose to participate in the regime's parliamentary elections, as it had done in 1946, it was not able to regain the dominance and the respect it had once had and instead lost an even greater number of followers. Nevertheless, Tudeh's main rival at the time, the National Front, was unable to fare better. The rivalry between the communist supporters of the Tudeh and liberal nationalists who follow the National Front is as old as the two parties themselves.[2] Undeniably, however, until the 1978 revolution the fates of the Tudeh and the National Front were almost completely intertwined and had direct bearing on one another, especially during the earlier phases of the two parties' development. Both parties remained largely inactive in the 1960s and the 1970s, mainly because of their suppression by the regime. Yet the increasing belittlement of both parties and their eventual insignificance were as much due to their own flaws as they were to the regime's obsessive and deadly intolerance of any sort of organized opposition.

The Tudeh's formation owed much to the activities of Taqi Arani, a German-educated intellectual of Turkish descent. Born in 1901 in the northern city of Tabriz, Arani attended the University of Berlin and received a doctorate in chemistry in 1930. While in Germany, he became an orthodox Marxist and formed a secret discussion group after his return to Iran. The group was uncovered in Tehran in 1937 and all of its fifty-three members were arrested. Of 'The Fifty-three', as they were to be remembered, all but Arani were released from prison in 1941, immediately after which they formed the Party of the Iranian Masses (Hezbe Tudeh-e Iran). Arani died in prison on 3 February 1942. From its formation in 1941 until after the 1953 *coup d'état*, the Tudeh party evolved into a powerful political organization and enjoyed widespread support among urban Iranians. The National Front, which at the time was the only other opposition party and which competed with the Tudeh for popular ideological acceptability, was composed of a coalition of several smaller parties and therefore lacked Tudeh's monolithic and solid organizational apparatus. The turbulent and uncertain political climate in which the Tudeh was initially formed and in which it operated also accounted for most of the party's early successes. The Anglo-Soviet occupation of Iran during the Second World War, the absence of central authority and the relaxation of government repression that followed Reza Shah's abdication in 1941, and the heightening of xenophobic nationalism in Iran under Mussadiq from 1951 to 1953, all afforded scope to the Tudeh's ideological radicalism and enabled the party to consolidate its organization. Additionally, although the development of communist ideology in Iran dated as far back as the 1917 October Revolution, the Tudeh party was one of Iran's first communist organizations and was consequently perceived by many to be an appealing alternative to what was left of the traditional liberal opposition that remained from the days of the Constitutional Revolution.[3]

The Tudeh's initial successes were outstanding, but also temporary.

Within a few months after its formation, the party started to publish a central organ, *Siyasat* (Politics), and an 'anti-fascist' weekly called *Mardum* (People). In October 1942 it held its First Provisional Conference in Tehran, in which it outlined its programme and elected fifteen members to its central committee. Within a year the party was publishing four separate organs, and in 1944 it set up a 'Freedom Front' (Jebhe-ye Azadi), which was designed 'to protect and promote the freedom of the press'.[4] In August of the same year, Tudeh held its First Party Congress, in which three members were elected to the chairmanship of the party.[5] The party soon suffered a major setback, however. Having supported the Soviet-backed secessionist movement in Azerbaijan in 1945, many of Tudeh's members were arrested and imprisoned after the withdrawal of Soviet troops from Iran in December of 1946 and the subsequent quelling of the secessionists.[6] Following this fiasco, a number of moderates gained prominence within the party and started to advocate economic reforms and constitutional monarchy in preference to an all-out, proletarian revolution. The reformist intellectuals, headed by the socialist thinker Khalil Maleki, were soon frustrated and resigned from the party in protest in late 1947, and the Tudeh once again reoriented itself towards a Moscow-dictated line of communism.[7] The party's popularity once again rose and its membership and strength reached unprecedented proportions. In 1949 the Shah decided to clamp down on opposition activists following an unsuccessful attempt on his life and banned all political parties. The ban, however, was to no avail and by 1951 the Tudeh had once again become a popular and powerful party.

In 1951 Dr Mohammed Mussadiq started his popular but brief tenure as prime minister, during which he nationalized the country's oil industry. While Mussadiq never lifted the legal ban on the Tudeh, the party became intensely active from 1951 to 1953 and initiated several popular campaigns to aid the nationalisation campaign. A number of front organizations were set up, such as the Democratic Youth Club, the Iranian Peace Committee, and the National Action Committee, through which the Tudeh attracted new recruits and expanded its propaganda network of publications and meetings.[8] The party organized several strikes and demonstrations in Abadan in 1951 and staged massive May Day celebrations in Tehran in 1953. Throughout Mussadiq's premiership, however, friction between the cabinet, which was dominated by the National Front, and the Tudeh persisted.[9] Despite the myths that surround his character, Mussadiq was never able to overcome his anti-communist bias. Had he permitted the Tudeh to participate in his cabinet, it is possible that he could have significantly strengthened his own position and expanded his power base. Some of the Tudeh's leaders were eager to join Mussadiq's government, if only to share the credit for the nationalization of oil.[10] The party was instead continually harassed by both the National Front and the clerical establishment. The Tudeh itself saw Mussadiq as a 'national politician' and respected his 'anti-imperialism', but accused him of underestimating the zeal and strength of post-Second World War US imperialism and the ambitions of the United States for 'international hegemony'.[11] The Tudeh went so far as to allege that many National Front members were 'American lackeys'.[12] Towards the end of his premiership, even Dr Mussadiq himself was branded as an 'imperialist stooge'.[13] Dr Mussadiq was overthrown in 1953 through a US-sponsored military *coup*. The Tudeh later claimed it had had inside information regarding the *coup* and that it had continuously informed Mussadiq of the unfolding developments.[14] The 'inside information' had been furnished by the Tudeh's secret Officers' Organization (Sazman-e Afsaran), which comprised the party members on active military duty at the time. This organization was uncovered only a few months after the *coup* and its members were either executed or imprisoned.[15] It is not exactly clear whether the Tudeh's army units could have prevented the military from launching a *coup*, or whether they could have staged a counter-*coup* immediately afterward. The party itself later argued that the small size of its army units and their inaccessibility from one another would have doomed any initiatives they might have taken.[16] Nevertheless, even if the Tudeh could have prevented the *coup*, there were few ideological or even political reasons for it to do so. Mussadiq was no more sympathetic to the Tudeh than the Shah had been. Furthermore, as its units had already infiltrated into the military, the party might have calculated on the possibility of later seizing power from the incoming military government after the *coup* by its own military units. If such were indeed the case, the Tudeh had grossly miscalculated.

The *coup* reversed the fortunes of the Tudeh and the National Front alike. After the *coup* some fifty members of the Tudeh who had escaped arrest fled to East Germany and set up a party in exile, while others sought asylum in the Soviet Union. The party remained inactive for some years, but in July 1957 it held its Fourth Central Committee Plenum in East Germany. The Fifth and Sixth Plenums, held in 1958, were aimed at 'rectifying the party's past mistakes', and in 1961 the party decided to opt for parliamentary participation.[17] Such a moderate and compromising stand led to the development and later the separation of a Maoist faction from the main party. In 1965 the splinter group formed its own party, the Revolutionary Tudeh Party (Hezb-e Engelabiye Tudeh), but later changed its name to the Marxist-Leninist Organization of Tufan (Storm) (Sazman-e Marxist Leninisti-ye Tufan).[18] Prior to the 1978–79 revolution, however, Tufan never gained any real significance and hardly anyone knew it even existed.

Meanwhile, as most of its leaders lived abroad, Tudeh's rank and file inside Iran was heavily infiltrated by SAVAK agents. In 1969 the Central Committee's general secretary, Dr Reza Radmanesh, was blamed for SAVAK's infiltration. He was removed in 1971 and was replaced by Iraj Eskandari, who remained in his post until 1978. On the eve of the revolution Dr Nurredin Kianouri, who had been a professor at Moscow University while in exile, became the party's new secretary general.

Initially, the Tudeh's general leadership cadre mainly comprised professionals and other members of the intelligentsia such as university professors and men of letters. The party's rank and file, however, was not as elitist in its composition. While the mid-level echelons were mostly occupied by the salaried middle class, the bulk of the rank and file was composed of urban wage-earners.[19] During the 1960s and the 1970s the social composition of the Tudeh's top ranks was not extensively altered. Most of the party's leaders such as Eskandari and Kianouri had started their active careers as early as the 1940s and the 1950s. The rank-and-file configuration of the party, however, which was naturally more susceptible to the ramifications of social change and economic growth, changed from initially being dominated by urbanized industrial workers to primarily embodying wage-earners and members of the salaried middle classes. The main causes of such a shift in the orientation of Tudeh's social base appear to have been the government's curtailment of independent trade unions and worker syndicates and the concurrent growth of extensive bureaucratic networks in all urban centres. The actual size of the Tudeh's rank and file inside Iran, meanwhile, greatly decreased in the 1970s as did the influence of its leadership operating from exile.

The National Front

All through its life prior to the revolution, the Tudeh was faced with political and ideological competition from the National Front. The National Front was established in October 1949, when a group of intellectuals and political activists marched into the grounds of the royal palace in Tehran in protest over the absence of basic civil liberties and the monarch's lack of accountability to the constitution. The group was headed by Dr Mohammad Mussadiq, whose opposition to the regime dated as far back as the Reza Shah era, and was mainly composed of staunchly nationalist intellectuals who believed in the workability of the 1906 Constitution. Eager to offer a non-communist alternative to the Tudeh, this group of demonstrators later issued a statement in which they announced the formation of a National Front (Jebhe-ye Melli). The

Front was soon joined by four parties: the Iran Party (Hezb-e Iran), The Iranian Nation's Party (Hezb-e Melli-ye Iran), The Society of Islamic Combatants (Jame'e-ye Mujahadeen-e Islam), and the Toilers' Party (Hezb-e Zahmatkeshan), all of which had similar, nationalist orientations, but none of which was individually strong enough to compete with the Tudeh. Once formed, the coalition soon evolved into a major source of opposition to the regime and threatened not only the Tudeh's monopoly over opposition activities but the very foundations of the monarchy as well. The National Front reached the peak of its popularity and strength when Mussadiq became prime minister in 1951, but was never able to regain it after the premier was ousted from office in 1953. Nevertheless, even after the military *coup*, the Front managed to maintain an oppositional voice throughout the rest of the Shah's reign, and eventually it emerged as the only formal political party to make significant contributions to the revolutionary movement in 1978. Not unlike other opposition parties, after the early 1950s the Front merely lingered on, and, especially in the 1960s and the 1970s, its tactics and even its strategy appeared to the public to be outdated and largely ineffective. While members of the Front preferred to see themselves as constitutionalists rather than as liberals, a growing number of younger and more militant students thought the Front's moderate and featureless opposition was useless against the regime's despotism. Yet at the same time the militant guerrilla organizations were no more popular than the National Front.

Initially, the political line-up of the National Front coalition included a number of small and not very different parties. The Iran Party, which officially excluded non-Moslems from its membership, advocated a return to constitutional monarchy and called for the abolition of feudalism and its replacement with equality and social justice. The Toilers' Party was formed by two noted intellectuals, Mozzafar Baqai, a French-educated professor of aesthetics at the University of Tehran, and Khalil Maleki, who had previously broken away from the Tudeh. Maleki left the Toilers' Party in 1953 and formed a new party called the Third Force (Khatte Sevvom).[20] The Iranian Nation's Party, which was formed by a law student in Tehran named Dariush Foruhar, had a chauvinistic nationalist platform and called for the restoration of all Iranian territory lost since the 1800s. The Society of Islamic Combatants, headed by Ayatollah Kashani, drew most of its members and sympathizers from among theology students and Bazaari merchants. Once these groups coalesced as the National Front, the coalition rapidly grew into a significant political force and gained considerable popularity, owing mainly to Mussadiq's personal charisma and the Front's advocacy of the nationalization of the country's British-controlled oil industry. Candidates from the coalition successfully participated in the Majlis elections of 1949, and gained the majority of seats in 1951. The Front's leader, Dr Mussadiq, became prime minister and appointed a cabinet from members of the coalition.

As soon as he became prime minister, Mussadiq quickly initiated a number of popular measures. He curbed the powers and privileges of the royal family, to the extent that the unpopular twin sister of the Shah, Princess Ashraf, was temporarily forced to leave the country. He also reduced the national budget's heavy dependance on oil revenues.[21] But what turned Mussadiq into an almost legendary hero for all Iranians, and what has since become a milestone for the Iranian nationalist movement, was his stubborn and uncompromising determination to nationalize the country's oil industry. Until its nationalization, Iran's oil industry was owned and operated by the British-controlled Anglo-Iranian Oil Company (AIOC).[22] While talk of nationalizing the oil industry had been circulating among Iranians for some time before 1951, Mussadiq sought to realize this task at a time when other Iranian politicians were either procrastinating or merely indulging in rhetoric, and when the British government was most reluctant to surrender further interests in the Middle East after 1945, especially because oil had become essential to Europe's post-war revival. Given the incompatibility in the levels of economic and technical capabilities of the Iranians and the British to refine and market the oil, it is doubtful whether the nationalization campaign was realistically in Iran's immediate interests. Whether the public understood this is open to debate. What mattered was that such an act symbolized the regaining of national self-respect, the termination of British influence in Iran, and, by implication, the start of more drastic measures against the oligarchical political establishment. Britain's intransigence throughout the nationalization campaign further added to the elation of Iranians and to the popularity of their prime minister as a hero when they eventually emerged victorious. However, neither the largely symbolic national victory of Iranians nor the premiership of Mussadiq had any lasting permanence. Mussadiq was overthrown in 1953, by which time he had already alienated many of his former supporters and was even beginning to lose some of his personal popularity.[23] The Tudeh remained banned and its members were frustrated by Mussadiq's refusal to co-operate with them. The armed forces and the clergy had also become disenchanted with the premier's policies. The clergy, of whom Ayatollah Kashani and his Society of Moslem Combatants were best representative, were at first supportive of Mussadiq but were soon angered by his rigid secularism.[24] More importantly, Mussadiq had never had any real support within the military, which was generally loyal to the Shah, as was demonstrated during the *coup d'état*. In an attempt to neutralize the army, Mussadiq forced most high-ranking officers who were noted for their loyalty to the

Shah into early retirement.[25] These very officers subsequently became even more determined to oust the prime minister and to restore full power to the Shah. The international situation that had emerged after the nationalization of the AIOC, meanwhile, offered the perfect opportunity for the United States not only to take over Britain's interests in Iran but also to gain further advances in its cold war against the Soviet Union. Thus came the CIA's *coup* of 1953, ending a brief but tumultuous and highly significant chapter of Iran's modern political history.

Following the *coup*, a number of National Front members including Mussadiq were detained and put under house arrest. Dr Mussadiq's former associates made several attempts to revive the coalition, but none had any degree of success. In 1954 Dr Karim Sanjabi, who had been the minister of education in Mussadiq's cabinet, formed the National Resistance Movement (Nehzat-e Muqavemat-e Melli), but in 1956 the regime once again arrested most of its members on charges of undermining constitutional monarchy.[26] A Second National Front (Jebhe-ye Melli-ye Dovvum) was formed in 1960 and initially generated considerable enthusiasm among the growing university student population and the Bazaari merchants. *Bakhtar-e Emroz* (Today's Orient), the Front's central organ, was widely circulated and read on most university campuses.[27] By 1963, however, the National Front was once again on the verge of collapse as the regime renewed its campaign to intimidate political activists following the unrest that had occurred after the passage of the Land Reform bill. Meanwhile, some party activists were becoming increasingly attracted to religious ideology and were coming into growing disagreement with the more secular members of the Front. A split occurred within the coalition, and the Third National Front (Jebhe-ye Melli-ye Sevvom) was subsequently formed. The new coalition comprised the Iranian Nation's Party, the Society of Iranian Socialists (Jame'e-ye Sosiyalist-haye Iran), and, perhaps the most significant of the three, the Liberation Movement (Nehzat-e Azadi) The Front remained active throughout the 1970s, although most of its propaganda activities were carried out outside of Iran. It was not until 1977, when the Shah was pressured by the United States to ease some of the restrictions imposed on opposition activities, that the National Front was once again reactivated and briefly became prominent in the revolutionary movement.

From among the political parties that formed the Third National Front, the Liberation Movement was the only organization that remained relatively active in the 1970s. Inside Iran the activities of the Liberation Movement consisted almost entirely of sponsoring lectures, debates, and discussions. The lectures, which were often given by the party's leader, Dr Bazargan, were mostly designed to develop a theoretical synthesis between Islam and politics (see p.73). A more significant feature of the Liberation Movement, however, was the intense propaganda campaign it launched against the Iranian regime outside of the country. Such anti-regime activities abroad, especially in the United States, where there was a large community of Iranian students and expatriates, gained increasing significance in the late 1970s as the Shah became particularly concerned about his image in the international press and among world leaders. Iranians who were studying in Western countries had for some time been active in trying to 'expose the crimes of the regime'.[28] A Confederation of Iranian Students (CIS) had long existed in the United States and had by the 1960s become formidable enough not to be ignored. CIS was an umbrella organization that included virtually all anti-regime activists and students. By the mid-1960s, however, some of its members had become interested in Maoism. A number of religiously inclined members withdrew from the Confederation and subsequently set up the Islamic Students' Society (ISS) (Anjoman-e Daneshjoyan-e Islami). The ISS soon became an affiliate of the Liberation Movement and later served as a vital link in co-ordinating the activities of the revolutionaries in Iran and in the West. Most of the original founders and activists of the ISS had travelled to Iraq in the 1970s to visit Khomeini. Some of these visitors were later to receive government portfolios in the first post-revolutionary cabinet. Bazargan, the leader of the Liberation Movement, became the provisional prime minister; the ministries of Defence and Foreign Affairs were given to Chamran and Yazdi, respectively, both active in the ISS; and the powerful post of heading National Iranian Radio and Television went to Qotbzadeh, also one of the main figures of the ISS.

The Mujahadeen

Whereas the Tudeh and the National Front were suppressed after the 1953 *coup*, the 1960s and the 1970s marked the emergence of Iran's two guerrilla organizations, the Mujahadeen and the Fedaiyan. The People's Mujahadeen Organization of Iran (Sazman-e Mujahadeen Khalq-e Iran) was established in 1965. Its founders, Mohammad Hanifnezhad and Saeid Mohsen, had previously been members of the Liberation Movement but had left the party after becoming frustrated with its tactics. They had concluded that fighting the regime was 'impossible without weapons', and that 'the struggle had reached a deadlock and the only way out was to choose new methods'.[29] In fact, the regime's heavy-handed response to the 1963 unrests had left the traditional opposition in disarray. Members of the Tudeh had mostly been imprisoned or exiled and the clerical establishment had become fearful for its very survival. Furthermore, the Mujahadeen's founders were heartened by the conclusion that 'the heroic Iranian masses have demonstrated great readiness to wage struggles.... Our people, when they find a trustworthy leader, will not hesitate even to shed their blood in order to destroy the reactionaries'.[30] The new party's name, People's Mujahadeen (Crusader), reflected both the militancy of its leaders and the religious orientation of their ideology. In order to publicize their existence, the Mujahadeen hurriedly printed a pamphlet entitled 'What is Struggle?' (*Mubarezeh Chist?*), in which they outlined their short-term strategic goals, and soon afterwards formulated the party's ideology in a book called *Imam Hossein's Movement* (*Nehzat-e Hosseini*).

Initially the organization concentrated most of its efforts on forming cadres and solidifying a sound ideological framework. Recruitment procedures followed rigid guidelines at first and new members were subjected to an intense programme of ideological indoctrination. Such procedures were later relaxed as the party began to grow in the late 1960s.[31] In 1969 the organization completed the formulation of its strategic goals and tactics. It concluded that the Land Reform Programme had changed Iran from a 'feudal-bourgeois' society to one of 'dependent bourgeoisie', and that land distribution to peasants had neutralized the revolutionary potential of the countryside.[32] What was needed was to 'shatter the police atmosphere' and to demonstrate to the urban public that armed action against the regime was not impossible. Strategically, the main 'contradiction' in Iran was seen to be between the 'masses' and the 'imperialists'. The 'revolt' would have to begin in the urban centres at first, but would then naturally spread to the rural areas as well. The 'final victory' and the attainment of revolutionary success was seen to be possible through the formation of a 'liberation army' and by waging guerrilla warfare.[33] Additionally, the party decided to increase its contact with the 'revolutionary petit-bourgeois', establish links with other revolutionary organizations, and encourage more women to take part in its revolutionary activities.

Following its new policy, the Mujahadeen managed, with great difficulty, to send some members to Lebanon in 1969, where they received military training from the Al-Fatah organization. In 1971, however, some Mujahadeen members inside Iran were exposed to SAVAK and the regime subsequently arrested and imprisoned most of the party's leaders.[34] As most of its leaders and theoreticians were serving prison sentences, the party's already shaky ideological amalgam of Islam and socialism began to come unstuck and some of its leading members became increasingly oriented towards Marxism. This trend continued and became so extensive that in the mid-1970s there were two distinct camps of 'Islamic' and 'Communist' Mujahadeen within the party. The two factions split in May 1975, with the Communists adopting, but not until after the revolution, the name Peykar (Struggle), short for Sazman-e Peykar dar Rah-e Azadi-ye Tabaqe-ye Kargar (The Organization for the Struggle to Liberate the Working Class).[35] The break between the two factions was not peaceful, and the infighting led to the murder of one member and the arrest of two others by SAVAK. Years after the incident, the Islamic Faction, which had retained the name Mujahadeen, cited 'neglect of ideological education', the loosening of recruitment procedures, and the loss of competent leaders as the main causes of the split.[36] Peykar, however, saw it mainly as a result of the 'philosophical incompatibility of Islam with revolutions', and the subsequent need to replace it with communism.[37] Throughout the late 1970s neither of the parties was able to regain the growing momentum and significance they had gained prior to their split. The regime's security apparatus had in the meantime become even more effective and was able to prevent a regathering of strength by either faction. Until just before the revolution, both the 'Communist' and the 'Islamic' Mujahadeen were reduced to mere saboteur gangs. Their activities included bank robberies, assassination of US military advisors, and the bombings of the International Telephone & Telegraph and the Israeli Cultural Centre offices in Tehran.

The Mujahadeen improvised a grand theoretical synthesis between Islam and socialism. They argued that Iran's Shi'ite culture itself embodied 'great revolutionary potential'. Similar to Shariati and Banisadr, the Mujahadeen argued that original Islam, as practised by the Prophet Mohammed, would eventually lead to a *tauhidi* society, a society of 'unity', where man is united with the product of his labour, with nature, and with all of creation and ultimately with God. In a *tauhidi* society, 'all oppression and exploitation will crumble', and social solidarity based on Islamic principles will emerge.[38] In modern times, the Mujahadeen argued, the doctrinal distortion of Islam in Iran has taken place at the hands of the petty bourgeoisie, the very class with allegedly great potential for revolution.[39] Only with the 'correct' understanding of Islam could a *tauhidi* society be attained and mankind be liberated. The party was unable, however, effectively to propagate its ideology and to present it in a comprehensive form to the public. The organization's membership was almost exclusively confined to some university students and a limited number of middle-class professionals. The regime, meanwhile, had branded the Mujahadeen as 'Islamic-Marxists' and had effectively aroused general public scepticism regarding the underground organization. Unable publicly to defend its ideology and platform, the Mujahadeen remained increasingly misunderstood and mistrusted by a suspicious public throughout the 1960s and the 1970s.

Opposition to the regime

The Fedaiyan

The Mujahadeen were not alone in their efforts to wage guerrilla warfare against the regime. Unknown to the party, a gendarmerie post in the northern village of Siakal was attacked by a group of university students on 8 February 1971. The attack itself was a failure and most of the students were either killed or arrested, but out of the incident grew Iran's first communist guerrilla organization, the Organization of Iranian People's Fedaiyan Guerrillas (Sazman-e Cherik-ha-ye Fedai-ye Khalq-e Iran), the 'Sacrificial' Guerrillas or Fighters to the Death. Prior to the formation of the organization, the Siakal attackers had emerged out of a secret 'discussion group', which had focused on 'ideological education' in communism.[40] Adopting urban guerrilla warfare as its main tactic, the Fedaiyan carried out 'revolutionary executions', explosions, and attacks against selected targets throughout the 1970s. Such attacks were not part of an outlined and orchestrated programme, but were generally designed to present the party as a 'revolutionary vanguard force' that needed to use violence in order to 'shatter the police atmosphere' that prevailed in the cities (Table 3.1).

Table 3.1 Fedaiyan activities before the revolution

Type of Activity	Target	Reason given	Date
'Revolutionary executions'	Fateh Yazdi	Owner of Jahanchit factory in Karaj	11 August 1973
	Captain Norouzi	Guard at Tehran University	14 March 1973
	Captain Niktab	SAVAK agent	29 December 1973
Explosions	Roudsar Governor's Office	'Injustice to peasants'	February 1974
	Khorasan Employment Bureau	'Injustice to workers'	May 1975
	Shahrery Mayor's Office	'Demolishing the houses of destitutes'	Winter 1976
	Iran-American Society in Tehran	Pres. Carter's visit	December 1976
	Qom Police Station	Anniversary of Siakal	8 February 1977
	Qom Rastakhiz Party H.Q.	Anniversary of Siakal	8 February 1977
Attack	Tabriz Police Station	'Massacre of people'	17 March 1977
Explosion	Police patrol unit	'Suppression of demonstrations'	1 April 1978

Source: Compiled from Fedaiyan, *Tarikhche-ye Sazman-e Cherik-haye Fedai-ye Khalqe Iran* (A History of the Iranian People's Fedaiyan Guerrillas), pp. 4–5

While adhering to a generally communist-oriented doctrine, the Fedaiyan did not have a specific ideology. Party members relied mostly on the writings of Lenin, Mao, and Guevara. Initially, two of the party's original founders, Jazani and Ahmadzadeh, wrote a number of important theoretical works. Their efforts, however, were largely ignored by other party leaders soon afterwards. Jazani, writing while serving a prison sentence for his part in the Siakal attack, attempted to develop an indigenous communist ideology that would be applicable to Iran. In two of his most important works, *The History of Thirty Years of Politics (Tarikh-e See Saleh-ye Siyasi)* and *How Does Armed Struggle Become Mass Strike? (Cheguneh Mobarezeh-ye Mossalahaneh Tudeh-ii Mishavad?)*, Jazani argued that the Land Reform Programme had not only 'neutralized' the countryside but had in fact turned it into a base of support for the regime. A 'peasant revolution' was therefore impossible and the party needed to concentrate its activities in urban centres. Furthermore, dependent capitalism had evolved in the cities, owing its very subsistence and growth to the West.[41] Ahmadzadeh formulated the party's overall tactics, arguing that 'guerrilla warfare is necessary not only for military victory, but also for mass mobilization'.

> To smash the enemy's army, there must be a people's army. To create a people's army, there must be a prolonged guerrilla war .... On the one hand the mobilization of the masses is the condition for military and political victory. On the other hand mass mobilization is not possible without armed struggle.[42]

Because of the 'absence of class struggle in the countryside', the movement would have to be launched in the cities. The revolution would have an 'avalanche effect' and would eventually spread into peasant-dominated areas as well.[43]

While both the Fedaiyan and the Mujahadeen were gifted with some highly talented and energetic activists, neither organization was able to evolve into a major source of opposition to the regime. To a great extent, their failure was due to the lethal efficiency of SAVAK and the regime's determination to eliminate all opposition groups and elements. Yet both organizations were also responsible for their failure and for their lack of popularity among the public. Neither the Mujahadeen nor the Fedaiyan ever made extensive and co-ordinated efforts to familiarize the public with their respective ideologies and as a result both were viewed with general scepticism and suspicion. Fearing infiltration by SAVAK agents, the two guerrilla organizations remained highly elitist in their approach towards potential recruits and were consequently unable to gain a meaningful foothold among the people. For much of the 1960s and 1970s, both organizations operated in a social vacuum and remained grossly out of touch with prevailing political currents. Concurrently, however, another segment of the society, the intellectuals, were becoming increasingly important not only in their vociferous opposition to the regime but also in giving direction to the prevalent social and cultural values of the time.

The intellectuals

Intellectuals have been defined as those 'qualified, and accepted as qualified, to speak on matters of cultural concern'.[44] They are, however, inherently different from academics and scholars. While intellectuals 'predicate societal action', academics focus on the 'seminal diffusion of ideas to students'.[45] There is also a distinction between intellectuals and the intelligentsia. Intellectuals are usually a part of the intelligentsia: while the intelligentsia are simply better educated, intellectuals trade in ideas and reflect on them. The intellectual, therefore, is essentially defined by virtue of his or her relationship to social and cultural values. Through the utilization of ideologies, intellectuals elicit, guide, and form the expressive dispositions of a society,[46] thus either reshaping or reinforcing certain norms and values around which matters of social and political controversy revolve. Intellectuals speak against their society's dominant cultural frame of reference and choose deliberately to estrange themselves from the cultural superstructure. Such estrangement often arises out of the intellectuals' alienation from their surrounding environment and from other social groups with whom they cannot communicate and for whom they remain enigmatic and little understood. Social alienation and psychological frustration often lead intellectuals to be politically oppositional and to view themselves as the future leaders of a political movement. The role that intellectuals play in modernizing societies differs from that of intellectuals in more advanced, industrially developed countries. As modernization requires the transformation of both the industrial infrastructure and the cultural values that govern a society, intellectuals in such a polity acquire a special relationship to the rapidly changing body of social and cultural values. In modernizing societies, intellectuals' support for or opposition to the values at hand is at a more fundamental and grass-roots level. Such values have either not been fully adopted by the general public, or their adoption and popular social acceptance can be easily challenged by other contending values. In modern societies, in contrast, where values have long been widely adopted and form an integral part of the accepted norms of society, the intellectuals' support for or opposition to such values is not as fundamental to their popular acceptability or rejection as is the case in modernizing societies. In modernizing countries, therefore, intellectuals exert a higher degree of social influence. As the contention between varying values is more polarized in countries that are undergoing rapid modernization, so is the influence of the intellectuals, owing to the nature of their position in relation to those values. The more polarized the divergence among values, and the more fragile the acceptability of such values in a society, the greater is the significance of intellectuals.

In Iran, as in virtually all other modernizing societies, segments of the intellectual elite, even if at times minute in size, had consistently voiced opposition to the political system and the social and cultural values that the regime was trying to promote. In fact, the 1978 revolution initially started as an intellectual movement. In 1977 the Iranian Writers' Association sponsored a series of meetings called the Nights of Poetry, in which open opposition to the regime was voiced for the first time. But political opposition from Iranian intellectuals was not a new phenomenon. Intensified social change and economic growth, starting especially in the 1960s, had resulted in the flourishing of intellectual fervour. The political activism of the clergy immediately prior to the revolution also coincided with that of the intellectuals, although the two groups were broadly distinguishable by the nature of their opposition. The clergy generally tended to oppose social change and political absolutism on grounds of the ensuing infringements of the religious establishment as a whole and of certain fundamental tenets of Islam in particular. The intellectuals, however, challenged the social and political orders on grounds that Iran's society as a whole was 'being led in the wrong direction'. Ironically, the main intellectual current in Iran in the 1960s and the 1970s aimed at 'politicizing' Islam, therefore reducing the contrast between the secular and the religious opposition to the regime. The politicization of Islam was attempted within the camps of both the clergy and the intellectuals, a task that was in the end successful, with the establishment of the theocratic system of an Islamic republic. Immediately prior to the outbreak of the revolution, the intellectuals and the clergy had come to form an almost united body of opposition to the regime. Nevertheless, significant differences between the two groups persisted. While a general doctrine of political Islam did in fact exist, its origin was neither unified nor was its theoretical exposition universally agreed upon. Meanwhile, the intellectuals who adhered to ideologies other than or opposed to political Islam were either active within their own parties, or if on their own, they were generally not as vocal in expressing their opposition to the regime as the others were. To analyse Iranian intellectuals prior to the revolution, therefore, it is necessary to study that category of intellectuals who expounded on a doctrine of political Islam. These were highly influential socially although they were few in number. Most representative of this group of intellectuals were Jalal Al-e Ahmad, Mehdi Bazargan, Ali Shariati, and Abolhassan Banisadr.

Besides representing the dominant intellectual trend in Iran in the 1960s and the 1970s, the writings of Al-e Ahmad, Bazargan, Shariati, and Banisadr, especially in that order, signify the important evolution of Islamic ideology into a decidedly political doctrine. The groundwork was prepared by Al-e Ahmad, who discovered that Iranian society and culture had become 'Westoxicated' and pointed to religion as the necessary remedy. Bazargan and Shariati tried to make Islam compatible with twentieth century life, the latter going further by trying to revolutionize Islamic ideology. Lastly, Banisadr theorized about the nature of the society that would be established after an 'Islamic revolution'. The writings of each successive author represent stages through which political Islam evolved and eventually dominated the intellectual atmosphere of the country prior to the revolution. In the case of the writings of Shariati and Banisadr, the evolution of political Islam was orchestrated. In 1962 in Paris, where both Shariati and Banisadr resided at the time, they decided jointly to work on the theoretical development of political Islam. Shariati's task was to criticize the present, 'morbid' nature of Islam as it had developed throughout history. Banisadr, on the other hand, was to propose an alternative system of Islamic government for the future.[47] A comparison between the works of the two theorists is indicative of such an arrangement. Shariati's most important and controversial books include *Islamology, Ali's Shi'ism versus Safavid Shi'ism, Shi'ism: The Religion of Protest*, and *Return to the Self*. Banisadr's main works, meanwhile, are *Tauhidi Economics, The Manifesto of the Islamic Republic*, and *The Main Guidelines and Principles of Islamic Government*.

It is important to see why political Islam and not other ideologies gained widespread endorsement by most Iranian intellectuals in the late 1960s and the 1970s. Shariati and Banisadr might have planned together to theorize about the same subject. But why did the only other notable intellectuals who had anything worthy to say choose Islam as well? Why did Shi'ism dominate Iran's pre-revolutionary intellectual trend? Shi'ism became popular as a field of intellectual investigation in Iran only after Iranian intellectuals had experimented with its antithesis. During the 1930s and 1940s, a number of prominent Iranian intellectuals came to view Iran's pre-Islamic history as providing the core of Iranian nationalism. This older generation of intellectuals included such noted figures as Ahmad Kasravi, Dehkhoda, Ali Dashti, and Sadiq Hedayat. Often having fiercely anti-Islamic sentiments and views, these intellectuals consistently tried to alleviate the influence of Arabic from Persian literature and even raised questions regarding the very validity of Islam as a credible religion.[48] For some time, particularly in the 1950s and up until the early 1960s, this trend towards the adoration of pre-Islamic Iran was somewhat popular and its proponents were praised by educated professionals and other members of the intelligentsia.[49] Nevertheless, the trend never gained much of a hold over the public. Two reasons underlied this failure. First, these intellectuals were criticizing something to which most Iranians were deeply attached, namely their religion. Underestimating the strength of Shi'ism as a pervasive social and cultural force, most of these intellectuals merely engaged in academic debates over the superiority of Persian versus Arabic literature or Zoroastrianism versus Islam.[50] Second, the anti-Islamic intellectual trend failed largely because it was in concert with the official doctrine of the Pahlavi regime. While none of the older-generation intellectuals necessarily supported the regime, their glorification of Iran's pre-Islamic history lent support to the regime's justification of monarchy as a historically sound political system for Iran.[51] After the 1953 *coup* most Iranians, particularly the urban middle classes, were apprehensive of supporting intellectuals who appeared to be in collusion with a regime that most people considered to be a puppet of the CIA.[52]

Within this context a growing number of younger intellectuals began to look toward Shi'ism as a general frame of ideological reference. While Shi'ism was not necessarily thought of as a convenient doctrine for the formulation of Iranian nationalism, it was gradually looked upon as a political ideology. To most intellectuals, not only was this ideology widely accepted throughout society, but, if interpreted properly, it could also embody the right political message. They found Shi'ism appealing because it was distinctly Iranian in that it differed from the religion of the rest of the Islamic world. It was also something to which most Iranians were deeply attached, emotionally, culturally, and historically. Shi'ism was not alien or imported, while practically all other ideologies were. Most importantly, concern with politics had been a historically salient feature of Shi'ism.[53] It was these characteristics that prompted a growing number of Iranian intellectuals to pay more attention to Shi'ism in the 1960s and the 1970s. With the works and the writings of each intellectual, Shi'ism changed more and more from a religious sect into a political and, in fact, a revolutionary ideology.

Al-e Ahmad

One of the very first intellectuals to detect the need to change his anti-religious views and to embrace Shi'ism was Jalal Al-e Ahmad. Al-e Ahmad himself argued that his experiences as a child and later as a young man and his observations of the events that occurred during these years attracted him first to communism, then to socialism, and eventually to Shi'ism. For this reason it is necessary to present a rather detailed account of Al-e Ahmad's life in order to understand the transformation of his ideals.

Al-e Ahmad was born in a village near Qazvin in 1923 into a family headed by a 'despotic' religious father.[54] Despite the objections of his father, who wanted his son to become a cleric, Al-e Ahmad enrolled in a secular school and graduated in 1943. By that time Iran's official neutrality in the Second World War had been ignored and the Allied powers had occupied the country. The war had a profound effect on the young Al-e Ahmad. He recalled the war as having 'had for us no killing and destruction and bombs. But it had famine and typhus and chaos, and the painful presence of occupation forces.'[55] In 1943 he entered Tehran's Teacher Training College. Largely in rebellion against his father, he joined the Tudeh Party the following spring. He rose quickly in the party's ranks and edited and published several studies and short stories in the Tudeh's numerous publications. Disenchanted with the party's pro-Stalin policies, Al-e Ahmad and a group of reformists resigned from the Tudeh in 1947. He also grew disillusioned with communist ideology and became attracted instead to socialism. After an unsuccessful attempt to establish a party that would rival the Tudeh, he refrained from political activity and for some time concentrated on translating works by European authors such as Gide, Camus, and Sartre.[56] This 'period of silence' ended with the events of 1951–53, when with Maleki's co-operation he formed a small party called the Third Force (Niru-ye Sevvam) and joined Musaddiq's National Front Coalition. In the spring of 1953 Al-e Ahmad 'withdrew to the sidelines' because of a difference of opinion with the Third Force Leadership.[57] To his frustration with party politics was added the bitter disappointment of Musaddiq's overthrow later in 1953 and the subsequent reversal of most of the late prime minister's policies. 'The upshot of defeat in that struggle', he wrote in his autobiography, 'lay like sediment at our feet.'

> The defeat of the National Front and the victory of the companies ... brought about a second enforced silence that proved an opportunity for a serious self-look and in the reasons for those defeats for getting exact about oneself ... And this is how a young religious man who ran away from home and survived the confusion of war and its politics became aware of the essential contradictions of traditional Iranian social underpinnings, watching Western countries changing it to suit their needs and perhaps making another colony of it. These were the things that prompted *Westoxication* in 1962.[58]

By writing *Westoxication*, Al-e Ahmad intended to produce a social commentary directed against the cultural and technological domination of Iran by the West. The book itself is confused in some parts, poorly argued, and often reflects Al-e Ahmad's naive hopes. Yet the importance it had in discovering and analysing a new social phenomenon and its influence among Iranian students and professionals alike can hardly be exaggerated. It was a book that most educated Iranians had at least heard about, if not read. Its attraction lay in the originality of its topic as well as in its style of writing. It was one of the first books written by an Iranian author who was sharply critical of Iranian society and culture. Furthermore, it was written in Al-e Ahmad's characteristically lucid and plain style. It was not a translation of what a foreigner had said about Iran. Neither was it one of those domestic works whose complicated language and disguised message could only be understood and deciphered by a few.[59] *Westoxication* was sharp and direct, sparing no time in telling Iranians that they had a 'diseased' society on their hands.[60] It was, in fact, largely because of the provocative nature of *Westoxication* that the intellectual flurry that had been put to rest by the 1953 *coup* was once again reactivated.

In *Westoxication*, Al-e Ahmad argued that Iran is dominated by the West in two areas: in its technological and industrial development and in its culture. He argued that while modernization is a desired objective in itself, its imposition on Iran by Western companies had resulted in the 'Westoxication' of the country.[61] Western economic concerns, particularly the oil cartels, according to Al-e Ahmad, control Iran's economic and political destiny.[62] To combat this domination, Iranians need to produce machines and factories themselves instead of merely importing the tools and the goods they need. In discussing the social ramifications of 'Westoxication', Al-e Ahmad concentrated on the individual rather than on the society as a whole. He described the 'Westoxicated' person as relatively well-educated, nominally religious, 'hippy-like', inattentive to the needs of his society, and instead interested in what goes on in Europe and the United States.[63]

Another topic that Al-e Ahmad discussed in *Westoxication* was the question of democracy in Iran. He argued that none of the types of freedom essential to a democratic system – freedom of speech, assembly, and voting – existed in Iran, despite the government's insistence that the regime was indeed democratic.[64] True democracy, he claimed, could only be possible when all feudal relations had been obliterated, when the mass media became completely free of government control, and when SAVAK and the police forces stopped harassing political activists.[65]

Four years after *Westoxication*, Al-e Ahmad wrote a second book called *On the Service and the Disservice of Intellectuals*. Except for the publication of a few of its chapters in different journals, this latter book was not published in its entirety until the government eased its censorship restrictions before the revolution in 1978. Although the book was not necessarily directed against the political establishment, the government appears to have prevented its publication because of Al-e Ahmad's reputation as a bold and controversial social commentator after his publication of *Westoxication*. Quite contrary to the government's apparent assumption, *On the Service and the Disservice of Intellectuals* is far from being another social commentary similar to *Westoxication*. Al-e Ahmad wrote the two works with completely different purposes in mind. The earlier work was intended for the consumption of the public at large. Whoever was literate enough to read could read *Westoxication*, understand it, perhaps even identify with the Westox- icated or traditional characters that Al-e Ahmad critiqued, and form an opinion on the subject. *On the Service and the Disservice of Intellectuals* was written for a much smaller circle of readers, namely the intellectuals. To begin with, the book's style of writing is not as simple and as easily understandable as in Al-e Ahmad's previous works. Some of its chapters are also direct translations of works that Western authors such as Gramsci and Sartre have written on the subject of intellectuals. If *Westoxication* was 'the diagnosis of a disease' written for a mass of patients, *On the Service and the Disservice of Intellectuals* was a prescription written for a handful of physicians Al-e Ahmad wished to put in charge of curing the society.

In analysing Iranian intellectuals, Al-e Ahmad claimed that they had failed completely to fulfil their responsibilities to their people and to their society. To begin with, Iranian intellectuals needed to realize that they live in a semi-colonial society and they thus needed to stop looking at Iran as if it were a Western country.[66] Moreover, Al-e Ahmad argued, since most Iranian intellectuals were educated in the West, they cannot understand and appreciate the complexities of their own culture and most are alienated from their society.[67] Al-e Ahmad accused Iranian intellectuals of either becoming 'agents of imperialism' and helping to expedite the country's 'Westoxication' or going into academia and concerning themselves with the study of abstract Western philosophies.[68] In one way or another, Al-e Ahmad claimed, Iranian intellectuals ignore the problems of the society in which they live.

While Al-e Ahmad's analyses of culture and intellectualdom were laid out in sociological works, his views on Islam and Shi'ism were expressed mostly through his short stories. Although he tried to 'rebel' against the religious orthodoxy that his father subjected him to in his early childhood,[69] he endorsed religion shortly after his break with the Tudeh. His widow later claimed that Al-e Ahmad's 'relative return to religion ... was a way toward deliverance from the evil of imperialism and toward the preservation of national identity ... Jalal had need of such religion.'[70] Al-e Ahmad's increasingly uneasy awareness of cultural Westernization led him to discover Shi'ism as the one element that could revive the country's cultural and national identity. Frustrated with communism and socialism, he turned to religion. But he was unwilling to endorse the orthodox Shi'ism of the kind his father practised. Although he never specified it in his writings, he wanted a new Shi'ism, one that would be free of the morbid and the inhibiting rituals that had become such an ingrained part of that religion. A 'progressive' Shi'ism, he believed, could be the country's salvation in the face of rampant 'Westoxication'.

'The Pilgrimage' is one of Al-e Ahmad's short stories in which he endorsed and glorified Shi'ism. In a number of other stories, he qualified his endorsement of Shi'ism by criticizing its overwhelming ritualistic and static nature. 'The Untimely Breaking of the Fast', 'Seh'tar', and 'The Sin' are representative of the stories in which Al-e Ahmad criticized the way Shi'ite institutions, regulations, and customs can become barriers to the progress of most Iranians.[71] He valued Shi'ism not necessarily as a religion as such but rather as a force capable of putting an end to Iran's 'Westoxication'. His recognition of the importance of Shi'ism was demonstrated by the preponderance of religious themes in his stories and essays. However, he went no further than to criticize the possible adverse effects that Shi'ite rites can have on the people and stopped short of formulating a doctrine of political Islam. What Al-e Ahmad did was to lay the groundwork for others to build on in devising a doctrine of political Islam. This task was partially fulfilled by Mehdi Bazargan.

Mehdi Bazargan

Similar to Banisadr and Shariati, Bazargan attempted to lay the theoretical foundations of a political Islam. He saw the Islamic doctrine, as elaborated in the Koran, as deliberately ambiguous in its details in order to retain a persistent but metaphoric applicability throughout history while still maintaining its basic guidelines and principles.[72] Historically, he argued, 'Moslemhood' has itself come to be the Moslems' greatest source of misery and backwardness. 'Islam, a religion of action, trials, crusades, and justice has turned into a worshippers' religion only good for verbal protestation.'[73] The perversion of original Islam, 'a disservice of our ancestors',[74] must be corrected through a 'renaissance' based on the logic of the Koran.[75] This renaissance, according to Bazargan, must be consonant with Iranian culture and cannot take place without an understanding by the Iranians of their own history and society. Bazargan criticized the Iranian mentality, which he said was meek, untidy, and unstable.[76] Iranians must realize their 'historic flaws', re-think their life styles, and become more industrious.[77] Within the political sphere, majority rule, which was practised by prophets Mohammad and Ali, is inviolable,[78] and personal freedom is a divine right.[79] Freedom is not confined to men, for Islam guarantees equality and freedom for women as well.[80]

Bazargan's main essays and lectures were directed at creating a general framework within which a 'rejuvenated' Islam could once again be politicized and would regain its compatibility with the culture of today. He saw Islam as an ideology through which technical progress, political independence, and personal freedom would become obtainable. Nevertheless, perhaps largely due to harassment by the regime, Bazargan was unable or unwilling to write a single and coherent theoretical work expounding on his ideas. While his writings are within the general framework of political Islam, they appear uncoordinated and scattered. Unlike Al-e Ahmad, who had access to a somewhat larger audience through his books and short stories, Bazargan had a much more limited forum through which he could present his ideas. Very few people, such as those who remembered his alliance with Mussadiq and some university students who knew him because of his position as the dean of the engineering college at Tehran University, had actually heard of Bazargan's name or were aware of his ideological stands. The fragmentary nature of most of Bazargan's writings, coupled with their inaccessibility to the public at large, resulted in Bazargan's general recognition as a political activist rather than as an ideologue or a theorist. None the less, an increasing number of intellectuals gradually began to gain access to Bazargan's writings and became familiar with his views. Among the small circle of university instructors, essayists, and politically minded students, Bazargan was a noted figure. To most of these intellectuals Bazargan's writings were at least intriguing if not necessarily appealing. One such intellectual, Shariati, shared Bazargan's belief that Iran's moral and socio-cultural salvation could be found in religion. While Shariati's Islamic ideology did not directly grow out of what Bazargan had said earlier, his writings complemented Bazargan's works and helped further construct a theoretical frame of reference for political Islam.

Shariati

Ali Shariati was born into a religious family in 1933 in a village in the province of Khorasan. After graduating from the Faculty of Letters at Ferdowsi University in Mashhad, he was sent to France on a state scholarship in 1960, where he studied sociology at the Sorbonne under the orientalist Louis Massignon. Writing his doctoral dissertation on Persian philology, Dr Shariati returned to Iran in 1964. He was arrested at the Turkish border, however, as he had been active against the Iranian regime during his student years in France. He was released the following year and received a teaching position at Ferdowsi University in 1966. In 1969 he was either dismissed or compelled to leave his post and joined a newly established informal religious institute in Tehran called the Hosseini-ye Ershad. The institute, which sponsored lectures and seminars on Islam, was closed down by government authorities in 1973 and many of its officials, including Shariati, were imprisoned. Shariati was released in January 1975, but was kept under house arrest in his native village until 1977. In June of that year he was permitted to leave Iran for Britain, where shortly after his arrival he was found dead on 19 June 1977. While an autopsy determined heart attack to have been the cause of his death, opponents of the regime saw it as the work of SAVAK.

Similar to Banisadr, Shariati argued that the original *tauhidi* religion of Islam had been corrupted and abused and had been replaced with a system of rites designed to manipulate and to maintain the social and political status quo. Shariati defined *tauhid* (unity), literally meaning monotheism, as a religion of revolution, a means by which man can escape from the void of his self and can instead attain a divine zenith.[81] *Tauhid*, he argued, is a 'revolution of enlightenment', a whole system of life. It is a society in which there is unity among all social and economic classes. Today's Islam, Shariati claimed, is not the religion of *tauhid* that the prophet Mohammad originally practised, and it has become the concern of only the clergy. Islam has been 'depoliticized' and its revolutionary dynamism has been undermined. It has changed from a comprehensive ideology into a tradition.[82] In Iran the 'historic corruption' of Islam took place when Shah Ismail Safavi made Shi'ism the country's 'state religion' in 1501. To maintain power and to passify the opposition, the Safavids separated religion from politics and made Shi'ism a field exclusively concerned with jurisprudence and ethics. Several core Shi'ite principles were thus corrupted and the original Shi'ism of prophet Ali became contradictory to the Safavid Shi'ism. In a celebrated work, Shariati compared the two types of Shi'ism (Table 3.2).

Having thus differentiated between the Shi'ism of Ali and Safavid Shi'ism, Shariati then outlined solutions to what he saw to be the ills of Iranian society. He claimed that 'the most urgent task' in Iran and in other 'backward' countries is to bridge the gap between the intellectuals and the masses.[83] Echoing one of Al-e Ahmad's main concerns, Shariati asserted that intellectuals must become 'socially responsible': they must inject a sense of self-awareness into their society and must lead its people in the direction of *tauhid*. In their task, intellectuals must refrain from all the 'isms' and must instead seek shelter in their religion and nationality. To counter Western cultural imperialism, they must

Table 3.2 Comparison of the two types of Shi'ism

	Ali's Shi'ism	Safavid Shi'ism
Visayat (appointment as trustee)	The prophet's appointing, by God's command, the most suitable and right people in his family, on the basis of knowledge, to leadership.	The principle of government by designation, based on dynastic inheritance founded on descent and kinship alone.
Imamat (leadership)	Pure, revolutionary leadership for guiding the people and the true construction of society, leading to the latter's awareness, growth, and independence of judgement of human beings who incarnate the religion.	Belief in 12 pure, sacred and supernatural souls, superhuman beings who are the only means of approaching and having recourse to God; of meditation; 12 angels to worship, hidden creatures akin to deities.
Intizar (Awaiting)	Spiritual, ideational, and practical preparedness for reform, revolution, changing the world situation, decisive belief in the elimination of tyranny, victory of justice, and the coming into its own of the deprived class, the masses' inheritance of the earth, in tandem with true, self-made men of the world revolution.	Being at spiritual, ideational and practical ease in submitting to the status quo; explaining away corruption; fatalism about everything; rejecting responsibility; despair about reform; prior surrender before taking any step.
Ijtihad (Exegesis)	A factor for the movement of religion through time; the companion of history; permanent revolution and integrative revolution in the outlook of religion; a legal perfection and reconciling in changes and development of the system.	A factor of stultification and ossification; a block to progress, change, and transformation; a means of blasphemy and perfidy; an absolute censure of any new act on the path of religion, system, life, thought, knowledge, society, everything.
Taqlid (Imitation)	A logical, scientific, natural, and necessary link between a layman or non-specialist with an aim of religion on practical and legal questions that have a technical or expertise aspect to them.	Blind obedience to a clergyman; absolute subordination, with no questions asked, to the mind opinion, or decision of clergymen; or, in the words of the Qur-an: worship of a religious man of the spirit.

Quoted in Shahrough Akhavi, *Religion and Politics in Contemporary Iran* (Albany, NY: SUNY Press, 1980), pp. 231–33.

embrace the principle of 'return to the self'.[84] The Shi'ism of Ali, meanwhile, must destroy and replace Safavid Shi'ism.[85] Islamic personalities such as Mohammad, Ali, and Fatimeh must all be studied and emulated as role models for Iranian men and women. The supernatural and magical characteristics that have been attributed to these figures must be discarded, and instead their attitudes and responsibilities toward their society must be scrutinized and learned from. Islam must once again become all-embracing.

Abolhassan Banisadr

Similar to Shariati, Banisadr was educated in France, although he deliberately delayed the submission of his doctoral dissertation to Sorbonne University in order to avoid having to return to Iran and facing possible imprisonment. Born in 1933 into a religious family in Hamadan, Banisadr at first attended the University of Tehran where he became active in the National Front. He moved to France in 1962 and intensified his activities against the Iranian regime. It was at this time that he met Shariati and started closely to collaborate with him. In an effort to lay down the theoretical foundations of a future Islamic society, Banisadr wrote a number of important works, among them *Tauhidi Economics*, *The Manifesto of the Islamic Republic*, and *The Main Principles and Guidelines of Islamic Government*. In such works Banisadr formulated the foundations of a government that would excel man in a '*tauhdi* direction' and which would be based on Islamic tenets. His works also include *The Cult of Personality*, a study of social and psychological traits that lead to despotism and autocracy; *Equilibriums*, an outline of how the main pillars of Islam lead to the divine ascension of man; and *Petrole et Violence*, co-authored with the French sociologist Paul Vielle, which is an analysis of the dependent economies of some Third World oil-producing states.

The Manifesto of the Islamic Republic, written in 1971, comprises two main sections. In the first, Banisadr gives a critical analysis of Iran's economic, political, and social conditions under the Shah. In the second section, he outlines how such conditions would differ in a system of government he calls the 'Islamic republic'. Banisadr's main critique of Iran in the 1960s and the 1970s is not too different from that of most other contemporary Iranian intellectuals: 'Westernism' has overwhelmed Iranian socio-cultural traits; the country's industrial and technological infrastructure is a mere reflection of the society's orientation towards consumerism; political freedom is totally unattainable; and the country's national independence is at risk of being overrun by Western (mainly American) imperialism.[86] The system to replace this ruinous, despotic rule will be an Islamic republic, one based on the principles of *tauhid*.

In the second section of *The Manifesto of the Islamic Republic*, Banisadr lays down the theoretical foundations of a political system based on Islamic doctrine. It was not until his next major work, *The Main Principles and Guidelines of Islamic Government*, published in 1974, that Banisadr outlined in detail the characteristics of the political system he had previously proposed for Iran. The publication of this work appears to have been a direct result of Banisadr having reached the conclusion by 1974 that the collapse of the Pahlavi regime was inevitable.[87] Yet the originality and the innovative mastery of the *Manifesto* have gained it more recognition and attention than the latter work. Nevertheless, both works are of fundamental importance in understanding the principles of an 'Islamic republic'. Such a government, Banisadr proposed, would pursue an active foreign policy, 'departing from the global power system' and extending assistance to movements of national liberation.[88] Political power within the Islamic government would be dispersed among the masses, at the base of the society, and authoritarian centres in which power might be concentrated would be abolished. The government is responsible for the defense of the population, while its powers must be kept under the supervision of the public at all times. Economically, the government must guarantee to provide basic necessities for the general public and it must redirect economic production towards those needs that facilitate the attainment of a *tauhidi* society. Socially, culture and education must be re-oriented in accordance with the tenets of Islam and away from Westernism.[89]

Tauhidi Economics (Eqtesad-e Tauhidi) is another major book by Banisadr and forms an important part of his overall thesis. The book is divided into two sections. In the first section Banisadr outlines a general sketch of political economy in broad and at times ambiguous terms. The second section, which is more central to Banisadr's main argument, outlines an economic system based on the principle of *tauhid*. Banisadr argues that in Islam neither private nor communal ownership is absolute. God has absolute ownership and all temporal ownership is only relative. Consequently, economic and political power may not be concentrated within any one source that is outside of God.[90] Private ownership, meanwhile, is permissible since individuals have ownership over the products of their own labour, which must also be directed towards the attainment of a *tauhidi* society.[91] In fact, the main goal of the Islamic government's economic production will be the manifestation of a *tauhidi* society. The individual does, however, have 'relative' ownership over the products of his labour before the *tauhidi* society is attained, while the Imam, who is the leader of the Islamic community, has only limited ownership over the accumulated economic production of society.[92]

The Ulema

The desire to politicize Islam was not exclusive to the intellectuals. Concurrent with the writings of Shariati and Banisadr, there were moves within the clerical establishment itself to once again turn Islam into an active political force. The clerical initiative to 'reactivate' Islam came in 1960, when Ayatollah Merteza Mottahari established a Monthly Religious Society (Anjoman-e Mahan-e Dini) in Tehran. Mottahari, a professor at the Faculty of Theology in Tehran University, along with a number of other notable clerics and religious scholars, gave a series of lectures at the Society on the theme of Islam's role in politics and society. The group published a journal entitled *Monthly Lectures (Guftar-e Mah)*, and later published a book called *Considering Leadership and Clericalism (Bahsi Darbare-ye Marjaiyat va Rouhaniyat)*.[93] The book, which included essays written by members of the Society, was an attempt to project into Islamic principles new meanings and implications which, taken in totality, would form a dynamic, self-reliant system of social, political, and Islamic values. The book urged the clergy to concern themselves with temporal as well as theological matters and to become active in social and communal affairs. Furthermore, it argued that the clerical establishment was too hierarchical, and that the *marj'a taqlid*, the highest source of Shi'ite authority until the hidden Imam Mahdi returns, was too centralized and needed to allow for greater participation by other clerics. Owing much to the credibility of its well-known figures and the popularity of their proposals, the Society soon generated considerable public enthusiasm, especially among religious students and the younger clergy. However, its activities came to a sudden end in March 1963, when as a result of the disturbances in Qom the government cracked down on active *ulema* and closed down most religious centres.

Tensions had originally broken out in Qom on 6 September 1962, when newspapers announced the passage of a bill in the Majlis that gave voting rights to women and to religious minorities.[94] The ayatollahs in Qom reacted quickly by sending telegrams to the Shah and the prime minister, arguing that the law undermined the integrity of Islam and the independence of the country. Among the ayatollahs who sent such telegrams, Khomeini's were most poignant and sarcastic.[95] He suggested that the prime minister travel to Qom, 'so that if there are any misunderstandings which cannot be put into writing they be verbally discussed'. The government finally repealed the law on 22 November 1962, after which Khomeini thanked the Shah in a telegram but reminded him that 'of course, the protection of Islam is what the Moslem people of Iran expect from Your Excellency'.[96] Nevertheless, Khomeini did not stop his attacks against the regime and continued to preach against the Shah from the Feyziyeh religious seminary in Qom. In March 1963 the government retaliated by occupying the seminary and arresting Khomeini. During the occupation some theology students died, thus inciting the *ulema* to launch a vociferous propaganda campaign. Khomeini was soon released, but was detained again on 4 June after he renewed his sharply critical sermons against the regime. The news of his arrest for a second time triggered off riots and demonstrations in Qom, Tehran, Shiraz, Marshhad, and Kashan, during which several people were killed or wounded.[97] After a few days the unrest finally subsided as the presence of government troops in the streets deterred further demonstrations. From his subsequent release in August 1963 to the day of his exile on 4 October 1964, Khomeini spent another seven months in detention, this time for urging people to boycott the upcoming Majlis elections. He was at first exiled to Turkey, but in 1965 he moved to the Shi'ite holy city of Najaf in Iraq.

The events of 1963 had two important consequences. First, they threw Khomeini into the scene of national political activity. His 'struggle' against the regime introduced a practical axiom, albeit in a much more radical form, into the theoretical framework for political Islam that the Monthly Religious Society was trying to formulate. There is no evidence to suggest a direct association between Khomeini and the Monthly Society, although the ayatollah's inclination towards political activism had been known as early as 1944, when he had published a polemic against Reza Shah's despotism entitled *The Discovery of Secrets (Kashf al-Asrar)*. A further development arising out of the events of the early 1960s was a diversification in the clergy's area of expertise within Islamic theology. This diversification of specialities was one of the original proposals put forward by the Monthly Society, but its application was not put into effect until after the death of Grand Ayatollah Borujerdi. Borujerdi had been the sole *marj' a taqlid* (Source of Emulation) up until his death in 1961. His death led to the delegation of relatively higher authority to other ayatollahs. Nevertheless, it was mainly the intellectuals who in the 1970s spearheaded the politicization of Islam, while most clerics focused on religious ethics and philosophy. From his exile in Najaf, however, Ayatollah Khomeini formulated and published the principles of his *Islamic Government (Velayat-e Fagih)* in 1971.

In 1978–79, according to one estimate, there were some 180,000 clerics in Iran.[98] Most were low-ranking clergymen such as *wa'izin* (preachers) and *shayks* or *akhunds*, commonly known in English as mullahs.[99] Most of these clerics served as foot soldiers for the more prominent *mujtahids*, who were themselves divided into the ranks of Hujjatoleslam (Proof of Islam) and Ayatollahs (Light of God), the latter being more senior than the former. Because of the government's growing curtailment of *sharia* (religious) law, most *akhunds* and *mujtahids* engaged in delivering sermons in mosques or were primarily concerned with the administration of local religious institutions such as *howzehs* (centres of Shi'ite learning).¹⁰⁰ Among the ayatollahs, ten to fifteen had achieved prominence and fame throughout Iran, either because of their scholarly contribution to Islamic philosophy or due to their political activities against the regime, or, as in the case of Ayatollahs Mottahari and Taleghani, because of a combination of both. The most notable of these included Mahmud Taleghani, Hussein Ali Montazeri, Mohammad Baheshti, Morteza Mottahari, Baha al-Dir Mahalati, Hussein Dastgheyb, and Abdullah Shirazi-Qommi.¹⁰¹ Even more senior than these ayatollahs were the six *marj'a taqlids*: Ayatollahs Abulqassem Khoi and Ruhollah Khomeini, both residing in Najaf, Kazem Shariatmadari, Mohammad Reza Golpaygani, and Shahab al-Din Mar'ashi-Nujafi, all of whom lived in Qom, and Ahmad Khonsari, a resident of Tehran. The question of exactly how a leading ayatollah becomes a *marj'a taqlid* is unclear. The consensus of the other living *marj'as* appears to be an important determinant.¹⁰² The administration of charitable endowments and the sponsorship of seminary students are equally significant factors in becoming a *marj'a*. The amount of funds at the disposal of a ranking ayatollah generally signifies the people's vote of confidence in his religious eminence and his ability to administer *howzehs*. Khoi, Khomeini, Shariatmadari, Golpaygani, and Mar'ashi-Najafi all headed their own *howzehs* and most sponsored the building of public projects such as schools, libraries, and hospitals. Most Iranians knew the names of the *marj'as*, often due to their exalted position and at times because of their political stands against the regime.

In the 1970s the Iranian *ulema* were generally divided into three groups. Some *ulema* members, of whom Khoi and Dastgheyb were noted examples, remained largely aloof of politics and concentrated mostly on various aspects of Islamic theology such as ethics and jurisprudence. A second group of *ulema* held the view that clerics should be politically aware and needed to act as the 'guardians' of the political system.¹⁰³ This group included Mottahari, Golpaygani, Khonsari, Mar'ashi-Najafi, and Shariatmadari. Finally, there were those who advocated political activism and who argued for the direct assumption of political responsibilities by the clergy. They included Beheshti, Montazeri, Taleghari, and Khomeini. Significantly, Ayatollah Khomeini was the only *marj'a taqlid* among this latter group. Along with Shariatmadari, these politically active *ulema* formed the core clerical leadership of the revolution. Because of their growing significance in the mid- and late 1970s, this group of *ulema* must be studied in further detail.

Ayatollah Khomeini

Within the clergy, Khomeini's activities and publication in the 1970s stand out. His first major work, *Discovery of Secrets (Kashf al-Asrar)*, published in 1944–45, was a polemic against the 'decadence and corruption' of Iran's social life and political situation. The book was written as a reply to another work, entitled *One Thousand-Year-Old Secrets (Asrar-e Hezar Saleh)*, which was representative of the anti-religious intellectual trend in Iran during Reza Shah's reign. This trend was personified by Ahmad Kasravi, a veteran politician of the constitutional era and a historian who had at one point sponsored book burning sessions in an effort to eliminate Arabic and Islamic influence from Persian culture.[104] Kasravi was assassinated in 1944 by the Fedaiyan-e Islam. In his first book Khomeini directed most of his attacks against Reza Shah and Kasravi and called on the people 'to wipe out these shameless sinners with an iron fist'.[105] He accused Reza Shah and those who supported his forceful unveiling of women as being 'lustful animals ... guilty of great tyrannical acts'.[106]

For all its revolutionary aura and uncompromising rhetoric, however, Khomeini's book does not appear extraordinary when considered within the context of the time in which it was written. At the time, Iran was occupied by the Allied Forces, and the country's twenty-four-year-old monarch wielded little real authority. Reza Shah's sudden abdication and the dismantling of his forced secularization of the country had the natural consequence of provoking the retaliation of the *ulema*. As criticism of 'past mistakes' and wrongdoings had become the order of the day, Khomeini's work seems to have attracted little popular attention and was apparently not greatly influential even within the religious establishment. In fact, Khomeini was not thought to be a significant figure in Qom prior to 1963, partly because of his lack of scholarly contribution to Islamic theology and partly because he taught the less popular and more suspicious subject of philosophy.[107] The 1963 disturbances served to familiarize and popularize Khomeini among the public at large and to give the ayatollah an opportunity to crystallize his vociferous anti-establishment rhetoric. His exile the following year once again caused his name to fade from the public's memory. Once in Najaf, he is said to have initially suffered from a lack of sufficient funds and reportedly underwent a period of seclusion as the two other ayatollahs there, Hakim and Khoi, did not pay him the traditional homage.[108] Only by 1968 was Khomeini able to pay stipends to students and to resume his seminary. His 1971 publication of *Islamic Government (Velayat-e Faqih)*, more accurately meaning The Governance of the Religiously Learned, evolved out of his lectures in Najaf. It was in this second work that Khomeini outlined his grand theory of an Islamic system, rejected monarchical government as blasphemous, and prepared the groundwork, at least theoretically, for a political system called the Islamic Republic.

Velayat-e Faqih is a guideline for the establishment of a political system based on a universalist view of Islam. It is undoubtedly one of the most significant efforts aimed at formulating a workable theological political system, outlining in detail the functions of the executive, judicial and legislative branches of an Islamic government. Khomeini argued that the monarchical constitution, 'devised out of an amalgamation of British and French laws, is fundamentally opposed to Islam's basic tenets'.[109] He outlined an alternative political system 'for the Moslem community', to be headed by a *kalif* or a *faqih* (someone learned in religious sciences). Such a community would be governed by Islamic judicial and financial laws and regulations, the applicability of which Khomeini claimed to transcend the limitations of time and culture. The legislative functions of the Islamic government need to be performed by a planning council instead of a parliament, which would be responsible for determining the specific functions of the various government ministries. In such a system, 'governance [*hakemiyyat*] is only that of God and His commands will be the law'.[110] The *faqih* will lead the Islamic community until the return of Imam Mahdi and is responsible to see that Islamic justice is implemented in the meantime. Piety, a sense of justice, and adequate knowledge of law are the prerequisites of becoming a *faqih*, and those claiming to meet such conditions are to be followed and obeyed by all other Moslems. The *faqih* must not only be an administrator, he must also be a legislator, a judge, and an army commander. He must be both a ruler and an onlooker over the whole system.[111] To establish such an Islamic political system, the clergy must not only lead the masses to revolt against the tyrannical establishment, but they must at first purge themselves of corrupt and 'Court-tied' elements. They must also invite the passive *ulema* to become active. In return for their popular respect the *ulema* owe it to the public to revolt and to protest in the name of Islam.

> Even if you have not attained political power yet, do not sit quiet. Yell and scream if they hit you over the head. Protest, deny, cry out loud. You must create a propaganda apparatus to counter the lies of the regime.[112]

Furthermore, in apparent reference to other ayatollahs, Khomeini wrote: 'These impotent characters, who are merely sitting in their religious seminaries, are such parasites that they cannot even put their pens into fruitful use.[113]

Shariatmadari

Another influential cleric who gained prominence in the revolutionary movement was Shariatmadari. Ayatollah Shariatmadari was a native of Tabriz and one of the six *marj' a taqlids* who were alive in the late 1970s. His senior rank and influence among Turkish-speaking *Azerbaijanis* led some foreign journalists incorrectly to identify Shariatmadari rather than Khomeini as the leader of the brewing unrest.[114] However, throughout the 1960s and the 1970s, Shariatmadari had concentrated on supervising the funding and the administration of schools and hospitals in Qom.[115] He was briefly interned in July 1963 for protesting against the government's attack on the Feiziyeh seminary. For a considerable length of time after that, however, he did not concern himself with political issues and was generally considered to be conservative in orientation.[116] He was in fact said to have earned the widespread disapproval of other clerics for an 'effusively loyalistic' message he had once sent to the Shah.[117] Nevertheless, he became vocally critical of the government following the Qom and Tabriz riots of January and February 1978. In a statement issued after the Qom incident, Shariatmadari said: 'We strongly condemn these acts, which are directed against humanity and religion, and we are assured that God will punish the perpetrators of such crimes.'[118] In a similar statement after the riots in Tabriz, he called on people to observe 'the painful tragedy of the massacre' by holding 'orderly' memorial services in mosques or in other gathering places.[119]

Throughout the rest of the revolutionary movement, Shariatmadari continued to issue statements and communiqués condemning the regime's heavy-handed response to the unrest. He also remained readily accessible to foreign journalists and was repeatedly interviewed in the Western press. These interviews strengthened Shariatmadari's image abroad as one of the main leaders of the movement against the regime. However, two important factors separated Shariatmadari from the rest of the emerging leaders of the revolution. First, his role in the movement was largely reactive rather than active: he issued statements in support of certain incidents but he did not call for anti-regime activities himself. In contrast, Khomeini and his associates in Paris were preoccupied with devising ways to expedite the regime's collapse and to augment the popular discontent against the establishment. Second, there were indications that Shariatmadari was opposed to an all-out revolution. As late as December 1978 he called on the government to 'obey the [1906] Constitution'.[120] This amounted to endorsing the monarchy rather than seeking its overthrow. In an interview with a foreign newspaper he stated:

Revolution in Iran

> We are deeply attracted to the idea of an Islamic government. But the present circumstances are not ready for such a system. For now, an Islamic government is a distant dream. Before anything else, we want the regime to obey the present constitution.[121]

In the same month, in another interview Khomeini said: 'Our ultimate goal is an Islamic government. We must, therefore, first overthrow this oppressive regime.... The regime we will establish will not be a monarchy.'[122] Shariatmadari became less vocal in expressing reservations about an Islamic government as the revolution progressed.[123] However, when the Shah's overthrow and the revolution's success began to look inevitable, Shariatmadari's relatively moderate opposition found fewer enthusiastic supporters. He continued to urge the government to stop the killings and expressed solidarity with the wishes of the 'Moslem people'.

Montazeri and Taleghani

Ayatollahs Montazeri and Taleghani were also prominent clerics in the revolutionary movement, although their rise to political prominence occurred largely after the success of the revolution. Taleghani was a radical clergyman with deep political convictions and a long prison record. Born in 1911, he studied theology in Qom and began preaching in a Tehran mosque in 1939. His sermons were politically provocative and were consequently well attended by young political activists. In the late 1940s and the early 1950s he collaborated with Dr Mossadiq's National Front and continued his activities after the 1953 *coup* until he was arrested in 1957. Released soon afterwards, in 1961 he formed the Freedom Movement with Bazargan but was imprisoned again the following year for a period of five years. In 1970 he was arrested once more for continuing to preach against the regime and was sent into internal exile in 1971. After his return to Tehran, he was interned for a fourth time in 1975 but was released in October 1978 as part of the regime's amnesty to political prisoners. During his many years in prison, he wrote several books on Islam and forged close ties with the founding members of the Mujahadeen organization, namely Rezai and Hanifnezhad. The important books he wrote in this period included a multi-volume commentary (*tafsir*) on the holy book of Islam, called *Lights from the Koran* (*Partow-vi az Koran*), and *Islam and Ownership* (*Islam va Malekiyyat*), which still remains one of the few books on economics by Islamic scholars. Taleghani's close affinity with the Mujahadeen led the party's members to view him as their 'spiritual guide' and to refer to him as their 'Father'.[124]

Montazeri's activities before the revolution were very similar to those of Taleghani. He was born in 1925 in a village near Isfahan and received his early religious education in Qom under Ayatollahs Borujerdi and Khomeini. A relentless political activist, he was arrested four times and was once sent into internal exile, in spite of which he still managed to visit his old teacher, Khomeini, in Najaf and to maintain contacts with him throughout the years.[125] His final release from prison, similar to that of Taleghani and many other political prisoners, came in October 1978.

Both Taleghani and Montazeri were incarcerated from 1975 to 1978 and did not have any role in the agitation that began in late 1977 and early 1978. By the time they were released, the revolution had already gained full momentum: anti-government riots and marches occurred on a daily basis and the revolutionaries had successfully paralysed Prime Minister Sharif-Emami's cabinet of 'national reconciliation'. Montazeri travelled to France and personally met with Khomeini. Although he soon returned to Iran, very little is known about his exact activities from after his trip to February 1979. It is significant to note that he did not become a member of the Council of Revolution although his credentials made him a prime candidate for such a position. He was also not a signatory to any of the declarations against the regime that joint groups of the *ulema* repeatedly issued.[126] He was, however, reported to have been in regular contact with Khomeini via telephone.[127] Soon after the Islamic Republic was established, Khomeini named Montazeri the Friday Prayer Imam of Qom and eventually designated him as his successor.

Taleghani maintained a more active profile after his release. He resumed his close co-operation with Bazargan's Freedom Movement and openly expressed support and sympathy for the Mujahadeen. He also became the chairman of the Council of Revolution and personally led street marches and rallies. After the revolution he was elected to the Assembly of Experts, which was charged with drafting a new constitution. He died on 7 September 1979.

Beheshti

Last, there was Ayatollah Mohammad Beheshti. He had been one of the few clerical leaders of the revolution who had not been imprisoned or exiled by the regime. Born in Isfahan in 1928, he studied theology in Qom but later moved to Tehran and earned a doctorate in theological sciences from Tehran University. In 1951 he returned to Qom and taught English at a high school. In the early 1960s he supported Ayatollah Mottahari's efforts to reform and politicize Islam.[128] In 1964 he went to Europe, reportedly on Ayatollah Borujerdi's orders, in order to propagate Islam among Iranian students studying abroad. After founding a mosque in Hamburg, he returned to Iran in the early 1970s and served as an advisor on religious matters to the Ministry of Education. In 1978 he visited Khomeini in Paris and became an influential figure in the Council of Revolution upon his return to Iran.

As the above study shows, only one of the politically active clerics, Ayatollah Khomeini, who resided outside Iran, could freely denounce the regime in press interviews or issue statements and declarations against the government. For his part, Shariatmadari did give extensive interviews to the foreign (mainly US) press. But he was unwilling to go as far as Khomeini and call for a complete overthrow of the regime. Shariatmadari's 'liberalism' gradually widened the distance between him and the revolutionary movement. Taleghani and Montazeri had been active in the opposition in the 1960s and 1970s, but because of their activism they had almost always been either imprisoned or exiled. Their release in October 1978 came too late to give them the opportunity to lead the revolution. Last, there was Beheshti. Beheshti was neither 'revolutionary' nor significant enough among the *ulema* to emerge as their leader in opposing the regime. Khomeini, on the other hand, had the best opportunities and the uncompromising determination to topple the regime.

For all of the *ulema*'s revolutionary rhetoric, nevertheless, it was at first the intelligentsia who voiced open and orchestrated opposition to the regime in the late 1970s. While a number of intellectuals had voiced opposition to the regime and to the general social and political conditions of the country in the late 1960s and early 1970s, their activities had never been part of a co-ordinated effort to overthrow the Pahlavi state. The essays and speeches of Shariati and many other intellectuals were philosophical rather than political, and although at times they vehemently attacked the general state of culture and society under the Pahlavis, monarchy as a political system and the person of the Shah as its ruler were never directly mentioned or challenged. The only individual activist who had vociferously advocated the overthrow of the monarchy and of the Shah, and who had already devised a theoretical blueprint for a future political system, was Ayatollah Khomeini. Banisadr had also formulated the principles of an 'Islamic Republic' while in self-imposed exile in France, but he continued to remain largely unknown in Iran until after the revolution. The two guerrilla organizations, meanwhile, had always operated underground and could not at any rate mount effective attacks against their targets due to SAVAK's growing efficiency. By the summer of 1977, however, co-ordinated measures to criticize and oppose the regime were initiated by a number of intellectuals inside Iran.

Opposition activities

The intellectuals' reformism

As early as April 1977 a group of lawyers and civil rights activists of the Mussadiq era had established the Iranian Society for the Defence of Freedom and Human Rights. Although the society's activities were mostly confined to giving interviews to foreign and some Iranian journalists, the very establishment of such an organization was in itself unprecedented and was considered to be a revolutionary feat. Even more significant, however, was the reactivation of the Writers' Association in June of the same year. For the first time ever, the Writers' Association sent an open letter to Prime Minister Hoveida. The letter, signed by forty prominent writers, poets, and essayists, protested against the brutalities of SAVAK, accused the government of abrogating the main principles of the 1906 Constitution, and called for an end to literary censorship. Another open letter also appeared in June, this time addressed to the Shah and signed by three well-known members of the hastily reactivated National Front. The signatories of the letter, Sanjabi, Bakhtiar, and Forouhar, were to play significant roles in the development of the future course of events. The letter urged the Shah to 'restore individual freedoms, re-establish national cooperation, ... submit to the principle of constitutionality, abandon the single-party system, and respect the people's rights'.[129] Twenty thousand copies of the letter were privately circulated as it became the symbol of the intellectuals' opposition to the regime. As another member of the National Front later revealed, however, there had been serious disagreements over the contents of the letter, which was originally designed to be signed by a far greater number of opposition figures.[130] The intellectuals' movement grew throughout the autumn, none the less, and its expression of dissent acquired a progressively more determined and more radical posture. In October the Writers' Association held a nine-day symposium called the Nights of Poetry, in which well-known novelists and poets read inspirational poems against the regime and the prevailing circumstances. One such poet was Saeed Soltanpour, a member of the Fedaiyan guerrillas, whose poem 'What Has Happened to My Country!' was a captivating and emotional plea calling on the people to revolt and to overthrow tyranny. One estimate put the number of those who attended the symposium at between 5,000 and 6,000 people.[131] Although this estimate appears to be exaggerated, such an unprecedented occasion at the time demonstrated open and revolutionary opposition against the regime. In November a symposium similar to the Nights of Poetry was attended by students at Tehran's Aryamehr University, but violent demonstrations broke out when the authorities prevented Soltanpour from delivering a speech.

Revolution in Iran

Two significant characteristics stand out in the intellectuals' activities against the regime in the summer and autumn of 1977. The intellectual movement in Iran followed a pattern that was parallel but not identical to that headed by *philosophes* and *physiocrats* in France in the 1770s and 1780s. The *philosophes* were philosophers and theoreticians whose arguments formed the premisses for which the French masses demonstrated. They included individuals such as Bayle, Montesquieu, and Rousseau, whose theories and ideologies became the very slogans and principles of the revolution.[132] In Iran, however, there was no similar class of *philosophes*, no 'ferment of ideas', while it was indeed the intellectuals who initiated what eventually turned into a revolutionary movement. Of the hypothetical *philosophes* of the Iranian revolution, Khomeini was in exile and little was known of him inside Iran in 1977, Shariati had been arrested in 1975 and had later died in England in 1977, and Banisadr was only known by some exiled political activists. Yet the activities of groups such as the Iranian Society for the Defence of Freedom and Human Rights and those of the Writers' Association served to trigger the first expressions of popular discontent against the regime, similar to what had resulted from the *philosophes*' writings in France in the eighteenth century. Also of significance was the fact that virtually all the demands of Iranian intellectuals centred around the restoration of basic personal liberties (freedom of speech and publication, for example) and the honouring of the principles of the 1906 Constitution. The movement, therefore, at first aimed specifically towards reforming the system rather than overthrowing it. The proponents and the opponents of the regime alike thought that the government was invincible and that the Shah's overthrow was impossible. Furthermore, many intellectuals who were active in the initial phases of the opposition movement were willing to go only so far as to demand the regime's reform rather than its overthrow. Such intellectuals included Ahmad Bani-Ahmad, a Majlis deputy from Tabriz, and Bakhtiar, a signatory to the open letter to the Shah and eventually the monarch's last prime minister. Bakhtiar, who took pride in being a 'social democrat of the European tradition', remarked, 'I am not a man of revolution.'[133] Such intellectuals only wanted the government to promote greater civil liberties and to observe the 1906 Constitution.

Khomeini's activities

The intellectuals' largely reformist movement did not last more than a few months. By early December 1977 an entirely new cadre was emerging as the leaders of an increasingly radical movement. The shift was as much a consequence of the regime's own manoeuvres as it was the result of initiatives from within the opposition. A number of largely coincidental events had by late 1977 caused Ayatollah Khomeini's name to emerge as the symbol of the popular struggle against the regime. Despite all of his intense activities in the early 1960s and his radical theological approach to politics throughout his exile ever since, younger, urban Iranians knew little about Khomeini before 1976–77. The efforts of the *ulema* who had opposed the Shah's 'White Revolution' were remembered by only a small group of people, and many high school and university students did not know of Khomeini's past opposition to the regime. Many had never even heard Khomeini's name before. His name, nevertheless, spread throughout Iran in October 1977, when the ayatollah's oldest son, Mostafa, died in Najaf of an apparent heart attack. The exact cause of Mostafa's death has yet to be determined. When its news spread throughout Tehran, however, it was popularly perceived to be the work of SAVAK. When remembrance services were held in Tehran in November, some 3,000 people were reported to have attended.[134] Ayatollah Khomeini himself had meanwhile acquired somewhat of a mystical character for many Iranians, especially for those who were just beginning to learn about his anti-regime activities in the past. While Mostafa was seen as the victim of a regime that would resort to any measure to eliminate even its holy opponents, his father was popularly portrayed as a crusader who was determined to end oppression regardless of the costs and the sacrifices involved. Having thus emerged as the symbol of the struggle against the Shah, condolence messages were published in *Keyhan*, Iran's biggest daily newspaper, referring to Khomeini as the Great Ayatollah. For his part, Khomeini returned each message individually, often simply thanking the sender, but in many cases also calling for the overthrow of the regime.[135] Khomeini's proclamations against the Shah continued throughout most of 1977, but they were largely ignored by the political establishment and its opponents alike. The partial freedom of expression the press had been given since early 1977, meanwhile, had led to the appearance of occasional references to Khomeini in newspapers, often in flattering terms. The regime, meanwhile, saw itself increasingly threatened by Khomeini's unceasing attacks. To the regime, Khomeini was merely a 'crazy old man',[136] who could be 'eliminated' if necessary.[137] The Shah was hard pressed, however, to maintain a reputable international image in the face of the growing interest the Western media had taken in Iranian affairs. Furthermore, in compliance with President Carter's human rights policy, the Shah no longer wanted to appear authoritarian and despotic. The Iranian government decided to compel Khomeini to go to the West, where, it was thought, he would reveal his backward and primitive mentality through his exposure to the international media, therefore discrediting the opposition movement against the Shah.[138] In October 1978 the Iraqi government quickly reacted to Tehran's request and ordered the expulsion of Ayatollah Khomeini. Khomeini travelled to France on October 5 and took up residence in the Parisian suburb of Neauphle-le-Chateau. With Khomeini's move from Najaf to Paris, the movement against the Shah entered a new phase.

Khomeini's expulsion from Iraq proved to be a major miscalculation by the Iranian government. However, it was to be only the first of a series of costly mistakes the regime made in trying to deal with the incipient revolution. By late December 1977 the Shah, acting on the advice of an 'investigation committee', had pinpointed Khomeini as his principal enemy and had subsequently decided to wage an offensive campaign against the ayatollah.[139] In the 7 January 1978 issue of *Ittila'at* newspaper an article appeared that attacked Khomeini by name and branded him as a representative of the 'Black Reaction'. The article alleged that Khomeini was of Indian background and had only forged his Iranian nationality; that he had been a poet who had been driven to insanity by his romanticism during his youth; and that in 1963 he had acted as an agent of a foreign power when he opposed the 'progressive' programmes of the White Revolution.[140] The Court minister personally ordered the minister of information to publish the article.[141] This inadvertently resulted in the popular identification of Ayatollah Khomeini as the personal embodiment of the struggle against the Shah. Rumours of Mostafa Khomeini's death at the hands of SAVAK further reiterated an emerging picture of the ayatollah as the leader of a potentially revolutionary movement. Eventually, Khomeini's position as the 'leader' of the movement was solidified once he was forced to travel to France. The ayatollah's expulsion from Iraq amounted to a fearful admission by the Shah that Khomeini was the regime's most dangerous enemy. During the course of his four-month asylum in France, Khomeini did not repulse but rather attracted the overwhelmingly sympathetic attention of the international media. On his journey from Najaf to Paris, he was accompanied by Dr Ibrahim Yazdi, a naturalized US citizen and a successful oncologist in Texas for seventeen years, and one of the main founders and activists of the Islamic Student Society. A number of other intellectual activists also established close links with Khomeini once he was settled in Neauphle-le-Chateau, most notable of whom were Banisadr and Qotbzadeh.

The ayatollah's asylum in France facilitated the rapid formation of a nucleus of revolutionary activists who, with great success, co-ordinated and directed the mounting movement against the Shah. The Paris-based group soon developed a well-integrated structure for the numerous functions it had come to assume and rapidly evolved into the main centre of revolutionary agitation against the regime. The group comprised two amorphous 'fronts' that could not agree on whether an all-out revolution was feasible.[142] The majority believed that the Shah was too strong to be toppled and, even if the revolution was to succeed, a *coup* by the royalist military would be a certainty. They suggested that the situation at hand provided ample opportunity to gain as many concessions from the invincible Shah as possible. Members of the front, notably Bazargan, were predominantly those activists who had lived inside the country and who had closely observed the apparent strength and loyalty of the military to the Shah. The smaller front, meanwhile, which was made up of Banisadr and 'some friends', believed that the collapse of the Shah was imminent and that the army would disintegrate as soon as the Shah departed from the scene. The revolution, they maintained, must therefore be pressed until the Pahlavi dynasty was overthrown and defeated. There were at first acute differences between the two fronts, and Bazargan accused Banisadr of having become alienated from Iran's political realities as a result of his long exile in France. This disagreement over an appropriate revolutionary strategy was soon overcome, however, as the Shah's authority rapidly withered and desertions within the military grew.

Two other organizations also evolved from within the Paris-based group: a five-member 'commission', which served as a public relations committee for Ayatollah Khomeini; and a Council of Revolution (Shora-ye Enqelab), intended to serve as the revolutionaries' legislature. With members in Iran as well as in France, the Council of Revolution was designed to supervise the formulation and the subsequent implementation of decisions made by those revolutionaries who had gathered around Ayatollah Khomeini. The original idea to establish the Council was not that of any particular individual and was generally agreed upon by all members of the group. The methodology for selecting members to the Council, however, was debated between those who argued for popular elections and those who favoured appointments by Khomeini. Without consulting those who disagreed with him, Khomeini announced the names of his appointees to the Council in the autumn of 1978. The names of the members of the Council were never fully released to the public and little information has been made available as to its exact functions. Although at different times the membership of the Council varied by one or two, it never exceeded thirteen members. It originally included seven clerics, a retired brigadier general, and five members of the intelligentsia.[143] The Council's members were not all appointed at the same time, and, once appointed they continued to stay wherever they had been active prior to their appointment either in France or in Iran. Some members initially proposed that the Council's membership be augmented to include representatives of university students, Bazaari merchants, women, peasants, and industrial workers, but their proposals were never put into effect. When in February 1979 Khomeini appointed Bazargan as prime minister and asked him to form a cabinet, most members of the provisional government were drawn from the Council of Revolution.

There was also a more loosely defined commission that served as Ayatollah Khomeini's public relations agency. The group was made up of some of the individuals Khomeini had come to trust the most. They included the Ayatollah's son, Ahmad, Dr Yazdi, Banisadr, Qotbzadeh, and Hojjatal-Islam Musavi-Khoiniha, who was specifically brought in from Iran to make certain that the commission's activities had an Islamic flavour. The commission's primary task consisted of informing Khomeini of the day-to-day developments inside Iran, gauging and relaying to the ayatollah the state of international public opinion regarding the Iranian crisis, and preparing for him actual statements to make or general guidelines to follow in his numerous interviews with the international press corps. The commission frequently received written interview questions from journalists, and submitted written answers back to them after Khomeini had reviewed the answers that had been prepared for him. Certain issues, such as women's rights in Islam or the revolutionaries' views towards technological advancement, were seen by the commission as particularly necessary to be addressed by Khomeini in order to discredit accusations of backwardness and political *naïveté* made by the Iranian government. Therefore, the commission at times designed specific questions for the journalists who interviewed Khomeini regarding those very issues. It was thus guaranteed that the traditional religious views that the ayatollah might have had were replaced by an understanding of the modern times, thus giving him an impressive and progressive image. Three of the commission's members, Yazdi, Qotbzadeh, and Banisadr, had long been active in the West and were familiar with the Western public's biases and prejudices, thus using Khomeini's interviews and statements effectively to manipulate international support and sympathy. The Shah had originally thought that Khomeini would demonstrate a backward mentality and would therefore discredit the opposition movement against the regime. In actuality, however, Khomeini's brilliant performance and propaganda campaign in Paris greatly strengthened the opposition's international prestige and gave credence to the Iranian monarchy's image as despotic and brutal.

Another significant factor regarding the operations of the Iranian revolutionaries in Paris was the activity of Khomeini himself. The ayatollah had been conscious of his lack of adequate knowledge regarding matters such as diplomacy, economics, and military affairs. He therefore relied heavily on those around him whom he considered more knowledgeable in those fields. The intellectuals around him (namely Banisadr, Yazdi, and Qotbzadeh) served as the ayatollah's think tank by continually examining the situation and by providing for him options for appropriate courses of action. They submitted written analytical reports to Khomeini on a daily basis. These analyses were based mainly on the information gathered from the international media and from frequent telephone conversations with activists in Iran. Khomeini himself was also in close contact with another group of activists in Iran. Members of this second group were more concerned with immediate and short-term factors and made very specific recommendations to the ayatollah regarding the exact political manoeuvres they deemed advisable.

In retrospect, Khomeini's leadership position first among the *ulema* and then within the revolutionary movement was greatly strengthened by the help he received from other clerics. Almost all noteworthy members of the *ulema* approved of Khomeini's activities and by doing so legitimized his position as their leader in a movement that increasingly resembled a revolution. This approval came in the form of a vast number of declarations issued in Khomeini's favour not only by ordinary *akhunds* and *mujtahids* but also by highly influential figures within the clerical establishment. The repeated joint declarations issued by the *marj'a taqlids* in Qom were a case in point.[144] Although such declarations often fell short of lending unconditional support to Khomeini's calls for an Islamic republic, they amounted to nothing less than endorsing his position as the revolution's leader. The endorsements that Khomeini received from Ayatollahs Taleghani and Shariatmadari were especially instrumental in giving legitimacy to the leadership position he was beginning to assume. While both Taleghani and Shariatmadari had potential reasons to challenge Khomeini's leadership, they both gave their tacit approval to his initiatives by not challenging him and in fact often issued statements in his support. Shariatmadari, equal in rank to Khomeini as a *marj'a taqlid*, did not really favour an all-out revolution and merely wished to see a return to the 1906 Constitution. Taleghani, although not as imminent in Shi'ite hierarchy as Khomeini, had more impressive revolutionary credentials than did Khomeini and had the ready allegiance of an armed revolutionary organization, the Mujahadeen. Yet both he and Shariatmadari chose not to challenge Khomeini and instead rallied behind him, perhaps partly because they did not want to disturb the unity of the *ulema* and partly because they agreed with Khomeini's main goals if not necessarily with his methods. Beheshti and Montazeri, on the other hand, became Khomeini's vocal and dedicated lieutenants in Iran and carried out the instructions he gave them on the telephone. Khomeini, for his part, had both the opportunities and the determination to become the *ulema*'s revolutionary leader. Residing outside of Iran, he could freely denounce the regime in the international media. He also belonged to the highest rank of the *ulema*'s hierarchy and could therefore demand the following of all lesser-ranking clerics and the faithful, if not necessarily the obedience of other *marj'a taqlids*. There was no contest or disagreement among the *ulema* as to who would be their leading spokesperson in opposing the regime. What contest there was was between the *ulema* on the one hand and the political parties and the intellectuals on the other. Together, these three groups exploited the growing exigencies caused by the collapse of the regime. The *ulema*'s success over the other two groups in leading the revolution was facilitated not only by the nature of their own activities and by their opportunities but also by the social and cultural environment in which such activities took place.

Chapter four
Social change

Social and economic factors often play important roles in producing revolutionary circumstances. While revolutions are caused by the structural breakdown of the political apparatus, they can be and in fact often are considerably exacerbated by social and economic developments. In most revolutionary instances, the process and the consequences of social change provide the necessary and appropriate societal background in which popular revolutionary mobilization takes place. This chapter discusses the social and economic changes that took place in Iran before the 1978–79 revolution and examines the social and economic background in which the political collapse of the regime and the activities of the revolutionaries occurred. The exploitation of such socio-economic developments by the various revolutionary groups, and the socially determinant causes for the *ulema*'s hegemony over the revolutionary movement will be discussed in the next chapter. First it is necessary to review the process of social change in Iran before the revolution.

The process of social change

Social change is usually brought about as a result of the singular development or the combined interplay of four distinct sociological phenomena: modernization, diffusion, 'culture lag', and indigenously initiated alterations within the social system. Indigenous factors can lead to social change when a society becomes unable to cope adequately with the various forces that are engendered in it, therefore rendering structural and systemic changes inevitable. Both Marx and Parsons, for example, saw factors indigenous to the system as the main causes of social change; while Marx focused on 'contradictions' between the forces and the modes of economic production, Parsons examined the 'differentiations' and 'variations' of a society's 'sub-systems.'[1] Social change can also be induced by cultural diffusion. Few cultural items emerge independently from within a society. Rather, they are borrowed from other cultures, or are heavily influenced by them. The passage of traits native to one culture into another, to which they have heretofore been alien, causes changes in social systems. Some of the mechanisms of diffusion are ethnic movements, military conquests, missionaries, commerce, revolutions, and gradual infiltration.[2] With the overwhelming role played by the electronic media today, the cross-cultural diffusion of values and norms is made even more commonplace.[3] Once adopted, the borrowed culture traits must somehow be modified in order to fit into the existing cultural context.[4] The culture lag theory of social change, meanwhile, as pioneered by William Ogburn, argues that 'the various parts of modern culture are not changing at the same rate, some parts are changing more rapidly than others'.[5] This lag in the rate of change in the 'material culture' as opposed to 'adaptive culture' (i.e. customs, beliefs, laws, etc.) leads to cultural 'maladjustments' and social change.[6] Lastly, social change can result from modernization. Alterations in technology and the means of production, which characterize societies undergoing economic and technological developments, directly lead to changes in social institutions and cultural practices. Social change in societies undergoing modernization is often made easier by the formation of 'varied interest groups and social movements'. These groups make specific demands of change and often guide the integration of modern changes into the social system.[7] Modernization may lead to the development of different categories of elites, each of which may pursue the realization of specific demands arising out of their own positions in society at large.[8]

One of the effects of social change is the lack of persistence of norms (i.e. the expected pattern of behaviour). There are many conflicting varieties of accepted, or rather competing, modes of social behaviour in a society undergoing social change and it becomes impossible to detect a single and identifiably consistent set of norms. There is, therefore, conflict not only between the differing social values that prevail throughout society but also between norms. Rural immigrants, industrial labourers, wage-earners, the salaried middle class, and even the wealthy elite are all confronted with the enigmatic problem of how to behave properly in the presence of others with equal or superior social standing. The accepted and expected patterns of conduct and behaviour undergo such rapid changes, and new social groupings and segments develop at such rapid rates that the society as a whole cannot retain an interrelated set of norms. Each social group acquires its own set of norms, along with its attached values, and thus there often develops a vast gap between the value systems of one group as opposed to those of another.

Social change in Iran

In studying the causes and consequences of social change in Iran, all of the above-mentioned theoretical approaches need to be utilized. A society undergoing social change is likely to be affected by a combination of different factors, both indigenous and foreign. The 'Westoxication' (*gharbzadegi*) of Iran, as Jalal Al-e Ahmad saw and termed it, meant the diffusion within indigenous Iranian culture of alien, mainly Western, cultural traits. Rapid modernization, exemplified by the legal and institutional reforms of the early 1960s and the 'oil boom' of the early 1970s, also expedited social change in Iran. Furthermore, culture lag occurred, with the private values of people (i.e. religious values and symbols, attitudes concerning fertility rates, marital conditions, artistic and literary expression, etc.) being less easily susceptible to change than their public values (i.e. occupation, consumption and purchasing habits, clothing and housing, means of communication and transportation, and attitudes toward health, sanitation, medicine, etc.). Such maladjustments within the culture system itself increased the tension that the process of social change would in any event have caused. By 1978 social change had reached such proportions in Iran that not only were all sets of traditional values being challenged by newer ones, but the country had lost any meaningful degree of cultural homogeneity it had once had. Iranian culture, as such, was no longer clearly identifiable and had become highly metaphoric and transient. Apart from other ramifications, social change in Iran resulted in the general cultural disillusionment and disorientation of the public. Thus when the tide of revolution came, not only did it find disillusioned participants eager to search for their lost sense of identity in an extremist movement, it also assumed the rejection of the prevailing values and their replacement by alternatives to be one of its fundamental goals.

The White Revolution

Institutionally sanctioned social change under Mohammad Reza Pahlavi was officially launched in 1961 through a series of land reform bills that later became part of a broader 'White Revolution'. The overall plan of the government-sponsored revolution was to minimize the economic powers and thus the political influence of rural-based landlords by confiscating their land and distributing it among the peasantry.[9] This plan was intended to eliminate the power base of the landed proprietors and at the same time create a sizeable peasant-dominated base of support for the regime. The actual Land Reform Bill, which the government later augmented by other measures under the White Revolution, was officially signed on 9 January 1962. Largely a creation of Dr Hassan Arsanjani, the minister of agriculture at the time and formerly a member of the Tudeh party, the land reform programme was designed radically to alter the relations of economic production in the countryside. There were four main tenets in what was later to become only the first stage of the land reform programme. According to this first stage, (i) land holdings were limited to one village, (ii) the compensation to be given to the landlords was fixed on the basis of the taxable value of the lands forfeited, (iii) the land they had been cultivating was allocated to the peasants without upsetting the field layout of the village, and (iv) membership in a co-operative society became a condition for the cultivators' receipt of land.[10] Other points of the White Revolution included the nationalization of forests; the sale of state-owned enterprises to the public; workers' profit-sharing in 20 per cent of net corporate earnings; the formation of a so-called Literacy Corps; and the granting of voting rights to women and religious minorities.[11] To the regime, the 'revolution' was to achieve goals that were consistent with its programmes of social, economic, and even political development. Politically, the White Revolution was designed not only not to alter the political establishment but instead to secure its further consolidation by cultivating the support of the peasantry and by establishing a base of support among them. By literally handing out land deeds to peasants on highly publicized occasions, the Shah wanted to appear as their saviour (from feudal landlords) and to ensure their support for his regime and his personal self. The monarch's sudden egalitarianism was also intended to debase the arguments of intellectuals such as Al-e Ahmad, who criticized the regime for failing to upgrade the living standards of the village peasants and the urban poor. The very fabric of the country's social structure and the relations of economic production were also targeted for change. It was hoped that the White Revolution would expedite the socio-cultural modernization of the country, particularly in the rapidly growing urban centres. Economically, the revolution's land reform focused specifically on the countryside. It aimed at abolishing large landholding and feudal classes and at distributing their confiscated properties among a newly emerging class of landowning peasants. The government thereby hoped to complete the capitalist transformation of the country and to complement Iran's urban-based capitalism with a similar development in rural areas. The government was successful in achieving these goals, but only in the short term. The long-term ramifications (and significantly the eventual failure) of the White Revolution's promises proved fatal to the regime.

For social change to take place, *compatible* values and patterns of power relations need to occur concurrently. By giving full legal rights to women and non-Moslem minorities, an attempt was made to change the respective social positions of the two groups within society. But for changes in the patterns of relationships in the society to be effective, formal and legalistic measures need to be accompanied by changes in normative ethics and values. Alterations in traditionally accepted attitudes and relationships need more stimuli than mere reforms from above. What is exactly needed varies from culture to culture. In all cases, however, compatible elements indigenous to the culture itself – a kind of readiness to accept the changes envisaged – must already exist. Coercion or legal pressures, regardless of the degree of their rigidity and forcefulness, will not suffice unless the culture itself already embodies tendencies and proclivities that are consonant with the new transformations. Reza Shah's nationalist policies found far greater social receptivity than the Europeanization of Iran under his son. Iran's 'Westernization' was feverishly pursued and religiously accepted by most of the urban middle and upper classes under Mohammad Reza Pahlavi. Western values and social practices, however, coexisted side by side with more deeply rooted norms and values, which Reza Shah, who had never been further West than Turkey, understood better than his son, who despised them. While Westernism had a rival culture system to overcome, in Iran nationalism had none. Reza Shah's imposition of taxes on sugar and tea in order to finance railway construction in preference to subjecting the country to foreign debt aroused far less public resentment than his son's granting of voting rights to women and religious minorities. Family relationships in Iran had historically secured the domination of the male over the dependent female. Westernization of such a pattern – however humanely, socially, or economically desirable – ran contrary to age-old patterns of relationships and religious traditions. In the end, prejudices against women and the influence of religious minorities persisted and modernizing legal measures were largely abortive.

The same fate was shared by other programmes of the White Revolution. The land reform programme was broken down into three stages so that eventually much land was rechannelled to its original owners. The second stage of the land reform was initiated on 17 January 1962. The new provisions required that landlords either sell or rent their land to peasants (the rate of the rent to be based on the average income of the peasants), or divide the land between the peasants and themselves.[12] This was a further effort to break up the holdings of the landlords and to subsequently transfer the land over to the peasantry. But by early 1963 the growing independence of the peasantry and the popularity of the land reform programmes' main architect, Dr Arsanjani, began to appear as a potential threat to the regime. On 10 March 1963, Arsanjani was dismissed and was replaced by General

Riahi. In January 1966 Riahi announced a third stage to the land reform programme, intended for the 'full exploitation' of the country's agricultural resources.[13] Dr Valian, who replaced Riahi in 1968, was the actual engineer of this final stage of land reform. In October of that year, measures were introduced in the Majlis to abolish the sale of land to the occupying peasants and to establish joint stock agricultural companies, which were to be owned and operated by the government.[14] The agricultural companies were set up supposedly in order to expedite the mechanization of agriculture, reduce manpower inefficiency, and thus to increase output. The peasants, meanwhile, were to sell their newly acquired lands to the companies in return for a share of their stocks and employment in them as agricultural labourers.[15] The eventual failure of the rural co-operatives set up in the third stage of the land reform, however, not only caused many peasants to become landless, but also put many of them out of work. Some became wage-earning farm labourers while others migrated to the cities. One estimate put the number of the rural labouring class at more than 100,000 families.[16] Furthermore, one of the consequences of this third stage of the land reform was that former patterns of land ownership and rural social stratification were gradually reinstated. Nevertheless, domestic agricultural production did increase at an average rate of 3 to 4 per cent annually,[17] but urban-bound migration of landless and unemployed peasants also increased considerably. While the average population growth rate for the whole country was estimated at 2.5 to 3 per cent per year, cities of more than 50,000 grew at an average rate of 4 to 6 per cent.[18] Tehran's population, for example, grew in the 1950s and the 1960s by around 5.5 per cent per annum.[19]

The White Revolution was only one of the many attempts to 'modernize' the traditional fabric of Iranian society. What mainly differentiated it from other reforms launched by the regime was that it comprised a series of governmentally induced changes, deliberately orchestrated with extensive propaganda. The Shah repeatedly declared his dream of making Iran 'catch up' with Japan and other great powers by the year 2000 and saw his revolution as one of the means of reaching this goal.[20] Yet while the regime did not launch another orchestrated effort similar to the White Revolution, the government enacted numerous separate legal measures in order to alter the social norms that had resisted previous more sweeping attempts to change them. In 1966 a government-sponsored Women's Organization of Iran (Sazman-e Zanan-e Iran) was established, with the intention of promoting the social status of Iranian women – that is to Europeanize them.[21] In 1964 the Endowment Organization (Sazman-e Owqaf), which Reza Shah had originally set up to replace the financial functions and duties of the *ulema* as trustees of endowments (*owqaf*), was re-established. In 1967 and again in 1975 the government enacted two Family Protection Acts prohibiting polygamy and granting the right to women to file divorce suits.[22] Between 1960 and 1975 the city of Tehran lost nine of its thirty-two religious seminaries (*madresahs*) because of a shortage of theology students,[23] and the Endowment Organization and the Ministry of Education became increasingly influential in determining the quality of education and the overall curriculum of the remaining seminaries.[24] To further curtail the independence of the religious establishment and to bring more of the *ulema* under the secular control of the state, in August 1971 the Shah announced the formation of a Religious Corps (Sepah-e Din), to be sent into the countryside to provide the rural masses with religious education. The Religious Corps was complemented when a Department of Religious Propagandists (Muravvejin-e Din) was added to the Endowment Organization and put in charge of a number of social services programmes. The activities of the Religious Propagandists included religious instruction, health and development activities (e.g. caring for the sick, paving roads, etc.), and 'speaking on national policies' in rural areas.[25] The creation of the Religious Corps and the Religious Propagandists was a further attempt by the regime to reduce the independence of the clergy, block their access to rural masses, and to reinterpret Islamic values in keeping with government policy.

Aside from the institutional and legal measures the government took to alter established social practices and patterns of relationships, Iran's society underwent considerable social change due to industrialization and diffusion of other cultures. The decades of the 1950s, 1960s, and 1970s marked a period when the traditional fabric of Iranian culture was altered and replaced with foreign (almost always Western) values and norms. Such social transformations resulted mostly from cultural diffusion or industrialization, or from a combination of both. Cultural diffusion in Iran was accentuated in the decade of the 1950s and the early 1960s. The government's efforts to Europeanize Iran began especially in 1962 with the White Revolution. These reforms were complemented by the growing tendency of many Iranians themselves, mostly members of the expanding middle class, to adopt European values.

Not all Iranians, however, were willing to become Westernized and abandon most of the traditional values and principles they had long cherished. The result was a coexistence of traditionalism alongside Westernism, thus creating psychological difficulties and cultural contradictions for many urban Iranians who lived under a divided culture system (more of which below). There were two very different value systems in existence at the same time, and adherence to one necessitated the negation of certain principles in the other. To the economic differentiations of the society was added cultural classification – traditional versus 'modern' – which portended striking differences with, nevertheless, occasional overlapping. Consequently, prior to the 1978–79 revolution, Iranian society was divided economically as well as socially. Social stratification based strictly on the means of production would no longer suffice: the degree to which people had undergone cultural change also needed to be considered. Changes in cultural values and norms did not affect all members of an economic class at the same rate. Therefore no single economic class could be considered to be completely Westernized while others were labelled 'traditional', although it was mainly the middle-class Iranians whose cultural values showed the greatest susceptibility to change.

The division of Iranian society into the 'traditional' and the 'modern' segments, and the internal divisions of each of the social classes along parallel lines, resulted in one of the main social causes of the Iranian revolution. The confusion of the more traditionally oriented segments of society, and their resentment to the officially sanctioned programmes directed at Westernizing Iranian society were later translated into political opposition against the regime. At the same time, the popular identification of the regime as the main instigator of social change resulted in the growing attraction of those who were most resentful of social change towards those groups and individuals who not only opposed the regime politically but who rejected its social policies as well (i.e. the *ulema*). It is, therefore, necessary to study the various classes that existed in Iran prior to the revolution and to examine the degree to which they had been exposed to, and affected by, social change.

Classes in Iran

Five broad economic classes, distinguished by their respective positions in production relations, existed in the Pahlavi state. They included rural peasants and tribal masses; the urban-based working class; the *petite bourgeoisie*; the bourgeoisie, which was also inclusive of the Bazaari merchants; and an upper class that included tribal chieftains, urban-based landed magnates, wealthy merchants and businessmen, factory owners and industrialists, and the Crown.

Rural Inhabitants

According to the 1976 official census, 53 per cent of the Iranian population resided in rural areas.[26] These rural dwellers belonged to either of the two broad categories of cultivators and non-cultivators. Both groups included different strata that were classified according to the specific economic positions they had in relation to production means:

Non-cultivators

1. Absentee landlords, including the state, crown and *vaqf* trustees.
2. Large-scale renters from above, often absentee.
3. Village officials: head-men (*kadkhoda*), landlord's agents, field watchers, etc.
4. Non-cultivating small owners.
5. Non-cultivating leasers of productive equipment, usually cattle, sometimes water.
6. Non-cultivating heads of work-teams, providing at least one instrument of production.

Cultivators

7. Cultivating small holders.
8. Cultivator paying a fixed cash rental.
9. Cultivating head of work team.
10. Share cropper with some production equipment, usually oxen.
11. Share cropper with only his labour to sell, but with a regular position on a work team or on the land.
12. Labourer with regular wage, in cash or in kind.
13. Casual labourer without a place on a work team or land, often hired by the day only in peak season.[27]

The land reform programme effectively removed the top landlord stratum in many Iranian villages.[28] But the persistence of the rest of the stratification patterns – including, for example, competition for scarce work – led to the maintenance of social control by the top classes, to whom some of the power formerly held by landlords was transferred.[29] In 1966 a United Nations research team came to the following conclusions regarding land reform in Iran:

> There was nothing to prevent landlords from reordering the cultivation pattern in their villages before the land reform reached them in such a way as to ensure that the best land – or indeed any land at all – went only to their friends, relations, and loyal dependants. Again, landlords who exercised their option to retain a collection of parts of villages might contrive to retain the best parts and even, perhaps, those parts which dominate the water supply to the rest of the village.
>
> ....A second problem concerns the cost of land to the beneficiaries.... Many will find this too large a sum to pay off over fifteen years. Similarly it is doubtful how secure the new leasing system will actually be even if it can be enforced, since rents have not been reduced, they are to be fixed in cash at

pre-reform levels (thus exposing the tenant to the vagaries of market fluctuations) and the landlord may evict if the rent is not paid within three months of the due date.[30]

In addition to the land reform programme, in the early 1960s the government established its Literacy Corps (Seph-e Danesh), whereby educated conscript officers were sent into villages to introduce literacy via propaganda for the government, for religious values presented as part of those of a secular state, and for hygiene. A *sepah* [corps] to inculcate the virtues of hygiene was later established as a separate vehicle of government propaganda. The villagers were already familiar with the drive for Western-style sanitation and hygiene – it had previously been attempted under the US-sponsored Point Four Program. But while the Literacy Corps attracted them enthusiastically, hygiene was too personal a matter to be met with any response but ridicule – people did not want to be told by young men from Tehran how to go to the lavatory.[31] Consequently, in spite of the eagerness for literacy, in sum these attempts to alter the way of life of the villagers effected little change in the traditional environment of rural Iran. It was to be affected by the more radical interference with traditional patterns of cultivation that came with the major changes in land control and utilization, to which reference has already been made.[32] But so far as the minds and personal habits of the villagers were concerned, these 'reforms from above' did not penetrate.

The working class

The structure and characteristics of the Iranian working class prior to the revolution were heavily influenced by the economic policies and programmes the regime pursued. It was, in fact, largely due to the regime's economic development programmes that a phenomenal increase occurred in the size and significance of one of the segments within the working class, namely the rural immigrants, the lumpenproletariat. The relatively sudden appearance of huge numbers of rural immigrants in the cities was itself one of the sociological factors that directly contributed to the advent of the Iranian revolution (see p.127)

The government's modernization programme in the 1960s was widely augmented in the early 1970s due to a sudden rise in the rate of economic growth. Largely as a result of a dramatic increase in oil revenue, the country's economic growth reached unprecedented proportions in the early 1970s. During the 1973 oil embargo of the West by oil producing Arab countries, the Shah decided to continue the production and marketing of Iranian oil, though at a much greater price. The price of Iran's crude oil rose from US $2.6 per barrel (p.b.) in

Social change

January 1973 to US $11.9 p.b. in January 1974.[33] An 'oil boom' ensued, resulting in the expansion and intensification of the country's economic growth programmes. As compared with the 1971–72 average, oil revenues in 1973 jumped by 138 per cent to 587.5 billion Rials (b.R.).[34] The increase continued throughout the next year by 146 per cent, raising the revenues derived from oil to 1441.6 b.R. Between 1965 and 1971 the country's national income had grown at an average annual rate of 11.1 per cent. During the 'oil boom', the increase in the national income was some 36.1 per cent, going as high as 2152.2 b.R. Between 1973 and 1974 government revenues and expenditures nearly tripled, and the budget deficit of 13.2 b.R. in 1973 was turned into a 140 b.R. surplus in 1974. The country's economic growth was of unprecedented proportions and this dramatically influenced diverse economic, social, demographic, and even political developments in the succeeding years.[35] One such consequence was the growing share of oil in the gross national product (GNP) (Table 4.1). Oil and oil-derived products were recognized as the country's main source of revenue, and the government's economic development plans became almost exclusively dependent on the size of oil revenues. The Fifth Five-Year Development Plan, which began in 1973, was completely revised and augmented in order to account for the sudden jump in oil revenues. Furthermore, the government's estimated fixed total investment in the Fifth Plan was revised and extended by more than 90 per cent (Table 4.2). Inflation, meanwhile, nearly doubled. In 1973 consumer prices rose by 11.2 per cent as opposed to 6.3 per cent in the preceding year.

Table 4.1 Sectoral distribution of percentage of gross national product, 1963–78

Sector	1962–63	1967–68	1972–73	1977–78
Agriculture	27.4	21.6	10.3	9.2
Industry	17.8	20.7	12.6	18.5
Manufacture and mines	(12.8)	(14.2)	(8.5)	(12.6)
Construction	(4.3)	(4.8)	(3.5)	(4.8)
Water and power	(0.7)	(1.7)	(0.6)	(1.1)
Services	40.0	36.4	23.9	34.6
State services	(7.6)	(9.4)	(7.9)	(10.9)
Oil	12.3	18.0	50.6	34.7

Source: H. Katouzian, *The Political Economy of Modern Iran, 1925–1979* (New York: New York University Press, 1981), p. 257.

Table 4.2 Estimated total fixed investment in the Fifth Plan

	Original estimate		Revised estimate		
Sector	Sum (billion Rials)	%	Sum (billion Rials)	%	Percentage change
Industry and mines	552.4	22.4	846.4	18.0	53.2
Agriculture and natural resources	152.6	6.2	309.3	6.6	102.7
Transportation and communication	188.4	7.7	492.2	10.5	161.3
Housing	402.8	16.4	925.0	19.7	129.6
Oil and gas	461.9	18.7	791.2	16.8	71.4
Others	703.3	28.9	1,334.7	28.4	89.8
Total	2,461.1	100.0	4,698.8	100.0	90.9

Source: Iran, Plan Organization, Fifth Development Plan, 1975.

While the 1962 Land Reform had caused some rural–urban migration, it was during the 1970s that this process gained momentum and villagers flocked into the cities. The depressing economic conditions in which most immigrants found themselves after their arrival in the urban centres, the ramifications of their presence in the cities for the technological industrialization and the cultural Westernization of the country, and the peculiar socio-psychological orientation they developed after exposure to the mores of urban environment were all instrumental in creating conditions conducive to anti-government mobilization. Undeniably, rural–urban migration is often one of the inevitable side effects of modernization and industrial growth.[36] Also, unless there is an elaborate system for the provision of basic public necessities such as may be found in welfare states – which in most developing countries cannot – then most immigrants are likely to face harsh realities in trying to live an urban life. Finding adequate employment and accommodation in the cities, adjusting to the urban culture, and assimilating into the urban mainstream are some of the more acute problems that rural immigrants experience.[37] In Iran the agonies of this economic underclass were particularly compounded when the country's rapid economic growth in 1973–74 came to an abrupt halt in 1975 and continued its reverse trend all through the revolution (see p. 127). Widespread unemployment only accentuated the problems that the immigrants faced in adjusting to the cultural environment of the cities. Subject to economically and culturally disadvantageous circumstances, and painfully aware of it themselves, it was the rural immigrants who were readily taken by the revolutionaries' ethos as the intelligentsia's indolent opposition to the regime began to evolve into a mass movement. Had it not been for the immigrants' contribution to the opposition movement, the Iranian revolution might well have been of an entirely different nature altogether.

Domestic migration in Iran as elsewhere is most often due to economic factors. Most rural immigrants are young adults. They are often unmarried, but even if married, they have much less at stake than their elders. They frequently lack control over resources and are usually without power or significance within their own communities. They are generally at a transitional stage between adolescence and adulthood and are not yet firmly committed to an adult role in their village community. They therefore demonstrate greater adaptability to the urban environment and to its demands, and are less resentful of accepting marginal jobs, hoping eventually to find secure employment.[38] Often unable to find employment either in the formal or the informal economic sectors, migrants usually form a 'marginalized labour force', having to settle for whatever menial employment opportunities that are available.[39] In Iran this marginalized labour force was mainly composed of construction labourers, whose size grew from 710,000 in 1972 to 980,000 in 1977 (Table 4.3). Where the size of the labour force in all other major economic sectors grew between 1972 and 1973, the agricultural labour force did not increase during the same period, signifying the flight of most agricultural labourers into the cities. Construction in modernizing countries is by nature labour intensive and does not require a concentration of skilled labour. The construction industry is therefore often a main source of attraction to rural immigrants.[40] As housing and construction were given top priority in the Fifth Plan (Table 4.2), domestic immigration was further encouraged by greater occupational opportunities in the construction industry.

For the rural immigrant, the unexpected deficiencies of urban life are in most cases almost evenly divided into lesser economic opportunities than expected and the existence of greater social problems than originally anticipated.[41] The immigrants often face poverty in the cities, both materially and culturally. Yet research conducted among immigrants in Tabriz, Iran's fourth largest city at the time, indicated that their economic expectations had generally been met and in some cases even surpassed.[42] Housing was usually the immediate problem many urban-bound migrants faced. In fact, according to the nature of their accommodation in the urban centres, immigrants could be divided into two sub-groupings: those who resided in rented accommodation, composed mainly of unmarried wage-earning labourers with relatively secure jobs, and those residing in squatter settlements, made up mostly of families, whose head, the male, was often unable to secure a regular wage-earning position and was forced to settle for whatever jobs that were available. Those immigrant workers who could not afford to live either in squatters or in rented rooms often rented only one slot in a room to sleep in by the hour, and those working in construction projects usually slept at the site of the uncompleted buildings they worked on.[43]

Table 4.3 The Iranian labour force, 1956–77 (1,000s)

Sector	Annual totals			Increases	
	1956	1966	1972	1977	1972–77
Agriculture	3,326	3,774	3,800	3,800	0
Oil	25	26	40	55	15
Mining and manufacturing	816	1,324	1,820	2,500	680
Construction	336	520	710	980	270
Utilities	12	53	60	65	5
Commerce	355	513	650	725	75
Transport and communications	208	224	255	280	25
Government services	248	474	640	780	140
Banking, other services, n.a.d.*	582	650	900	1,040	140
Total fully or seasonally employed	5,908	7,558	8,875	10,225	1,350
Wholly unemployed	158	284	320	375	55
Total labour force	6,066	7,842	9,195	10,600	1,405

Source: Fred Haliday, Iran: Dictatorship and Development (New York: Penguin, 1979), p. 176.
*n.a.d. = Not adequately described.

It is difficult to detect a direct causal relationship between a state that can be best described as cultural disillusionment and social and political unrest. This disillusionment is particularly more acute among groups who perceive their norms to be less rooted in the urban setting and who thus feel greater alienation from the ever-changing cultural environment and the social mainstream. The young immigrant who comes into the cities looking for a job and for material prosperity often finds himself confronted with phenomena with which he had never had to deal before. Some of the problems with which immigrants have to contend are prostitution, illicit deals in drugs and stolen goods, alcoholism, and other similar problems often rampant in the low-income areas where most immigrants are often forced to reside upon entrance into the cities. The full analysis of the psychological effects of such an encounter are beyond the aims of this work. It is obvious, however, that the immigrants do not need to be excessively puritanical to be eventually disgusted and angered by the malfeasance they observe, even if they

Social change

themselves succumb to it. A more likely problem, nevertheless, and one with more intense ramifications for the social order, is the difficulty immigrants face in attempting to undergo urbanization: to assimilate into the urban mainstream and to adapt to the cultural environment of the cities. A would-be immigrant may envision the economic difficulties that await him in the city, but he is far less likely to anticipate culture shock and social segregation. Rural immigrants invariably find themselves unassimilated into the social mainstream. They have almost always been raised in conservative, traditionally oriented, and unsophisticated culture systems. Ethical values rigidly define good and bad in terms of black and white and often there are no values that fall in between. In the Middle East and Latin America, orthodoxy in religion and adherence to an accepted traditional code of conduct are features of most rural communities, while in most of Africa such rigidity is part of one's allegiance to tribal customs and beliefs. When rural immigrants are confronted with the urban culture, which is itself divided into a multitude of facets, they are unable to adjust to its complexities. Their powers of assimilation are also limited. The mores of city life are too commonly accepted as completely blasphemous, but they often remain entirely contrary to the principles to which the immigrants had been accustomed prior to migrating. The immigrants are incapable and, even if capable, often unwilling to assimilate into the urban culture and become urbanized.

There are two escape mechanisms with which rural immigrants tend to combat their alienation in the cities. They can, and often do, outwardly act and behave as if they understand and in fact enjoy the urban cultural environment that surrounds them. They often do not hesitate to enjoy the superficial pleasures of urban life, such as going to cinemas and to coffee-houses, usually in order to avoid seclusion from other peers or the embarrassment of meeting city folks, people with whom they feel at a disadvantage. Inwardly, however, they are troubled by a deep sense of guilt for their participation in what they generally consider to be a corrupt and decadent way of life. It was this very inner sense of repulsion towards the prevailing system of cultural conduct as displayed in Iran's modernized cities that facilitated Ayatollah Khomeini's mobilization of thousands of rural immigrants against the Shah and his regime.

Another method with which rural immigrants tend to compensate for their alienation in the city environment is through developing close links with other immigrants in similar circumstances and predicaments. Socialization takes place not at the level of the city community, but in a much more insular context, within the confines of a socially and culturally isolated caste existing only on the margins of active urban life. Once in the city, rural immigrants tend to stick together or, more out of necessity than out of desire, they often spend their free time in places where they feel a greater affinity, both valuationally as well as linguistically and culturally, to their native localities. Such local meeting places, besides the coffee-houses mentioned above, included in Iran mosques and other centres of religious activity.

Other noteworthy segments of Iran's urban-based working class included artisans and craftsmen, who specialized in traditional ornaments and handicrafts but who were destined for technological extinction; unskilled or semi-skilled employees of various jobs, active mostly in the informal sector of the economy; and industrial workers with modern skills. Beginning in the early 1970s, traditional craftsmen no longer occupied a significant portion of the economic labour force in Iran. Although they still retained their own bazaars in many Iranian cities, their social and economic significance was greatly diminished. The bulk of Iran's working class comprised workers with little or no educational or technical skills. They were often employed in small industrial complexes or in the labour-intensive segments of the informal sector of the economy. Mention has been made of construction workers. Also of this category were shop-assistants, people working with machines (not machinists), servants and maids, and handymen. A product of the urban labour surplus, these labourers were in reality mostly mis-employed or under-employed, if not in fact unemployed. While under-employment refers to occupations in which the task at hand could be satisfactorily carried out by far fewer persons, 'mis-employment' refers to jobs in which the goods produced or the services at hand contribute little to social welfare.[44] Skilled and educated industrial labourers comprised the smallest echelon of the working class and were therefore in high demand. Employed mostly in the oil refineries of Abadan, Tehran, Tabriz, Isfahan, and Shiraz, or in the steel plant in Isfahan, during the 1960s and the 1970s this segment of the working class grew rapidly (Table 4.3). Politically aware and socially more familiar with urban values (though not necessarily supportive of such values), the economic status of the skilled industrial working class often overlapped with the lower segments of the middle class (that of small shopkeepers, for example).

The development and expansion of a 'working class' in Iran was a direct product of the social change the country had been undergoing since the 1960s. The industrialization of the country's infrastructure had resulted in the development of an interdependent system of a few primary cities in which political life, social acculturation, and economic mobility were concentrated.[45] The price of rapid urbanization was rural–urban migration and its economic and sociological consequences: the development of shanty towns in the periphery of urban centres, the growth of newly developed economic classes (e.g. the landless, unemployed, and unskilled labourer), and subsequent alterations in social patterns of power relationships. Yet inasmuch as Iran's working class was itself an economic product of social change, it was alienated from the cultural and normative alterations that had resulted from industrialization and Westernization. Except for a small segment of skilled industrial workers, almost all labourers, despite residence and occupation in urban environments, still held traditional social norms and values. Labourers themselves strove to achieve economic mobility by acquiring a secure occupation, yet they often deliberately abstained from assimilation into the urban culture, which they viewed with cynicism and contempt. Social change in the 1960s and the 1970s altered the life of the Iranian working class economically far more than it did culturally.

The middle class

Prior to the revolution, the Iranian middle class was defined both in relation to its economic position in production relations as well as the degree to which it was affected by social change. Socially, there was a 'traditional' and a 'non-traditional' middle class, the former adhering to older values and cultural practices, while the latter, through industrialization and cultural diffusion, was oriented towards more recent social trends and power relations. Economically, the middle class was divided into the *petite bourgeoisie* (i.e. the salaried middle class), and the bourgeoisie (i.e. the upper middle class). Both the *petite bourgeoisie* and the bourgeoisie underwent varying degrees of social change, thus being distinguished not only by horizontal economic divisions but by vertical social differentiations as well.

The Iranian *petite bourgeoisie* comprised small entrepreneurs and the salaried middle class, most of whom were employed in the state bureaucracy. The economic mobility of the 'working class' into the ranks of the *petite bourgeoisie* was difficult, though it was made possible through the educational system and entrepreneurial innovation and hard work. The civil service and the labour-intensive informal sector employed the bulk of the Iranian *petite bourgeoisie*. Yet while upward economic mobility was not the main concern of the *petit-bourgeois*, it was made possible through several existing channels. Some were often deeply committed to nationalism and were concerned with social issues, while others, with neither deep convictions nor understanding, usually remained politically and socially passive.[46]

The Iranian bourgeoisie (upper middle class) included merchants, members of the professional intelligentsia, and high-ranking bureaucrats and army officers. Bourgeois merchants were mainly bazaar traders and a growing number of automobile and real-estate dealers.

There were also a number of import–export merchants, but their small size and economic insignificance in the face of the state's monopoly over foreign trade placed them in a relatively small minority. As the regime had adopted an industrialization/import substitution strategy of development, the well-being of Iranian merchants depended almost entirely upon the flow of foreign imports and investments.[47] High-ranking government officials and the professional intelligentsia comprised a further segment of the Iranian bourgeoisie. They included heads of bureaus and their deputies, physicians, university instructors, engineers, and high-ranking military officers. With the exception of those affiliated with the military, who were ostensibly dedicated to and dependent on the monarchy, the Iranian bourgeoisie before the revolution could be divided into three political groupings. The largest segment was made up of those who were politically passive and concerned mainly with economic mobility. A second group were opposed to the regime, composed mostly of men once deeply sympathetic to either the Tudeh or to the National Front in the early 1950s. Finally, a growing minority of the bourgeoisie were supportive of the regime. These wealthy and economically mobile members of the middle class were either historically close to the monarchy and the Court or were deeply aware that their economic standing directly depended on the stability of the government.[48] Beginning in the 1960s, when foreign and domestically educated Iranians became numerous enough to comprise a social stratum of their own, a further segment of professional intellectuals was added to the economic class of the bourgeoisie.

In addition to its division into the *petite bourgeoisie* and the bourgeoisie, the Iranian middle class was divided along socio-cultural lines into traditional and non-traditional segments. Iran's non-traditional middle class had developed as a direct result of social change (i.e. through industrialization, the expansion of bureaucracy, etc.). Traditional members of the middle class, on the other hand, had historically maintained their economic position in production relations. They included small property owners, bazaar merchants, and most real-estate dealers. For the most part, they had retained their economic positions regardless of the consequences of social change and did not derive their economic status from the society's infrastructural changes at large. The cultural and normative values they adhered to were mostly unaffected by social change and had remained consistent with traditional patterns of behaviour and power relationships. Such traditional values often included the persistence of large and extended families; art and the expression of other forms of communication (e.g. speech) through the usage of traditional idioms; deep respect for religion (Islam) and obedience to it in both personal feelings and in its formal rituals; and deeply personal relationships, usually with little regard for

Social change

formalities and legal proceedings. While these private values of the traditional middle class largely resisted the effects of social change, infrastructural and economic factors dictated greater flexibility in public values (purchasing and consumption patterns, clothing habits, housing, etc.). As a result, for instance, it was common for a traditional bourgeois merchant to own a house designed after Western architectural models but decorated in traditional Iranian taste.

Non-traditional middle-class Iranians generally included university instructors, physicians, engineers, and high-ranking civilian and military employees of the state. It was precisely as a result of social change that these economic classes had been developed and had expanded. Accordingly, their growth was directly dependent on the acceleration of social change: the more acute the process of social change, the greater the size of these groups. All such social segments were by-products of modernization, and thus the cultural systems they adopted were almost entirely non-traditional. Both their private and public values were shaped or deeply influenced by the Westernization of the country's infrastructure. Such groups tended to form nuclear families and felt less allegiance to more distant kin. Religion was a private matter for them; they felt a deep sense of emotional attachment to it but they did not regularly observe its rituals. Their acts and other forms of communication (e.g. songs) were modelled after contemporary Western styles. When required, their relationships were more formal, though informality in legal relationships still greatly prevailed among all strata of society. Finally, their general focus of cultural orientation was the West instead of the Iranian tradition. This non-traditional segment of the middle class dominated Iran's urban centres and was itself a medium through which further social change was attained.

The wholesale replacement of Iranian culture and values with those imported from the West by Iran's non-traditional middle class caused the anger of yet another segment of the middle class, the professional intelligentsia. Jalal Al-e Ahmad, who warned of the 'plague of Westoxication', and Ali Shariati, who urged Iranians to 'return to their own selves', were both representative of this group of intellectuals.[49] Such intellectuals were mostly members of the middle class, although some were also of upper-class backgrounds. Their educational skills usually enabled them to be in the same economic grouping as the bourgeoisie. Most Iranian intellectuals generally had at least one university degree and were therefore often in high technical demand. As a result, most were endowed with great social prestige. Unlike other economically well-off groups, however, they were usually aware, often with great unease, of the sharp divisions of the society, culture, and values that surrounded them. The intellectual could *choose* to become either non-traditional or traditionally oriented, but he was actively aware of his choice and critically assessed it in relation to his personal priorities and immediate surroundings. He was aware that on the one hand technological circumstances and social conditions necessitated the adoption of certain values and norms foreign to Iranian culture. On the other hand, his immediate cultural environment, which included religious values, interpersonal relationships, kinship ties, and so on, had a persistence not easily ignored. Different intellectuals opted for different priorities. Some, like Al-e Ahmad and Shariati, thought it necessary to preserve and in fact to nourish certain traditional aspects of Iranian culture, while others, like many constitutionalist liberals (e.g. Shapour Bakhtiar), gave priority to the adoption of foreign, mainly Western, norms and practices. This critical self-awareness of Iranian intellectuals rendered them potentially threatening to the monarchy, to political despotism, and to social Westernism. The regime was to some extent successful in assimilating most of these intellectuals into itself through lucrative positions and high salaries. However, as the 1978–79 revolution was to demonstrate, it was these intellectuals who initially spearheaded the movement against the Shah.

The upper class

Prior to the 1978–79 revolution, the upper class in Iran comprised three sub-groups: a non-landed aristocracy based in urban centres, which included bankers, merchants, army generals and cabinet ministers, financiers, and industrialists; tribal chiefs; and the Crown. Similar to the cultural dichotomy of the middle class, Iran's upper class was also stratified into the 'traditional elite', whose socio-economic standing was not conditioned by the process of social change, and the 'non-traditional elite', whose status resulted directly from social change. The Crown, tribal chiefs, and certain merchants, whose position within society was altered in form but not in substance because of social change, comprised the traditional elite. Bankers, financiers, industrialists, and army generals and cabinet ministers, on the other hand, were members of economic sub-classes developed primarily because of the modernization of the country. They would not have existed had it not been for social change and alterations within society's infrastructure. Being the direct products of – and in turn agents for – social change and modernization, the non-traditional elite adhered to the same exogenous culture systems and values that the non-traditional bourgeoisie readily adopted. The economic power of the upper class had in many cases given it more access to the products and processes of social change (through frequent trips abroad, for example) than even the non-traditional bourgeoisie. Tribal chieftains and khans, meanwhile, formed a very small percentage of the Iranian upper class. They usually resided in the provincial urban centres nearest to the geographic area where their tribe was located. Their economic and ethnic power base, however, had been reduced at the hands of the central government enough to nullify their significance.[50] While the Court was itself highly traditional in nature, under the Pahlavis it became perhaps the single most important institution in expediting social change in Iran. After the 1925 establishment of the Pahlavi dynasty under the dynamic and modernizing Reza Shah, the historically tradition-oriented institution of monarchy became determined to alter the very social and cultural values and power relationships that had secured its own foundations. The differential rates of change to which the social and political systems were subjected – social values drastically altered in the face of persistent, outdated political values that were no longer readily acceptable – had by the late 1970s reached contradictory levels. Grass-roots social change necessitated political alterations, though such political adjustments became increasingly unattainable as the establishment lacked the needed flexibility.

Social change and the revolution

The Pahlavi regime in several ways contributed to its own downfall. Political absolutism, bureaucratic inefficiency, naively optimistic economic expectations, and an unimaginably exaggerated sense of self-confidence characterized the Iranian regime and eventually were the main causes of its collapse. Through the promotion of social change the regime also played an equally important part in providing for the conditions that ultimately undermined it. The regime was more than capable of rectifying its policies and adjusting itself politically. Such structural and methodological reforms *appear* to have been easy to implement. Given the government's wealth even after the 'oil boom' was over, the regime might have sustained itself politically if it had curbed bureaucratic inefficiency and had adopted a measure of political realism. However, it lacked the conviction and the will to reform itself and to prolong its longevity. On top of such political misfortunes there were the additional adverse effects of social change and rapid modernization, which compounded the difficulties that the regime faced. The ever-expanding pool of immigrant villagers in the cities only increased urban unemployment and swelled the size of peripheral squatter settlements. In the cities, the only source of support and security the rural immigrants had were often kin or friends from the same village who had immigrated earlier. They were mostly left on their own, experiencing desolation, segregation, and the prejudice of the urbanites. If lucky, the younger ones could get jobs in the factories or become servants in the houses of the bourgeoisie and the *nouveaux riches*. For most, however, taking a manual job in a construction site or becoming a coolie was the only means of earning money. After the 'oil boom', even the coolies faced redundancies. The state, meanwhile, took no initiatives to improve the immigrants' conditions except occasionally to tear down their squatters in the hope of removing obstacles to urban development projects. At the same time, the growing university student population, the salaried middle class, and the bourgeoisie were becoming increasingly frustrated at their inability to participate in the political process. Most were also becoming resentful of the regime's insistence that they become socially and culturally Westernized. Instead of recognizing and appreciating the demands or at least the inclinations of the populace, the regime was too preoccupied with its dream of turning Iran into the 'Japan of the Middle East'. Whatever was 'traditional' about Iran and the Iranian culture, *except the concept and the institution of monarchy*, was to be discarded as outdated and obsolete regardless of its merits or substance. The political establishment was bent on modernizing Iran culturally as well as technologically. This objective was followed blindly and without any insight into its possible impact on the people. It did not take long for the political establishment to fall victim to the adversities of its naively conceived social policies.

Apart from the social and cultural ramifications of social change, economic factors also played an important role in the advent of the revolution. One of the most significant economic developments that expedited the revolutionary process was the abrupt reversal of the high rate of economic growth after 1974. The significance of this economic downturn lay not so much in its frustrating effects on aspiring middle and working classes as it did in expediting the structural collapse of the state. The government-engineered recession of 1977–78 did in fact put most rural immigrants out of employment and frustrated their aspirations for economic prosperity and security. However, they hadn't the political sophistication to organize and demand higher economic benefits nor, as the next chapter will show, was their cause effectively spearheaded by any of the opposition groups. The middle classes, as mentioned earlier, had generally acquiesced in living under inflationary circumstances and were generally affected very little by the government's budgetary constraints. Their response to the economic difficulties of the late 1970s was general apathy rather than political activism. When the disturbances occurred, the government mistakenly thought that they had originated because of economic frustration instead of social and political discomfort. It thus tried to quiet the middle classes by giving lucrative bonuses and salary rises to all civil servants. This effort proved to be completely fruitless and failed to slow down the growing momentum of the revolution. Among the upper classes, and even among the working class, the frustrating effects of the economic recession of the late 1970s were as equally ineffective in prompting them to revolt against the government. There were, indeed, several industrial strikes immediately before and during the revolution, the most significant of which were the closure of the Tehran Bazaar and the work stoppage at Abadan's oil refinery.[52] However, evidence suggests that in both instances the underlying motives for the strikes were primarily political rather than economic. The closure of the bazaar in Tehran and in other cities had been a symbolic act that Bazaari merchants had practised since the days of the Qajars as a way of expressing their displeasure with the government.[53] In the case of the Abadan oil refinery, its workers were uniquely politically sophisticated and were known to have been inclined towards communist ideology.[54] Yet they ended their strike when they were requested to do so by Khomeini's representative, Bazargan.[55] This also demonstrated that the oil refinery strike was more of a political gesture in opposition to the Pahlavi regime rather than an outburst of economic frustration.

The important conclusion to be drawn here is that while the social and cultural consequences of social change significantly increased the likelihood of the appearance of revolutionary circumstances in Iran in the late 1970s, its economic ramifications failed to produce similar effects. Through its deliberate and intense promotion of social change, Iran's monarchy delegitimized itself, or rather, it fostered policies whose results were explicitly contradictory to an authoritarian regime. Apart from its broader ramifications, social change affected Iranian society in two particular ways. First, city dwellers, regardless of their background and status, became socially and culturally disillusioned as they were for the most part unable or unwilling to conform to the often conflicting values that confronted them. Second, and a natural result of the first development, the public gradually refused to accept a despotic and highly conformist political system. While these two developments were in themselves not sufficient to produce a revolutionary movement, they were none the less instrumental in increasing the public's potential for revolutionary mobilization. What was needed was someone who would not only oppose the regime but who would also offer an appealing set of alternative values that the public could use as a remedy for its social and cultural disorientation. Khomeini was just the man, and Islam was his remedy. The public was longing to grasp values that rejected what was; it was not necessarily important whether they really understood the meaning and the depth of what they were grasping. Islam was deeply entrenched and respected in the Iranian psyche and its principles and values were whole-heartedly believed in, even if they were only superficially understood. When Khomeini came into the picture, he capitalized on and manipulated the disillusionment of Iranians, and, while perhaps not realizing it himself, he offered the one alternative the public was at the time most willing to follow.

Chapter five

Revolutionary mass mobilization

This chapter analyses the reasons for the emergence of the *ulema*, and within them Ayatollah Khomeini, as the leader of the Iranian revolution. Chapters 3 and 4 described the various opposition groups and the social classes respectively. It is now necessary to see what linkages developed between the revolutionaries on the one hand and the people on the other, and why one particular group of activists, the *ulema*, became the leaders of the revolutionary movement. To answer this question certain aspects of Iran's social and economic development prior to the revolution need to be examined. They include the extent and the nature of anti-state antagonisms throughout society, the role and significance of Islam as a social force, the viability of the different channels of communication with which the revolutionaries called on their followers to revolt, and more importantly, the cultural communicability of their revolutionary propaganda in relation to the masses. It will be argued that the convergence of all such factors facilitated Ayatollah Khomeini's rise to the leadership of the revolution.

In the 1970s there were three proximate causes for the articulation and expression of anti-state antagonisms by Iranians: economic, political, and socio-culturally originated grievances. The existence of such grievances among the population in turn created a reciprocal relationship between the politically aware – or rather, as it will be later argued, the politically manipulated – segments of the population on the one hand and groups competing for control over the state apparatus on the other. Apart from the Crown, Iran's urban society prior to 1978–79 was composed of five economically differentiated classes, namely the wealthy upper classes (e.g. industrialists and factory owners), the bourgeoisie (e.g. Bazaari merchants), the *petite bourgeoisie*, industrially based workers, and rural immigrants and other members of the lumpenproletariat. Except those in the upper classes, who were almost exclusively supportive of the establishment, all others were in one way or another disenchanted with the regime and could form potential blocks of revolutionary opposition. Concurrently, there existed various organized or quasi-organized groups that opposed the regime – the *ulema*, the intellectuals, and the political parties and guerrilla organizations – which, within their limited capabilities, levied political demands against the regime and competed against one another for greater popular acceptance and credibility. The convergence of the demands of the revolutionary groups with the predominant grievances among the different social classes, and the ability of one of those revolutionary groups effectively to articulate these grievances and to channel them into political activism, gave the Iranian revolution its doctrinal and ideological colouring.

Economic grievances

Economic grievances have long played an important role in political upheavals and revolutionary crises. More specifically, given that a sufficient level of consciousness exists, exploitation or infringement of economic privileges may result in political conflict. It is thus important to see whether any economically based grievances existed in Iran prior to the revolution, and if so how central to the demands of the revolutionaries they were. Two classes in Iran had reason to be economically disenchanted: the working classes, due to the exploitative nature of Iran's capitalist-style economic development, and Bazaari merchants, because of being targeted for elimination by the regime as a part of the government's drive to achieve social and economic modernity. Feudal landlords were similarly targeted by the White Revolution's Land Reform Programme. However, as it has been argued, most landed proprietors either eventually returned to their feudal estates or transformed their feudal privileges into capitalist ones by becoming urban-based industrialists.[1] Their potential for opposition against the regime was thus effectively undermined and was instead redirected into support for the status quo. Nevertheless, the working class, which was in fact subject to economic exploitation, did not demonstrate any significant degree of economically originated opposition to the regime either. The absence of political activism by the working class as such was partly due to the nature of its class structure and partly caused by the non-existence of opposition groups that could effectively address themselves to economic questions.

The greatly amorphous nature of Iran's industrial labour force under the Pahlavis prevented the development of political consciousness by Iranian workers. While a substantial portion of the population engaged in wage-earning employment, Iran did not have a homogeneous class of industrial labourers.[2] This heterogeneity was caused not only by the segregation of the working classes into different industrial sectors (i.e. oil, manufacturing, and construction), but more importantly, by the fact that only a small minority of industrial labourers worked in large-scale plants. In 1977 it was estimated that some 72 per cent of all Iranian workers were employed in units of fewer than ten persons.[3] The dispersion of industrial labourers throughout many small units effectively blocked the development of political consciousness among Iranian workers, a development further hampered by the nation's high rate of illiteracy and by the absence of independently active trade unions. All trade unions in Iran under the Shah were run by the state and all strikes were illegal.[4] Even if the trade unions were permitted by the government to express themselves politically, the high rate of illiteracy, which in 1976 stood at 62 per cent, would not have provided much opportunity for Iranian workers to formulate political demands. Furthermore, an unspecified portion of industrial labourers were actually construction workers with seasonal employment who were otherwise classified as rural immigrants.

In addition to the structural characteristics of Iran's working class, superstructural factors also prevented its politicization and muted its emergence as a revolutionary force. Mention has already been made of the high degree of illiteracy throughout the society. Concurrent with and in fact reinforcing this illiteracy was an exigency of opposition groups making serious and productive efforts to raise the level of consciousness among industrial labourers or to spearhead political campaigns on their behalf. The two oppositionally active political organizations that theoretically adhered to socialism, the Mujahadeen and the Fedaiyan, achieved little dialogue with or understanding of the working class they claimed to represent.[5] For its part, the Tudeh Party was at first successful in generating a measure of political activism among industrial labourers in the 1940s and the 1950s. But as most of its members were exiled in the 1960s and the 1970s, it too lost the marginal influence it had once had among industrial workers. Organized opposition groups failed ideologically to appreciate and utilize the supposedly revolutionary potential of the working class. The two groups were also blocked from access to one another by the absence of channels through which they could reciprocally communicate. Leaflets, tracts, and secret meetings and discussions were the only means through which the organized parties could propagate their ideologies among the working class, and among other social classes for that matter, and through which they could attract new recruits. This task was made all but impossible by a repressive political establishment and an overwhelmingly illiterate audience. Consequently, even if Iran's working class were structurally and organizationally capable of feeling the effects of economic exploitation, it was unable, either by itself or through those claiming to represent it, to translate those feelings and frustrations into a language of political protest. Therefore, the participation of the workers as an economic class in the Iranian revolution was conspicuously lacking. A rise in the level of unemployment did in fact lead to an increase in the size and frequency of street demonstrations and marches. But neither the demonstrators nor the organizers were specifically demanding more employment opportunities or a more just distribution of wealth (see below). Whatever contribution to the revolutionary movement members of the working class made, they did so not because of economic grievances but rather because they were urged to do so by the *ulema*.

A somewhat different role was played by the Bazaaris, who were in fact subject to economic coercion by the regime. Following the Rastakhiz party's price-controlling campaign in 1976, the regime targeted the Bazaaris for harassment in the hope of breaking down their economic power and thus reducing their socio-culturally conservative influence throughout society. By relying on commerce and trade, the Bazaaris had always remained politically independent of the government. Although they had at times opportunistically supported the regime (such as during the 1953 *coup*), most Bazaari merchants had remained close allies of the *ulema*. This alliance often took the form of a strong financial linkage between the two groups, with the Bazaari merchants paying their tithes, the *zakat*, to the *ulema*. Under the Shah this alliance was strengthened by the identification of the Shah as a common enemy determined to disgrace Islam and the Iranian tradition. Thus when the confrontation between the state and the *ulema* took place, the Bazaaris soon entered into the picture in support of the latter, a support greatly encouraged by the regime's own provocation of the Bazaaris.

The Bazaaris did not contribute to the revolutionary movement as an independent political or economic force. Instead, they rendered critical financial assistance to those who took part in revolutionary activities.[6] This financial support came in three forms. First, the Bazaaris gave massive sums of money to high-ranking clergy and particularly to Ayatollah Khomeini to finance their revolutionary operations and to spend as they deemed appropriate. According to one estimate, the Bazaaris donated £20 million to Khomeini when he was in Paris.[7] Second, Bazaari merchants financed strikes, either by directly paying the wages of those on strike or by generously contributing to special funds set up for that purpose. Work stoppages by reporters and journalists and by workers at Abadan's oil refinery, among the most damaging to the government, were two of the more celebrated instances when the Bazaaris substantially prolonged the duration of strikes by providing financial assistance to the striking workers. In this manner, the Bazaaris heightened the extent of revolutionary fervour throughout society and at the same time expedited the collapse of the government machinery. A third mechanism through which the Bazaaris contributed to the revolutionary movement was through hiring youths to take part in anti-government street demonstrations and thereby accentuating the apparent unpopularity of the regime. Those hired came from the vast pool of unemployed rural immigrants, who were easily accessible to the Bazaaris because of the latter's extensive financial and organizational network. It is not clear how extensive this practice was and how many of the demonstrators had actually been paid to demonstrate. It would be plausible to assume that this practice was prevalent only at the beginning of the revolutionary movement, when the intensity and the frequency of the uprisings and demonstrations were still at a low level and could easily be suppressed by the government. By mid-1978, however, when the government had almost completely lost its ability to exert any pressure on the revolutionaries, the number of those pouring into the streets in Tehran and in other cities in order to participate in street marches and demonstrations reached into the millions. This increase did not result from more hiring by the Bazaaris but was caused instead by a combination of developments arising out of the growing fragility of the regime and the subsequent progression of the revolutionary movement. Such developments included the growing feasibility of anti-state activities, the increasing predominance of one of the groups leading the revolution over others and the resulting doctrinal clarity of the revolutionary movement, and more significantly, the fact that the person emerging as the revolution's leader was a high-ranking member of the cleric class.

Political demands

There were two remaining domains for the appearance of antagonism, the political and the socio-cultural, exploited by secular intellectuals (some of whom were also members of political parties) and by the *ulema* respectively. At times the concerns of the two groups inevitably overlapped. Nevertheless, politically based antagonisms were only of secondary importance in spreading revolutionary sentiments among the people. As rampant as political corruption and the absence of freedom were during the Shah's reign, they did not constitute real causes for the participation of people in the revolutionary movement. There were two underlying reasons for this irony. First, political ideals such as democracy and justice had not been a major preoccupation of any of Iran's social classes in the 1960s and the 1970s, since the country as a whole was generally absorbed in the process of economic development and material progress. Even those who were most directly affected by the regime's political nepotism – the middle classes and especially the civil servants – were concerned mostly with economic gains rather than political ideals.[8] In fact, in addition to the government's deliberate economic programmes designed to expedite material prosperity, certain features of Iran's political dictatorship encouraged people to be more attentive to economic interests and be less concerned with politics. Corruption and 'log-rolling' (*parti-bazi*) were two such characteristics of Iran's political system that often fulfilled most economic aspirations of the middle classes and led to their subsequent political pacification.

This is not to assert that politically oriented complaints and provocations were completely unimportant in the appearance of the revolution's leaders and its followers. In fact, the very first group of activists openly to voice opposition to the regime, the intellectuals, did so in protest over the absence of political freedom and human rights. Political freedom and justice remained recurrent themes throughout the course of the revolution and were demanded by the *ulema*, the political parties, and the intellectuals alike. Nevertheless, such political demands did not have sufficient strength by themselves to prompt the masses to participate in the revolutionary movement. Not only were freedom and justice not the main preoccupation of the people, those who called for their realization had comparatively weak organizational support behind them and were for the most part alienated from the rest of the society.[9] The few Iranian intellectuals who had remained active in the 1960s and the 1970s could at the most publish essays or deliver protracted lectures to an audience of mostly university students and occasionally some of the more politically aware members of the middle classes. In 1977 groups such as the Writers' Association and the Society for the Defense of Freedom and Human Rights became active and started to call for an end to repression and the establishment of democracy. Despite the enthusiasm they generated, they did not have the extensive organizational network or communication channels necessary to arrange anti-government activities on a popular basis and to maintain their control over what was evolving into a revolutionary movement. Although the intellectuals had the nationwide support and sympathy of most writers, teachers, and other educated classes, they could only propagate their cause through the existing state-run media or publish manifestos and leaflets to distribute among the people, only 37 per cent of whom could read and write. The intellectuals also had no means through which they could systematically disseminate their demands and proposals. Thus their political activities occurred in a social vacuum from which substantial segments of the population were absent.

While neither the intellectuals nor any of the organized political parties were capable of adequately exploiting the political exigencies faced by the regime, the *ulema*, who were by far the best organized of the three groups, were. Four separate but interdependent developments concurred to result in the *ulema*'s hegemony over the revolutionary movement. First, the *ulema* benefited from a nationwide network of mosques, furnishing them with both organizational means at the local level as well as with extensive channels for communication and the dispersion of propaganda. Second, given the important role of Islam as a powerful social force throughout Iranian history, the *ulema*'s revolutionary message embodied a distinct and unique cultural communicability that made it understandable to all social strata. Third, the miscalculation of the regime as to where the real source of political opposition lay and its inability properly to suppress that opposition once it was detected further facilitated the *ulema*'s ascension as the revolution's leaders. Finally, this ascension was ultimately aided by Ayatollah Khomeini's personal leadership over the revolutionary *ulema*, both because of the circumstances that led to his leadership and because of his performance once he had reached that position. Together, such factors resulted in the *ulema*'s and in particular in Ayatollah Khomeini's leadership of the revolution.

Along with the bazaars, the religious establishment was the only social institution that the regime had not been able to co-opt within itself and which remained largely independent of government control. This independence arose as a result of the government's inability to absorb or to suppress effectively the informal and the overwhelmingly localized organizational features of the bazaars and mosques. The mosques provided informal networks whereby the *ulema* exerted influence and to some extent control at the local level in different communities and neighbourhoods. The *ulema* often exercised this influence by preaching sermons and by continuing to perform many of the juridical acts that the government was trying to secularize. Each local mosque was often used as a power base by a particular member of the clergy, who was in turn in close association with other clerics centered in other mosques. Bigger and more famous mosques, such as the Masjid-e Shah in Tehran, were usually used by different high-ranking *ulema* on special occasions and for important religious events. Mosques not only served as informal networks of local organization, they also provided for direct communication between the *ulema* and their audience. Because of the government's minimal control over what was said at the mosque, the *ulema* could (and after 1978 did) use the pulpit as a forum for discussing political issues and often did not hesitate to attack the regime. While none of the *ulema* were fully immune from the wrath of the regime, the mosques provided by far the easiest means by which a potentially oppositional group could have access to a wide spectrum of the population. First, capable of being used as a sanctuary, the mosques were to a certain extent immune from the danger of being stormed by army troops. The events of 1963, when the government attacked the Feiziyeh seminary in Qom, and its political consequences, still remained fresh in the minds of many Iranian leaders and made them reluctant to victimize the religious establishment once again and thereby heighten the *ulema*'s already soaring popularity. Furthermore, the mosques provided the only extensive and local source of direct, verbal communication between a group of revolutionaries on the one hand and large segments of the population on the other. While the political parties and the intellectuals could only propagate their cause via booklets or at the most through lectures and ideological debates least understood by most commoners, the *ulema* could present their views by merely preaching them in their mosques.

The *ulema*'s revolutionary propaganda was not only easily presented through the network of mosques; the language of their propaganda also enjoyed a distinct cultural communicability that made it most effective and widely understood. Before answering why the *ulema*'s revolutionary propaganda was so distinctly influential, it is necessary to see what role their domain of activity, Shi'ism, has played in Iranian society. There are two important historical features that distinguish the role of Shi'ism in Iran from that of other religions in other societies. First, Shi'ism has always been an important social force in Iran, affecting the people not only on the deepest personal level but also regulating and determining most legal and judicial matters that governed their lives. Shi'ite *ulema* are responsible to see that not only religious rites and functions are properly conducted and that Shi'ite ethics are observed, but also that the overall administrative aspects of running the community conform to Shi'ite principles. Second, because of the position of *ulema* within society and in relation to the political structure, Shi'ism has almost always served as a language of political protest.[10] More specifically, Shi'ism has served as a fertile ground for the formation of Iranian nationalism. While Shi'ism itself is not inherently opposed to the political order, Iran's historical experience before the revolution had repeatedly placed the *ulema* and the state in opposition to one another. The historical friction between the *ulema* and the state arose both as a result of the conflicting ideologies of the two and because both sides wished to maintain and to expand their spheres of social and political influence. The protests over the Reuter and the Tobacco Concessions, in 1870 and 1891 respectively,[11] and over the launching of the White Revolution in 1963, demonstrated instances when the *ulema* spearheaded the opposition to the regime because they considered their interests to be in jeopardy. On other occasions, the *ulema* took part in movements against the regime because they were genuinely concerned for the welfare of the country, as was the case in the 1905–1911 Constitutional Revolution and the 1951–1953 oil nationalization movement. In any event, up until the late 1970s the *ulema* had taken active part in every significant national uprising against the state, whether their participation was motivated by personal interests or by national concerns. Furthermore, in order to achieve maximum success in their opposition campaigns against the state, the *ulema* often resorted to Shi'ite doctrines and principles to justify and legitimize their stands and to acquire the support of the masses. The political opposition of the *ulema* and their use of Shi'ism as their doctrine left a lasting impression on the population at large, for whom the *ulema* appeared not only as the protectors of religion but as the historical defenders of Iran's national interests as well. In the 1970s, this doctrinal preparedness of the *ulema* was strengthened by the increasing politicization of Shi'ism by a growing number of intellectuals and clerics alike. Thus when the political crisis of the late 1970s began, Shi'ism was already equipped with doctrinal as well as political means to oppose the regime.

This is not to assert that Shi'ism and Islam in general are inherently revolutionary forces. It is often falsely assumed that Islam and Shi'ism are naturally dynamic ideologies that serve to undermine tyrannical political establishments.[12] Like all other ideologies, both Islam and Shi'ism have been used by their proponents in accordance to the needs of the time. In theory and in practice, both Islam and Shi'ism have been as quietist at times as they have been revolutionary.[13] Nevertheless, in 1977, 1978, and 1979, the quietist character that Shi'ism had developed in the 1960s and the early 1970s was rapidly overcome by a revolutionary dynamism representative of previous eras. In the late 1970s the radicalization of Shi'ism into a revolutionary social force was caused by several factors. After the events of 1963, and especially because of intensified social change in the 1960s and the 1970s, the *ulema* had felt increasingly coerced into submitting themselves to the secular powers of the regime and accepting the regime's official cultural programmes. Having retained their organizational capabilities through mosques, seminary schools, and the like, when the political structure started to break down in the late 1970s, the clergy began to retaliate by calling on the people to overthrow the regime. This revolutionism was considerably accentuated by the inability of other groups opposing the regime to be either organizationally strong or ideologically popular.

Socio-cultural grievances

Another factor benefiting the *ulema* over other revolutionary groups was the receptivity of the *ulema*'s audience to their revolutionary propaganda, and the significant size and social position of this audience in relation to other classes. Two groups dominated the *ulema*'s audience: rural immigrants and traditionally oriented middle classes. Both groups embodied a potential that made them significant contributors to the revolutionary movement. This revolutionary potential was caused by the growing social frustration of both groups, since frustration is a significant factor in increasing public discontent against an established order. Rural immigrants usually experienced frustration upon their very arrival in the urban environment as they were often unable to find adequate accommodation and were therefore forced to reside in slums, shanty towns, or in cheap *caravanserais*, where prostitution and other illicit activities were generally commonplace. With respect to finding jobs and earning wages, the immigrants did not face great difficulty, as a result of the rapid growth of labour-intensive industries throughout the country, especially during the 'oil boom' years.[14] With the artificial economic recession that Prime Minister Amuzegar engineered in 1977 and the first half of 1978, however, rural immigrants began experiencing frustration as their unemployment level rapidly rose and their economic position in the cities progressively deteriorated. At the same time, the aspirations of most members of the middle class were also frustrated. Their expectations of higher economic gains and social prestige were often affected by their own and by the system's overall limited capabilities. The rapid decrease in the rate of economic growth after 1974 was especially significant in polarizing the economic frustrations of many aspiring urban Iranians. Modernization and exposure to Western living standards through cinema and television or through trips abroad had led to an increase in the public's desire to be materially more prosperous. Such expectations were often either not entirely met or were not fulfilled with the desired speed. Within the middle class, the public sector experienced the greatest expectation gap as its salary rates generally lagged behind those of the private sector.

Furthermore, both groups, starting especially in the 1960s, began to confront newly introduced and intensely propagated social values and practices that were not only alien to them but often stood in sharp contrast to their traditional values. Rural immigrants were mostly unable to socialize within the urban environment. They were therefore alienated not only from the values they had traditionally held but also from the ones they had newly confronted in the urban centres. The traditional middle classes – mainly comprising small shopowners, wage-earning employees in the private sector, and clerks, secretaries, and other low ranking civil servants – were generally resentful of the growing Westernization of the country and were reluctant to accept the 'modern' patterns of social and cultural behaviour. Iranian heritage and traditional values, of which Islam was widely perceived to be an integral part, were seen by the traditional middle classes to have fallen victim to the regime's much publicized desire to Westernize the country. The political establishment, and specifically the person of the Shah, were generally blamed and resented for their campaign to degrade and ridicule Islamic principles and other traditional values and for trying to replace them by Westernism and other supposedly modern beliefs and practices.

Such resentment, albeit silent, was sufficiently intense and deeply rooted to have been the responsive chord that the *ulema*'s religious appeal struck among many urban Iranians. Despite the polemical lectures and essays of intellectuals such as Shariati and Bazargan, who were trying to develop a theoretical synthesis between Islam and modernity, the regime's unceasing efforts to Westernize the country had led to the division of Iranian culture between the traditional (Islamic) and the modern (Western). The *ulema*'s opposition to the regime was from the outset religious in tone and as such their propaganda found greater social receptivity among the public, for whom the ayatollahs and their crusade epitomized not only a political alternative but also a cultural self-realization and a 'return to the self'. Islam's development as the predominant ideological umbrella under which Iranians were mobilized against the regime was a result of that religion's symbolization of discontent and opposition to Iran's cultural Westernization and not because of inherent revolutionary dynamics that Islam is often said to embody. The traditional upper and middle classes, the latter mainly including Bazaari merchants, had until 1977–78 felt pressured into conforming to a social set-up that was increasingly parting from Islamic and other traditional values and which was adversely acquiring an anti-religious, Westernized nature. The apparent break-up of the political apparatus and the messianic image that Khomeini and his proclamations were beginning to acquire combined to increase the oppositional proclivities of a public that was already overwhelmingly discontented with the political process and alienated from the cultural orientation of the country.

Khomeini's leadership

Ayatollah Khomeini's personal domination over the leadership of the movement resulted from several independent variables. Once the general public had become familiar with his name and had acquired a vague notion of what his intentions were, it was the nature of his self-proclaimed mission that gradually heightened his appeal and popularity and which resulted in his eventual idolization throughout Iran. Significantly, Khomeini's appeal cut across social and economic stratifications and attracted individuals from diverse backgrounds. To the frustrated and culturally disoriented rural immigrants and the middle classes, Khomeini appeared as a Messiah battling on their behalf and on behalf of the values they cherished. His oppositional proclamations, embedded with Islamic allegory and metaphor, enabled him to capitalize on those values and beliefs about which the public had the most intense and personal feelings. Socially, his religious background and training enabled him to understand and communicate with the masses, a blessing no other opposition group could match. Khomeini was an ayatollah, the highest rank within the Shi'ite hierarchy and a stature achieved only after completing a treatise of solutions and answers for some 3,000 problems for which individuals had sought his counsel.[15] Unlike the intellectuals, whose knowledge of society was acquired mostly through books and essays, Khomeini had developed an appreciation for the people's problems and dispositions through his daily and personal dealings with them. His greatest advantage over others was his ability to communicate with the masses and then to project their feelings in ways most consistent with popular and deeply rooted values. His message was simple enough to be understood by all, rational enough to make common sense, and bold and daring enough to be intriguing. The Ayatollah also won much popularity and respect for appearing aggressively defiant of the regime and for being determined to continue the battle to the end regardless of victory or defeat. On a different level, to many intellectuals and the more educated groups Khomeini appeared to be the one source capable of breaking the political deadlock imposed by a seemingly invincible regime. He had speedily achieved a degree of success that many highly educated intellectuals had long tried for but had been unable to accomplish. Between 1963 and 1977, despite years of planning and activism both inside Iran and abroad, no individual or organization had been able to pose the slightest degree of serious threat to the regime. In only a few months, Khomeini, a clergyman, was beginning to rally the whole nation behind him and was even shaking the very foundations of the Iranian Crown. Many intellectuals, recognizing Khomeini's better chances of overthrowing the Shah, soon joined his circle of associates or became passively supportive of his leadership position within the opposition. Some others had already been in contact with him and become his chief advisors.

Naturally, Khomeini's leadership of the revolution would not have been possible without his own initiatives and manoeuvres. Khomeini's career as an opposition activist from 1962 to 1979 can be broadly divided into two phases. Initially, the Ayatollah's opposition stemmed from the regime's attempts to alter certain traditional Islamic practices and beliefs. The granting of voting rights to women and to religious minorities, for example, was a specifically religious issue over which Khomeini attacked the regime in 1962. Similar to many other religious figures at the time, it was a deep sense of conservatism that prompted Khomeini to oppose the 'blasphemous' regime that was bent on Westernizing Iran. By 1978, however, what was once a reactionary ayatollah had become a progressive and idealist saint. What caused this remarkable transformation is not fully clear. Perhaps Khomeini was merely enunciating what he thought the people wanted to hear. If so, he certainly said all the right things: the people must have freedom; men and women are equal; religious minorities can freely practise their religions; the clergy will not interfere in the political process; Iran's domination by the West and especially by the United States will be stopped; the toiling classes will no longer be oppressed; and so on. Those around him, and the entire Iranian nation for that matter, were convinced that the Ayatollah's proclamations vocalized only his deepest convictions. The depth of these convictions was questioned, however, soon after the revolution succeeded and Khomeini became the leader of the Islamic Republic. It is not that Khomeini was a brilliant manipulator, which he might have been, but rather because of a lack of other equally ingenious strategists and tacticians that he emerged as the undisputed leader of the revolution. Declaring the establishment of democracy as his prime objective, Khomeini vehemently attacked the Shah for having instituted a repressive and dictatorial regime in Iran. He claimed to represent the people's mandate to establish an Islamic regime that would 'safeguard independence and democracy'.[16] What this 'Islamic' democracy and independence really meant was hardly understood or questioned by anyone. Through his repeated assurances that the clergy cannot be involved in the political process and that he himself would 'have no role in the government',[17] Khomeini not only dispelled fears that the alternative he was proposing to the Shah's monarchy was a theocracy, he even appeared as a champion of democracy and freedom. The regime itself also contributed to the growth of Khomeini's popularity by slandering him in *Ittela'at* newspaper and by pressing for his expulsion from Iraq. Both incidents resulted in the legitimization of Khomeini's leadership within the opposition movement and further polarized his aggressive and revolutionary rhetoric. Contrary to what the Shah had hoped, Khomeini's proclamations from Paris and his performance before the international media did not discredit the opposition and in fact led to the exaltation of the revolutionaries and heightened the Ayatollah's prestige and charisma. Khomeini's striking humility and grace mesmerized his global audience as well as his closest associates.[18] The movement against the regime was gradually beginning to appear to the public as a crusade, a *jihad* (holy war), spearheaded by a saint and directed against an evil regime. To the millions of Iranians who were pouring into the streets to offer their sacrifices for the revolutionary cause, Khomeini's words were prophetic and his mission was divine. He was no longer a mere revolutionary, he *symbolized* the revolution. He was no longer a simple ayatollah, he was the Imam of the whole nation.

Chapter six
Conclusion

The immediate causes of the Iranian revolution of 1978–79 were in themselves distinctively political. The revolution was the result of the structural breakdown of the Pahlavi state on the one hand and the initiatives and manoeuvres of groups opposing the regime on the other. At the same time, the social situation in which such political developments occurred was of overwhelming importance in determining the character and the outcome of the revolution. The main body of this book has been devoted to analysing those causally important social and political developments that resulted in the Iranian revolution. The remaining pages will examine some of the questions regarding the revolution that were not previously raised. While such questions are mostly only hypothetical, they help sharpen our analytical understanding of the revolution. Was the Iranian revolution in any sense inevitable? Could it have had leaders other than the *ulema* and Ayatollah Khomeini? And, how much linkage has there been between the regime that has emerged after the revolution and the principles that the revolution stood for?

The occurrence of the Iranian revolution was inevitable because of its two prerequisites, the breakdown of the political apparatus and the subsequent activism of opposition groups. Given the nature of the regime's development over the decades – its heavy dependence on outside powers, its nepotistic and authoritarian organization, and its inability adequately to reform itself and to adapt to new circumstances – the collapse of the Pahlavi state structure was in fact inevitable. For the Pahlavi dynasty in general and for the Shah in particular, maintaining political power required a continuation of the Nixon-Kissinger doctrine, thus ensuring the regime of the international material and psychological support it needed, and a rapid rate of economic growth, in order to keep the public preoccupied with economic concerns rather than political considerations. The Pahlavi state was too fragile to withstand changes in the international status quo as well as those occurring internally. Had the Nixon-Kissinger doctrine been maintained, had

Revolution in Iran

international human rights organizations such as Amnesty International not called attention to the brutalities of SAVAK, and had oil prices continued to soar after 1974, perhaps then the Pahlavi regime would not have started to collapse. But these developments all did occur and the Pahlavis could not adequately deal with them.

Given the inevitability of the collapse of the regime, and given the fact that during the Pahlavi era there always existed groups that advocated the overthrow of the system, the Iranian revolution was in fact inevitable. As Chapters 3 and 5 demonstrated, the *ulema*'s leadership of the revolution was also inevitable, although it was facilitated to a great extent by the regime's own mistakes. The *ulema* had social and cultural hegemony and the resources for political mobilization that the other groups lacked. But the regime was ignorant of this truism and instead continued to harass the largely ineffectual guerrilla organizations and the intellectuals. When the government finally realized that it was the *ulema* who were the real source of opposition, it only took measures to facilitate their leadership of the revolution. The government insulted Khomeini by name in a newspaper article, pressed for his expulsion from Iraq to France, and appeased the revolutionary *ulema* inside Iran, hoping to quiet the disturbances and to silence the clerics. However, all such moves backfired and only polarized the *ulema*'s and Khomeini's revolutionism. Yet even if the government had not taken these measures, it would not have been probable that other groups could lead the revolution. The *ulema* had the overwhelming following of the two most important elements of the revolutionary movement, namely the middle classes and the rural immigrants. The social changes of the 1960s and 1970s had resulted in the widespread disillusionment and frustration of the middle classes, among whom the country's intellectuals stood up and cried for a sense of cultural identity. The lower classes, composed mostly of rural immigrants and industrially based workers, found themselves alienated from the rest of society and also began to search for something with which they could identify in the face of the foreign and seemingly hostile environment in which they found themselves. The one common denominator that both the middle classes and their intellectuals searched for and to which the lower classes had clung was Islam, the ideology of the *ulema*.

During the revolution's critical days in 1978 and early 1979, the question of what the post-revolutionary government would be was not raised in a serious manner and the issue was summarized in dogmatic slogans and protracted statements issued in Paris. The public only knew that they did not want the Shah, his regime, and his system of monarchy. It was commonly understood and generally agreed that the new system was to be a republic (since the revolution was seen to be directed against

Conclusion

2,500 years of monarchy), somehow Islamic (because of the *ulema*'s leadership), and independent of either of the superpowers (due to Iran's historic domination by Britain, the Soviet Union, and later by the United States). It would be erroneous to assume that the public would have endorsed any alternative to the Pahlavis. Yet the slogan 'Neither Eastern, nor Western; an Islamic Republic' summed up the crowd's understanding of the nature of the post-revolutionary system. It is doubtful whether any of the demonstrators really understood what that slogan really meant. The notion of an Islamic government had been raised and discussed in only two books: Banisadr's *Main Principles and Guidelines of Islamic Government* and Ayatollah Khomeini's *Islamic Government*. Neither of the books was ever extensively read or even widely heard of prior to the revolution. Banisadr's book was published in France and was read by only a handful of Iranian intellectuals living abroad, while Khomeini and his works remained obscure and unimportant even within clerical circles. When Khomeini and Banisadr became close associates following the ayatollah's asylum in France, their alliance crystallized itself in the theoretical foundation of an Islamic republic. The popular appeal of such a system was as much cultural as it was political. Politically, the new system was a republic, thus theoretically allowing everyone a chance to participate in the country's affairs and in the running of the government. Khomeini's repeated assurances that his incoming regime would be democratic further strengthened the public's belief in such a system. Socially, the system was to be Islamic, a characteristic generally assumed to mean opposition to the Shah's cultural Westernization of Iran. Any apprehension about the new system being a theocracy was put to rest by Khomeini's assurances that the *ulema* would remain aloof from politics. Until the revolution, the arguments of Banisadr and Khomeini were general and vague enough to avoid dissimilarities in their notions of an Islamic republic. Soon after the success of the revolution, however, it became clear that they had very definite and different ideas about the workings of such a system.

The question of how much consistency there has been between the revolution's promises and its outcomes depends on who that question is addressed to. Ayatollah Khomeini and his clerical colleagues running Iran today are likely to argue that they have kept the revolution's promise to establish an Islamic system in Iran and have remained true to their principles. Those who collaborated with Khomeini in overthrowing the Shah mostly feel betrayed, and those who have since escaped arrest and execution accuse Khomeini of establishing a dictatorship more brutal than the Shah's. Similarly frustrated are communist activists of the Tudeh and the Fedaiyan, who view the events of 1978–79 not as a revolution but rather as an 'unsuccessful revolt', unsuccessful because what occurred did not alter the relations and the means of economic production.

Because of an overall ambiguity about the nature and the form of the system intended to replace the Pahlavi monarchy, there is a measure of truth to all such answers. Clearly, however, Ayatollah Khomeini's system does not correspond to what he promised it would, namely democracy. Today's Islamic republic uses any means necessary to suppress political opposition. Post-revolutionary authoritarianism may be academically explicable,[1] especially since Iran has historically lacked the social and cultural norms necessary for the establishment of democracy. Iranian culture has not had any tradition of political co-operation and has embodied highly individualistic and sectarian tendencies. More importantly, Iranian society has suffered from a conspicuous absence of formal institutions embodying well-defined principles of goal attainment and co-operative efforts.[2] Throughout Iranian history, 'power has not flowed from institution to institution but rather from individual to individual'.[3] Given the absence of socially and culturally ingrained and accepted democratic institutions and principles, the replacement of the Shah's dictatorship with that of Khomeini was a strong possibility. Political actors make little difference; what constitutes a political system is its institutions. With democratic institutions non-existent in Iran prior to the revolution, there was every likelihood that the post-revolutionary regime would have also become dictatorial regardless of the names and the intentions of its leaders.

Appendix

On 6 November 1978, the Shah delivered a nationally broadcast speech. While the speech is greatly significant in providing insight into the political manoeuvres of the regime during the revolution, it is often either entirely neglected or is mentioned only in passing. Due to a national strike by Iranian newspapers at the time the speech was delivered, the full text of the speech is available in print in only one book. Bazargan has transcribed the speech from the archives of National Iranian Radio and Television. The following is a translation of the speech as printed in Bazargan, *Engelab-e Iran dar Dow Harkat* (The Iranian Revolution in Two Phases), pp. 207–9.

> In the political atmosphere which has been gradually developing over the past two years, you dear people of Iran have stood up against oppression and corruption. As King of Iran and as an Iranian, I cannot but to approve of the Iranian nation's revolution.
>
> Unfortunately, however, alongside this revolution are those who manipulate your feelings and your anger in order to create havoc and instability. The current wave of strikes, which are for the most part justified, has also lately become a tool for the disruption of the country's economic life. Even the flow of oil, which has direct bearing on the preservation of our nationhood, has been stopped and has therefore led to the halting of most economic activities. In some locations of our country, murders, insecurity, and riots have reached such proportions that our very national independence is endangered.
>
> Yesterday's unfortunate events which set the Capital on fire can no longer be tolerated by the people and the nation.
>
> Following the government's resignation, in order to prevent the disintegration of the country and the withering of national unity, for the sake of establishing law and order and to halt further bloodshed, I concentrated all of my efforts in forming a coalition government. When it became clear that the formation of such a

coalition would not be possible, We were forced to appoint a provisional cabinet.

I am aware that after the current anarchy ceases, past mistakes may recur and oppression may once again prevail. I am aware that the country's progress and interests may be used as justifications to reinstate pressure on the public and to once again permit financial and economic corruption.

However, as your monarch, who has sworn to defend the nation's territorial integrity, national unity, and the Shi'ite religion, I once again repeat my oath before the Iranian nation and promise that not only past mistakes, corruption, and lawlessness will not be repeated, measures will be taken to compensate for them. I promise that soon after law and order prevail, a national government will be appointed in order to establish political freedom and to initiate open elections. By doing so, the Constitution, which was hard won through the Constitutional Revolution, will be fully obeyed and respected.

I too have heard the message of your revolution.

I am the guardian of Constitutional Monarchy, which is a divine right and which has been conferred onto me by the People. That for which you have sacrificed, I will guarantee. Governance in Iran in the future will be based on social justice and national will, away from dictatorship and corruption, and in accordance with the Constitution.

In the present situation, the establishment of order and stability and the prevention of Iran's disintegration and collapse is the main duty of the Imperial Armed Forces. The Military has always retained its national identity, and through reliance on the people of Iran, has remained faithful to its oath.

Through the co-operation of you my dear compatriots, the needed order and stability must prevail as soon as possible. The subsequent national government, which would maximize liberties, execute reforms, and which will in particular hold free elections, can therefore expediently start to work.

You and I have in the past thirty and some years witnessed some important events, and have together safely passed through a great deal of dangerous events. I hope that in these delicate and fateful moments the Almighty Lord bless us so that we, alongside each other, can reach our main goals, which consist of tranquillity, comfort, freedom, and pride in our nationality and heritage.

I hereby request from grand religious scholars and the Ulema, who are the religious and spiritual leaders of the nation and the guardians of Islam and Shi'ism, to urge the people to restore order

Appendix

and stability so that the World's only Shi'ite country would be saved.

I ask of the society's intellectual leaders to invite people to stability and order, and to pave the way toward the principle struggle which is the establishment of democracy.

I ask you, Iranian fathers and mothers, who like me are worried for the future of Iran and that of your childrens' offspring, to prevent your children from joining the riots and thereby harming themselves and their country.

I ask of you, youths, who are the inheritants of Iran's future, not to engulf your country in blood and fire, and thereby not to damage your own present and Iran's future.

I ask of you, the political leaders of society, to neglect all your ideological differences, to consider the exceptional historical circumstances of our country, and to combine all forces to save our nation.

I ask of all of you, workers, peasants, and wage earners, whose efforts make the country's economy run, to actively try to preserve and to revitalize the national economy.

I ask of all of you, my dear compatriots, to think of Iran. In these great historical moments let us all together think of Iran.

Be assured that I accompany you in Iran's national revolution against oppression, injustice, and corruption. For the sake of preserving the country's territorial integrity and national unity, in order to safeguard the principles of Islam and to establish political freedom, to give realization to the desires and the slogans of the Iranian people, I will be with you.

I hope in the important days to come, the Great Lord gives us compassion and blessing, and continually be the saviour of our country and of the Iranian nation. May the glorious Allah be willing.

Notes

Chapter 1: Causes of revolution

1. Theda Skocpal. 'Rentier state and Shi'a Islam in the Iranian revolution', *Theory and Society* 2, no. 3 (May 1982): 265–83.
2. Chalmers Johnson, *Revolutionary Change* (London: Longman, 1982), p. 3.
3. Ibid., p. 62.
4. Ibid., pp. 57–58.
5. Ibid., pp. 93–94.
6. Ibid., p. 101.
7. Ibid., p. 107.
8. James Davies, 'Toward a theory of revolution', *American Sociological Review* 27, no. 1 (February 1962): 6.
9. Jerry Rose, *Outbreaks: The Sociology of Collective Behaviour* (New York: The Free Press, 1982), p. 86.
10. Davies, 'Toward a Theory of Revolution', p. 6.
11. Ibid., p. 19.
12. Ibid.
13. Ibid.
14. Ted Robert Gurr, *Why Men Rebel?* (Princeton, NJ: Princeton University Press, 1968), p. 24.
15. Ibid., p. 48.
16. Ibid., pp. 51–52.
17. Ibid., p. 53.
18. Ibid., p. 155.
19. Ibid., p. 247.
20. Ibid.
21. Charles Tilly, *From Mobilization to Revolution* (London: Addison-Wesley, 1978), p. 191.
22. Ibid., p. 192.
23. Ibid., p. 81.
24. Ibid., p. 202.
25. Ibid., p. 203.
26. Others who also examine political developments in pre-revolutionary staes include John Dunn in *Modern Revolutions* (Cambridge: Cambridge University Press, 1972), and Crane Brinton in *The Anatomy of Revolution*

(New York: Prentice-Hall, 1938). Brinton's work, similar to that of Skocpol, can be classified as one of 'historical sociology', particularly because of his extensive examination of the social and cultural conditions that existed before the English, American, French, and Russian revolutions. Nevertheless, he claims that those revolutions occurred when 'new conditions laid an intolerable strain on government machinery adapted to simpler, more primitive conditions' (p. 279).
27. Samuel Huntington, *Political Order in Changing Societies* (New Haven, CT: Yale University Press, 1968), p. 265.
28. Ibid., p. 142.
29. Ibid., p. 289.
30. Ibid., p. 265.
31. Ibid., p. 274.
32. Jerrold Green, *Revolution in Iran: The Politics of Countermobilization* (New York: Praeger, 1982), p. xiii.
33. Jerrold Green, 'Countermobilization as a revolutionary form', *Comparative Politics* 16, no. 2 (January 1984): 157.
34. Ibid., p. 160.
35. Ibid., p. 161.
36. Ibid., p. 163.
37. Ibid.
38. Theda Skocpol, *States and Social Revolutions* (Cambridge: Cambridge University Press, 1979), p. 47.
39. Ibid., p. 18.
40. Ibid., p. 285.
41. Ibid., p. 291.
42. Ibid.
43. Besides the works by Green referred to here, see also Green, 'Pseudoparticipation and countermobilization: roots of the Iranian revolution', *Iranian Studies* 18 (1980): 31–53.
44. For an insightful criticism of these and other theories of revolution see Rod Aya, 'Theories of revolution: contrasting models of collective violence', *Theory and Society* 8, no. 1 (July 1979): 33–99, especially pp. 65–66. Also see Michael Freeman, 'Review article: theories of revolution', *British Journal of Political Science* 2: 339–359.
45. Skocpol, *States and Social Revolutions*, pp. 18, 23–24.
46. In revolutions that are brought about as a result of guerrilla warfare (labelled 'eastern' revolutions by Huntington), states are weakened because of the activities and the attacks of revolutionary organizations. Revolutionary mobilization occurs before the state's collapse. In more spontaneous, 'western' revolutions, revolutionary mobilization takes place after the state has already collapsed or is about to collapse (Huntington, *Political Order*, Chapter 5). Skocpol correctly asserts that while Huntington's distinctions between 'eastern' and 'western' revolutions may be analytically useful, his labels need to be changed (Skocpol, *States and Social Revolutions*, p. 303, n. 99).
    Tilly's arguments closely fit the pattern of guerrilla-led revolutions.
47. Skocpol, *States and Social Revolutions*; Dunn, *Modern Revolutions*.

48. Skocpol, 'Rentier state and Shi'a Islam', p. 257.
49. Ibid., pp. 266-67.
50. John Dunn, *Rethinking Modern Political Theory* (Cambridge: Cambridge University Press, 1985), p. 77; Jerome Himmelstein and Michael Kimmel, 'Review article: states and revolutions: the implications and limits of Skocpol's structural model', *American Journal of Sociology* 86, no. 5: 1153-54.
51. For other criticisms of Skocpol's re-evaluation see 'Comments on Skocpol', written separately by Nikki Keddie, Eqbal Ahmad, and Walter Goldfrank in *Theory and Society* 11, no. 3 (May 1982): 285-92, 293-300, and 301-4, respectively.
52. Skocpol, 'Rentier state and Shi'a Islam', pp. 275-76.
53. Mostafa Rejai and Kay Phillips, *Leaders of Revolution* (London: Sage, 1979), p. 189.
54. Huntington, *Political Order*, p. 289.
55. Ibid.
56. Green, 'Countermobilization as revolutionary form', p. 156.
57. Ibid.
58. Ibid., p. 157.
59. For analysis and criticism of different definitions of revolution see Isaac Kramnick, 'Reflections on revolution: definition and explanation in recent scholarship', *History and Theory* 11, no. 1 (1972): 22-63, especially pp. 26-35; Dale Yoder, 'Current definitions of revolution', *American Journal of Sociology* 32, no. 3 (November 1926): 433-41, is also a useful (though by now outdated) review of mainly psychological approaches to the study of revolutions.
60. Skocpol, *States and Social Revolutions*, p. 16.
61. Skocpol, 'Rentier state and Shi'a Islam', p. 267.
62. In the case of Iran, U.S.- Iranian relations did not become strained but rather conditional: Washington made the continuation of Iran's privileged status *vis-à-vis* the United States dependent on certain conditions (e.g. greater civil liberties and the observance of human rights). See Chapter 2.
63. Dunn, *Modern Revolutions*, p. 235; Skocpol, 'Rentier state and Shi'a Islam', p. 267; Himmelstein and Kimmel, 'States and revolutions', pp. 1153-54; Tilly, *From Mobilization to Revolution*, p. 202.
64. Dunn, *Modern Revolutions*, p. 236.
65. The Iraqi regime was particularly weak from 1984 to 1986, suffering from both military losses to Iran and slackening oil prices in the international market. Since 1986, however, the state seems to have solidified itself and the economy has been improving.
66. Gramsci emphasizes this point most convincingly, arguing that a 'war of positions' among the different revolutionary groups is necessary in order to enable them to gain hegemony over the revolutionary classes. See Christine Buci-Glucksmann, *Gramsci and the State*, David Fernbach, trans. (London: Lawrence & Wishart, 1980), Ch. 8, and pp. 314-17.
67. John McAlister, *Vietnam: The Origins of Revolution* (New York: Alfred Knopf, 1969), p. 136.
68. Barrington Moore, *Injustice: The Social Bases of Obedience and Revolt*

(London: Macmillan, 1978), p. 459.
69. Johnson, *Revolutionary Change.*
70. Gurr, *Why Men Rebel?* and Davies, 'Toward a theory of revolution'. Eric Hoffer, in *The True Believer* (New York: Harper & Row), adopts a similar approach.
71. Stuart Schram, *The Political Thought of Mao Tse Tung* (New York: Praeger, 1969), pp. 241–46.
72. Herbert Matthews, *Revolution in Cuba* (New York: Charles Scribner's Sons, 1975), pp. 94–95.

Chapter 2: The Pahlavi state

1. President Carter, in a 1977 New Year Eve toast to the Shah. Quoted in Mohammed Reza Pahlavi, *Answer to History* (New York: Stein and Day, 1980), p. 153.
2. See Amin Banani, *The Modernization of Iran, 1921–1941* (Stanford, CA: Stanford University Press, 1961).
3. For the CIA's 1953 *coup* in Iran, see Kermit Roosevelt, *Counter-coup: The Struggle for Control in Iran* (New York: McGraw Hill, 1979); James Bill, *The Eagle and the Lion* (New Haven, CT: Yale University Press, 1988), pp. 72–97.
4. Richard Cottam, *Nationalism in Iran* (Pittsburgh, PA: University of Pittsburgh Press, 1979), p. 288.
5. Hossein Bashiriyeh, *The State and Revolution in Iran* (London: Croom Helm, 1984), p. 19.
6. Focusing on 'class analysis', Bashiriyeh identifies five (economic) 'foundations' for the regime: (1) state control of financial resources; (2) success of the economic growth programme; (3) creation of an 'equilibrium of classes through their economic control'; (4) patron–client relations with the upper bourgeoisie; and (5) expansion of the coercive forces of the state (*State and Revolution in Iran*, pp. 29–30). While these methods were in fact used by the regime to expand its economic control over society, they did not form the 'foundations' of the regime as such.
7. Bashiriyeh, *State and Revolution in Iran*, p. 19.
8. Khosrow Fatemi, 'Leadership of mistrust: the Shah's modus operandi', *The Middle East Journal* 36, no. 1 (Winter 1982): 51.
9. Confidential interview with a former cabinet minister.
10. Interview with Afkhami.
11. Abbas Gharebaghi, *Haqayeq dar-bare-ye Bohran-e Iran* (Facts about Iran's Crisis) (Paris: Soheil, n.d.), p. 31.
12. Interviews with Dariush Homayoun and Ali Amini.
13. Interview with Ali Amini. See also Ashraf Pahlavi, *Faces in a Mirror: Memoirs from Exile* (Englewood Cliffs, NJ: Prentice-Hall, 1980), especially Chapter 2.
14. Parviz C. Radji, *In the Service of the Peacock Throne: The Diaries of the Shah's Last Ambassador to London* (London: Hamish Hamilton, 1983), p. 9.
15. Interview with Amini.

16. Radji, *In the Service of the Peacock Throne*, p. 133.
17. Interview with Ali Amini; Anthony Parsons, *The Pride and the Fall, Iran 1974–1979* (London: Jonathan Cape, 1984), p. 141.
18. Interview with Afkhami.
19. Bill, *The Eagle and the Lion*, p. 166.
20. Interview with Amini.
21. Pahlavi, *Answer to History*, p. 149
22. Ibid.
23. Quoted in Robert Graham, *Iran: The Illusion of Power* (New York: St. Martin's, 1980), p. 74.
24. Pahlavi, *Answer to History*, p. 124.
25. For a rare and detailed analysis of the development and organization of Rastakhiz, see Gholam R. Afkhami, *The Iranian Revolution: Thanatos on a National Scale* (Washington, D.C.: Middle East Institute, 1985), pp. 66–75.
26. For the Land Reform Programme, see Chapter 4.
27. Interview with Javad Saeed, secretary general of Rastakhiz, *Ittela'at*, 5 Mehr 1357/27 September 1978, p. 4.
28. Interview with Daryoush Homayoun.
29. Ervand Abrahamian, *Iran Between Two Revolutions* (Princeton, NJ: Princeton University Press, 1982), p. 441.
30. Pahlavi, *Answer to History*, p. 124.
31. Hezbe Rastakhiz, *Falsafeye Enghelab-e Iran* (Philosophy of Iran's Revolution).
32. See, for example, Hassan Mohammadi-Nejad, 'The Iranian parliamentary elections of 1975', *International Journal of Middle East Studies* 8 (1977): 103–16, especially p. 105.
33. Homa Katouzian, *The Political Economy of Modern Iran* (New York: NYU Press, 1981), pp. 241–42.
34. See Chapter 5.
35. Interview with Rahim Safari, Rastakhiz official. *Ittela'at*, 5 Mehr 1357/27 September 1978, pp. 5, 9.
36. Pahlavi, *Answer to History*, p. 124.
37. For the 'King's dilemma' see Samuel P. Huntington, *Political Order in Changing Societies* (New Haven, CT: Yale University Press, 1968), Chapter 3, especially pp. 177–91.
38. Gholam R. Afkhami, *The Iranian Revolution: Thanatos on a National Scale* (Washington, D.C.: Middle East Institute, 1985), pp. 67–68.
39. See J. C. Scott, *Comparative Political Corruption* (Englewood Cliffs, NJ: Prentice-Hall, 1972).
40. Radji, *In the Service of the Peacock Throne*, p. 51.
41. Abolhassan Banisadr, *Sad Maghaleh* (One Hundred Articles) (Tehran: Payam-e Azadi, 1358/1980), p. 27.
42. Confidential interview with a former cabinet minister.
43. Afkhami, *The Iranian Revolution*, p. 85.
44. Ibid. Afkhami was a deputy interior minister under the Shah.
45. Interview with Admiral Abolfath Ardalan.
46. *Defense and Foreign Affairs Handbook* (Washington, D.C.: Copely & Assoc., 1978), p. 253.

47. Gharebaghi, *Haqayeq dar-bare-ye Bohran-e Iran*, p. 39.
48. Confidential interviews with a former brigadier general and a major general of the Imperial Iranian army.
49. Gharebaghi, *Haqayeq dar-bare-ye Bohran-e Iran*, p. 190.
50. Confidential interview with a former major general of the Imperial Iranian army.
51. Amnesty International, *Annual Report* (1977, 1978), London.
52. Afkhami, *The Iranian Revolution*, p. 186.
53. Mujahedin Organization, *Sharhe Ta'sis va Tarikhche-ye Vagaye-he Sazman-e Mujahedin-e Khalg-e Iran az Sal-e 1344 ta Sal-e 1350* (Explanation of the Establishment and the History of the Events of People's Mujahedin Organisation of Iran From 1965 to 1971) (Tehran: Mujahedin, 1358/1980), p. 84.
54. Ibid.
55. Interview with Dariush Homayoun.
56. Pahlavi, *Answer to History*, p. 150.
57. Dariush Hamayoun, *Dirouz va Farda* (Yesterday and Tomorrow) (United States: n.p., 1981), p. 59.
58. Bank Markazi Iran, *Annual Report and Balance Sheet* (2536/1977-78).
59. Pahlavi, *Answer to History*, p. 55.
60. Some other members of the former regime (e.g. Afkhami) also express doubts as to whether such money was ever paid to the opposition figures by the regime.
61. Shahrough Akhavi, *Religion and Politics in Contemporary Iran* (Albany, NY: SUNY Press, 1982), p. 141.
62. Afkhami, *The Iranian Revolution*, p. 87.
63. Ibid., p. 86.
64. See George Lenczowski, *Russia and the West in Iran: 1918–1948* (New York: Grunwood, 1968).
65. Pahlavi, *Answer to History*, p. 70.
66. For US aid to Iran after the 1953 *coup* see Richard Cottom, *Competitive Interference and Twentieth Century Diplomacy* (Pittsburgh, PA: University of Pittsburgh Press, 1967), Ch. 4; Fereydon Firoozi, 'The United States economic aid to Iran, 1950–1960', Ph.D dissertation, Dropsie University, 1966; Bill, *The Eagle and the Lion*, pp. 113–20, 133.
67. Robert Litwak, *Detente and the Nixon Doctrine: American Foreign Policy and the Pursuit of Stability* (Cambridge: Cambridge University Press, 1984), p. 135.
68. Ibid., p. 78.
69. Mohammad Reza Pahlavi, *Mission for My Country* (London: Hutchinson, 1960), pp. 294–296.
70. Gary Sick, *All Fall Down: America's Tragic Encounter with Iran* (New York: Random House, 1985), p. 18.
71. Quoted in Litwak, *Detente and the Nixon Doctrine*, p. 141.
72. Jimmy Carter, *Keeping Faith* (London: Collins, 1982), p. 143.
73. Michael Ledeen and William Lewis, *Debacle: The American Failure in Iran* (New York: Alfred Knopf, 1981), p. 77.
74. Ibid.

Revolution in Iran

75. Ibid., p. 85.
76. Bill, *The Eagle and the Lion*, pp. 219–20.
77. John Stempel, *Inside the Iranian Revolution* (Bloomington, IN: Indiana University Press, 1981), p. 32.
78. Bill, *The Eagle and the Lion*, p. 232.
79. Carter, *Keeping Faith*, p. 435.
80. Bill, *The Eagle and the Lion*, pp. 229–30.
81. Stempel, *Inside the Iranian Revolution*, p. 78.
82. Bill, *The Eagle and the Lion*, p. 228.
83. *Iran Political Digest*, no. 174. (19 April 1978), p. 2.
84. Figures given for the numbers of dead vary, but were usually put between six and eight.
85. See, for example, *New York Times*, 7 May 1978, p. 25; 10 May 1978, p. 6.
86. *New York Times*, 21 August 1978, p. 20.
87. Pahlavi, *Answer to History*, p. 163.
88. Ibid., p. 116.
89. Robert Graham, *Iran: The Illusion of Power* (New York: St. Martin's, 1980), p. 238.
90. Amir Taheri, *The Spirit of Allah: Khomeini and the Islamic Revolution* (London: Hutchinson, 1985), p. 229.
91. Gharebaghi, *Haqayeq dar-bare-ye Bohran-e Iran*, p. 24.
92. Ibid., p. 31.
93. Afkhami, *The Iranian Revolution*, p. 95.
94. Gharebaghi, *Haqayeq dar-bare-ye Bohran-e Iran*, pp. 39–40.
95. *London Times*, 12 September 1978, p. 1.
96. Gharebaghi, *Haqayeq dar-bare-ye Bohran-e Iran*, p. 41.
97. Interview with Dariush Homayoun. Homayoun was among those who were arrested.
98. *Iran Post* (London), 19 Aban 1357/10 November 1978, p. 1. Newspapers in Iran had at the time gone on strike in protest at the government's censorship.
99. Dariush Homayoun, *Negah az Biroun* (Looking from Outside) (United States: Iran va Jahan, 1984), p. 63 n. 1.
100. Gharebaghi, *Haqayeq dar-bare-ye Bohran-e Iran*, p. 73.
101. Ibid., pp. 73–74.
102. Ibid., p. 91.
103. Ibid., p. 92.
104. Interview with Banisadr.
105. Confidential interview with a former official at the National Iranian Oil Company.
106. Pahlavi, *Answers to History*, p. 166.
107. Gharebaghi, *Haqayeq dar-bare-ye Bohran-e Iran*, p. 108.
108. William Sullivan, *Mission to Iran* (New York: W. W. Norton & Co., 1981), pp. 211–12.
109. *New York Times*, 12 December 1978, p. 1.
110. See, for example, a lengthy interview with Khomeini in *Impact International*, 24 November – 7 December, 1978, pp. 6–9.

111. Interview with Admiral Ardalan; Barry Rubin, *Paved with Good Intentions* (Oxford: Oxford University Press, 1980), p. 223.
112. Interview with Amini.
113. Confidential interviews with a former major general and a brigadier general of the Imperial Iranian army; Robert Huyser, *Mission to Tehran* (New York: Harper & Row, 1986), p. 119.
114. For details of the planned *coup*, see Ibrahim Yazdi, *Akharin Talash-ha dar Akharin Rouz-ha* (Last Attempts in the Last Days) (Tehran: Qalam, 1363/1984), pp. 249–295.
115. Gharebaghi, *Haqayeq dar-bare-ye Bohran-e Iran*, pp. 135–150.
116. Ibid., p. 129.
117. Radji, *In the Service of the Peacock Throne*, p. 284.
118. Pahlavi, *Answer to History*, p. 168.
119. Carter, *Keeping Faith*, p. 435.
120. Bill, *The Eagle and the Lion*, p. 243.
121. Cyrus Vance, *Hard Choices: Critical Years in America's Foreign Policy* (New York: Simon & Schuster, 1983), p. 316.
122. Interview with Ambassador Sullivan; Bill, *The Eagle and the Lion*, p. 247.
123. Carter, *Keeping Faith*, p. 435.
124. Quoted in ibid, p. 438.
125. Rubin, *Paved with Good Intentions*, p. 209.
126. Gary Sick, *All Fall Down* (New York: Random Books, 1985), p. 46.
127. Rubin, *Paved with Good Intentions*, p. 203.
128. Vance, *Hard Choices*, p. 325.
129. Interview with Ambassador Sullivan.
130. Zbignew Brzezinski, *Power and Principle* (New York: Farrar, Straus, & Giroux, 1985), p. 358.
131. Sick, *All Fall Down*, p. 61.
132. Ibid., p. 71. For a detailed analysis of the growing cleavage between the NSC and the State Department during this period, see Bill, *The Eagle and the Lion*, pp. 243–57.
133. Sullivan, *Mission to Iran*, pp. 170, 171.
134. Anthony Parsons, *The Pride and the Fall: Iran – 1974–1979* (London: Jonathan Cape, 1984), p. 122.
135. See, for example, Pahlavi, *Answer to History*, pp. 161–62.
136. Brzezinski, *Power and Principle*, p. 371.
137. Sullivan, *Mission to Iran*, p. 167.
138. Interview with Ambassador Sullivan. Ambassador Parsons, who accompanied Sullivan in the almost daily audiences to the palace, describes the Shah's mood as somewhat less gloomy, although he does mention that the Shah did not appear as strong-willed as before. See *The Pride and the Fall*, pp. 84, 86, 114.
139. Sullivan, *Mission to Iran*, pp. 193–96.
140. Quoted in Brzezinski, *Power and Principle*, p. 365.
141. Sullivan, *Mission to Iran*, p. 182.
142. Interview with Ambassador Sullivan.
143. Brzezinski, *Power and Principle*, p. 358.

144. Ibid., p. 371.
145. Ibid., p. 373.
146. Interview with Ambassador Sullivan; Sick, *All Fall Down*, p. 126.
147. Carter, *Keeping Faith*, p. 444.
148. Bill, *The Eagle and the Lion*, pp. 252–53.
149. Brzezinski, *Power and Principle*, p. 375.
150. Sick, *All Fall Down*, p. 126.
151. Sullivan, *Mission to Iran*, p. 213.
152. Sullivan, *Mission to Iran*, p. 213; Parsons, *The Pride and the Fall*, p. 125.
153. Interview with Bakhtiar.
154. This scenario was suggested by Ambassador Sullivan and was implicitly mentioned by Admiral Ardalan. There was also congruency between this scenario and Washington's four suggestions to the Shah on 28 December, Bakhtiar's subsequent actions, and Brzezinski's messages to Iranian military leaders.
155. Pahlavi, *Answer to History*, p. 171.
156. Interview with Ambassador Sullivan; Sick, *All Fall Down*, p. 82.
157. Brzezinski, *Power and Principle*, pp. 385–86.
158. Gharebaghi, *Haqayeq dar-bare-ye Bohran-e Iran*, p. 190.
159. Ibid., p. 80.
160. Interviews with Banisadr and Ambassador Sullivan; Afkhami, *The Iranian Revolution*, p. 140.
161. Gharebaghi, *Haqayeq dar-bare-ye Bohran-e Iran*, p. 173.
162. Ibid., p. 140.
163. *Keyhan*, 16 Day 1357/6 January 1979, p. 1.
164. *Ittela'at*, 19 Bahman 1357/8 February 1979, p. 1.
165. *Keyhan*, 26 Day 1357/16 January 1978, p. 1.
166. Interview with Bakhtiar.
167. Gharebaghi, *Haqayeq dar-bare-ye Bohran-e Iran*, p. 136.
168. Huyser, *Mission to Tehran*, p. 7.
169. Ibid., p. 18.
170. Ibid., pp. 14–15.
171. Ibid., p. 16.
172. Zbignew Brzezinski, personal correspondence, 10 August 1987.
173. Brzezinski, *Power and Principle*, p. 371.
174. Huyser, *Mission to Tehran*, p. 96.
175. Ibid., p. 50.
176. Ibid., p. 71.
177. Ibid., pp. 73–74.
178. Ibid., p. 123.
179. Ibid., p. 200.
180. Ibid., p. 224.
181. Gharebaghi, *Haqayeq dar-bare-ye Bohran-e Iran*, p. 200.
182. Ibid., pp. 153–55.
183. Shapour Bakhtiar, *Yekrangi* (Honesty) (Paris: n.p. 1982), p. 228.
184. Gharebaghi, *Haqayeq dar-bare-ye Bohran-e Iran*, pp. 431–39.
185. Ibid., p. 464.
186. Bakhtiar, *Yekrangi*, p. 235.

Chapter 3: Opposition to the regime

1. Richard Cottam, *Nationalism in Iran*, (Pittsburgh, PA: University Pittsburg Press, 1979), p. 211.
2. See, for example, Rasoul Mehraban, *Barresiy-e Mokhtasar Ahzab-e Bourgeoisi Melli Iran dar Moqabeleh Ba Jonbesh-e Karegari va Engelabi-ye Iran (A Brief Analysis of Iran's National Bourgeois Parties in Comparison with Iran's Workers' and Revolutionary Movement)* (Tehran: Peyk-e Iran, 1359/1980).
3. For an account of the early history of communism in Iran, see Tulsiran, *The History of the Communist Movement in Iran* (Bhopal, India: Grafix, 1981), Chapters 1–3.
4. Abdolhassan Kambakhsh, *Nazari beh Jonbesheh Karegari va Komonisti dar Iran (An Account of the Worker's Communist Movement in Iran)* (Stassfurt, Germany: Hezb-e Tudeh, 1972), pp. 186–87.
5. Ervand Abrahamian, 'Communism and communalism in Iran: the Tudeh and the Firgah-i Dimukrat-e Azarbayjan,' *International Journal of Middle East Studies* (1970): 300.
6. For a detailed account of the Tudeh in this period see Evrand Abrahamian, *Iran Between Two Revolutions* (Princeton, NJ: Princeton University Press, 1982), pp. 398–415.
7. Ibid., p. 311.
8. Kambakhsh, *Nazari beh Jonbesheh Karegari va Komonisti dar Iran*, pp. 168–69.
9. Cottam, *Nationalism in Iran*, p. 280.
10. Abrahamian, *Iran Between Two Revolutions*, p. 321.
11. Nureddin Kianouri, *Hezb-e Tudeh-e Iran va Doctor Mohammad Mussadiq (The Tudeh Party of Iran and Dr Mohammed Mussadiq)*. (Tehran: Hezb-e Tudeh, 1359/1981), pp. 5–6. Kianouri was at the time a Central Committee member and later became its chairman.
12. Ibid., pp. 17-26.
13. Abrahamian, *Iran Between Two Revolutions*, p. 322.
14. Kianouri, *Hezb-e Tudeh*, pp. 36–42.
15. Abrahamian, *Iran Between Two Revolutions*, p. 338.
16. Kianouri, *Hezb-e Tudeh*, p. 45.
17. Tulsiran, *The History of the Communist Movement in Iran*, p. 143.
18. Abrahamian, *Iran Between Two Revolutions*, p. 453.
19. Ibid., p. 327. For an analysis of the Tudeh's 'class base' see ibid., Chapter 7.
20. Cottam, *Nationalism in Iran*, pp. 264–65.
21. Sepehr Zabih, *The Mossadegh Era* (Chicago, IL.: Lake View Press, 1982), pp. 29, 68.
22. For the AIOC's role in the Iranian economy, see Homa Katouzian, *The Political Economy of Modern Iran, 1926–1979* (New York: New York University Press, 1981), pp. 182–85.
23. Cottam, *Nationalism in Iran*, p. 283.
24. Zabih, *The Mossadegh Era*, p. 86.
25. Abrahamian, *Iran Between Two Revolutions*, p. 273.

26. Ibid., p. 457.
27. Ibid., p. 460.
28. See, for example, Confederation of Iranian Students (US), *Report* 1, no. 2 (July 1977).
29. Mujahedeen-e Khalq, *Sharh-e Ta'sis-va Tarikhche-ye Vagaye' Sazman-e Mujahadeen-e Khalq-e Iran Az Sal-e 1344 ta Sale 1350 (Explanation of Foundation and a History of the People's Mujahadeen Organization of Iran From the Year 1965 to the Year 1971)* (Tehran: Sazman-e Mujahedeen, 1358), p. 16.
30. Ibid., p. 19.
31. Ibid., p. 49.
32. Ibid., pp. 43–46.
33. Ibid., p. 45.
34. For a full account of the arrests, see ibid., pp. 58–72.
35. See the Communist faction's *Bayaniye-he I'lam-e Mavaz-e' Ideolozhik (Manifesto of Ideological Stands)* (Tehran: 1975).
36. Mujahedeen, *Ettela'iye I'lame Mavaze-ye Sazman-e Mujahadeen-e Khalq-e Iran dar Barabar-e Jaryan-e Aportunistha-ye [Enherafi-ye] Chap-nama (Manifesto of the Stands of the People's Mujahadeen Organization of Iran Against the [Deviatory] Leftist – Pretending Opportunist Affairs)* (Tehran: n.d.).
37. Mujahedeen, *Bayaniye-he I'lam-e Mavaz-e' Ideolozhik*
38. Interview with Masoud Rajavi, Mujahadeen leader, *Keyhan* 18 Bahman 1357/7 February 1978.
39. Mujahedeen, *Varshekastegi-ye Tarikhi-ye Dark-e Khorde Bourgeoisie az Eslam (The Historical Bankruptcy of the Petty Bourgeoisie's Perception of Islam)* (Tehran: n.d.), pp. 10–11.
40. Sazman-e Fedaiyan, *Tarikhche-ye Sazman-e Cherikehaye Fedai-ye Khalg-e Iran (A History of the Organization of Iranian People's Fedai'i Guerrillas)* (Tehran: Sazman-e Cherikha-ye Fedaiye Khalq, n.d.), p. 19.
41. Bizhan Jazani, *Capitalism and Revolution in Iran*, Iran Committee, trans. (London: Zed Press, 1980), p. 19.
42. Masoud Ahmadzadeh, *Mubareze-ye Mosalahaneh, Ham Estratezhy Ham Taktik (Armed Struggle, Both a Strategy and a Tactic)* (Tehran: Sazman-e Cherikhaye Fedai-ye Khalq, 1358/1979), pp. 28–29.
43. Mansour Eskandari, *Mas'aleh-e Arzi Janbesh-e Dehganan va Siasat-e Ma (The Land Issue, Penants' Struggle, and Our Policy)* (Tehran: Sazman-e Cherik-ha-ye Fedaiye Khalq-e Iran, 1363/1984), p. 40.
44. S. P. Nettl, 'Ideas, intellectuals and structure of dissent', in P. Rieff, ed., *On Intellectuals* (New York: Anchor Books, 1970), pp. 89–90.
45. Ibid.
46. Edward Shils, 'The intellectual and the power', in *On Intellectuals*, p. 30.
47. Interview with Banisadr.
48. Mangol Bayat-Phillip, 'Tradition and change in Iranian socio-religious thought', in N. Keddie and M. Bonine, eds., *Continuity and Change in Modern Iran* (Albany, NY: SUNY Press, 1981), p. 50.
49. Some of the popular books of this category included Hadayat's *Charand-o-Parand (Nonsense)*, Kasravi's *Shi'egary (Shi'ism)*, and Dashti's

Bist-o Se Sal (Twenty-Three Years).
50. Bayat-Phillip, 'Tradition and change in Iranian socio-religious thought', pp. 50–51.
51. See, for example, Mohammad Reza Pahlavi, *Mission for My Country* (London: Hutchinson, 1960), p. 11.
52. Cottam, *Nationalism in Iran*, p. 291.
53. See, for example, Ali Shariati, *Islamshenasi (Islamology)*. vols. 1–2; Abolhassan Banisadr, *Dar Jostejuyeh Charjubi bara-ye Andisheh va Amal (In Search of a Framework for Theory and Practice)* (Paris: n.p., 1971).
54. Interview with Jalal Al-e Ahmad's brother, Shams, printed in *Keyhan Havii*, 25 Shahrivar 13661/16 September 1987, pp. 16–17.
55. 'An autobiography of sorts', in Al-e Ahmad, *Iranian Society*, Michael C. Hilmann, trans. (Lexington, KY: Mazda Publishers, 1982), p. 14.
56. Ibid., p. 16.
57. Ibid.
58. Ibid., p. 17.
59. Complicated language and double meanings were often used by popular authors in order to evade government censorship. Hedayat's *Blind Owl* is a classic example. Another example was Kasravi, who used 'pure Persian' in order to alleviate the influence of Arabic from Persian literature.
60. Jalal Al-e Ahmad, *Gharbzadeghi (Westoxication)* (Tehran: Ravaq, 1341/1962), Chapter 1.
61. Ibid., p. 35.
62. Ibid., p. 87.
63. Ibid., pp. 144–47.
64. Ibid., pp. 170–71.
65. Ibid., pp. 172–73.
66. Al-e Ahmad, *Dar Khedmat va Khianat-e Roushanfekran* vol. 1 (*On the Service and the Disservice of Intellectuals*) (Tehran: Khawrazmi, 1357/1978), p. 47.
67. Ibid., p. 40.
68. Al-e Ahmad, *Roushanfekran*, vol. 2, p. 234.
69. Interview with Shams Al-e Ahmad, *Kayhan Havaii*, 25 Shahrivar 1366/16 September 1987, p. 16.
70. Quoted in Al-e Ahmad, *Iranian Society*, p. xi.
71. These stories, along with some other writings by Al-e Ahmad, are translated in *Iranian Society*. Some of Al-e Ahmad's other stories are translated in Minou Southgate, *Modern Persian Short Stories* (Washington, D.C.: Three Continents, 1980).
72. Mehdi Bazargan, *Be'sat va Ideolozhi (Prophetic Mission and Ideology)* (Tehran: n.p., n.d.), p. 161.
73. Mehdi Bazargan, *Serr-e Aqaboftadegi-ye Melal-e Mosalman (Secret of the Moslem Peoples' Backwardness)* (Tehran: n.p., n.d.), p. 18.
74. Ibid., p. 10.
75. Mehdi Bazargan, *Zarre-ye Bi Enteha (The Infinite Particle)* (Tehran: n.p., n.d.), p. 24.
76. Mehdi Bazargan, *Sazegari-ye Irani (Iranian Mentality)* (Tehran: n.p., n.d.), pp. 26–38.

77. Ibid., p. 72.
78. Bazargan, *Be'sat va Ideolozhi*, pp. 144–63.
79. Ibid., p. 133.
80. Ibid., p. 143.
81. Ali Shariati, *Mazhab Alayhe Mazhab (Religion versus Religion)* (Tehran: n.p., n.d.), p. 17.
82. Ali Shariati, *Ideolozhi (Ideology)* (Tehran: n.p., n.d.), p. 17.
83. Ali Shariati, *Az Kuja Agaz Konim? (Where Do We Begin From?)* (Tehran: n.p., n.d.), p. 8.
84. Ali Shariati, *Bazgasht Beh Khish (Return to the Self)* (Tehran: n.p., n.d.), pp. 132–33.
85. Shariati, *Mazhab Alayhe Mazhab*, p. 47.
86. Interview with Banisadr.
87. Ibid.
88. Abolhassan Banisadr, *Osule Paye va Zabete-haye Hokumat-e Islami (The Main Principles and Guidelines of Islamic Government)* (Paris: n.p., 1974), pp. 54–55.
89. Ibid., pp. 60–68.
90. Abolhassan Banisadr, *Eqtesad-e Tauhidi (Tauhidi Economics)* (Paris: n.p., 1974), p. 152.
91. Ibid., pp. 276–77.
92. Ibid., p. 355.
93. S. Akhavi, *Religion and Politics in Contemporary Iran*, pp. 118–19. For the names of the lecturers at the Monthly Religious Society see p. 229, n. 31.
94. Ali Davani, *Nehzat-e Rouhaniyon-e Iran*, vol. 3 *(The Struggle of the Iranian Clergy)* (Tehran: n.p., n.d.), offers a fully documented account of the 1963 disturbances.
95. Other ayatollahs included Shariatmadari, Golpayegani, Morteza Haeri, and Abdollah Haeri.
96. Quoted in Davani, *Nehzat-e Rouhaniyon-e Iran*, vol. 3, p. 91.
97. The number of the dead is generally put at 'several hundred'.
98. Paul Balta and Claudine Rulleau, *L'Iran Insurge* (Paris, 1979), p. 152. Although the accuracy of this figure cannot be attested, it appears to be a generally correct estimation of the *ulema*'s population.
99. Michael Fischer, *Iran: From Religious Dispute to Revolution* (Cambridge, MA: Harvard University Press, 1980), p. 100.
100. For a discussion of the *howzehs* see Akhavi, *Religion and Politics in Contemporary Iran*, p. 126.
101. This is not a conclusive list and does not include some of the *ulema* who were primarily influential in the cities and the provinces in which they lived. Fischer also includes some of the famous preachers such as Rashed, Falsafi, and Hejazi. Two additional ayatollahs also became highly influential outside Iran, although they did not achieve the same status inside the country. They were Musa Sadr, who became the main *marj'a* in Lebanon after he moved there in 1959, and his cousin Mohammad Baqir al-Sadr, born in Nujaf, who was the *marj'a taqlid* of Iraqi Shi'ites. For more on Musa Sadr, see Fouad Ajami, *The Vanished Imam* (Ithaca, NY:

Notes

Cornell University Press, 1986). For more on Mohammad Baqir al-Sadr, see Hanna Batutu, 'Iraq's underground Shi'ite movement: characteristics, causes, and prospects', *Middle East Journal* 35 (Autumn 1981): 578–94.
102. Fischer, *Iran: From Religious Dispute to Revolution*, p. 88. After the revolution, Montazeri was generally considered to have become a *marj'a taqlid* after Khomeini referred to him as a Grand Ayatollah (Ayatollah Uzma), which is a title usually reserved for *marj'as*.
103. Akhavi, *Religion and Politics in Contemporary Iran*, p. 170.
104. See Ervand Abrahamian, 'Kasravi: the integrate nationalist of Iran', in E. Kedouri and S. Haim, eds, *Towards a Modern Iran* (London: Frank Cass, 1980), pp. 96–131.
105. Rouhollah Khomeini, *Kashf al-Asrar (Discovery of Secrets)* (Qom: n.p., 1944), p. 73.
106. Ibid., p. 282.
107. Akhavi, *Religion and Politics in Contemporary Iran*, p. 101.
108. Amir Taheri, *The Spirit of Allah: Khomeini and the Islamic Revolution* (London: Hutchinson, 1985), pp. 157, 160.
109. Rouhollah Khomeini, *Velayat-e Faqih (Islamic Government)* (Tehran: n.p., n.d.), p. 10.
110. Ibid., p. 47.
111. Ibid., p. 80.
112. Ibid., p. 126.
113. Ibid., p. 167.
114. See, for example, 'The gentle scholar of Qom', *Time*, 18 September 1978, p. 39.
115. For a full, mostly anthropological account of the activities of the Qom *ulema* see Fischer, *Iran: From Religious Dispute to Revolution*, Chapter 3, especially pp. 86–97.
116. Akhavi, *Religion and Politics in Contemporary Iran*, p. 102.
117. Quoted in ibid. p. 224, fn. 34.
118. Davani, *Nehzat-e Rouhaniyon-e Iran*, vol. 7, p. 46.
119. Ibid., p. 112.
120. Ibid., p. 98.
121. *Libération*, 12 May 1978.
122. *Le Monde*, 6 May 1978, p. 4.
123. For Shariatmadari's statements in the latter stages of the revolutionary movement see Davani, *Nehzat-e Rouhaniyon-e Iran*, vol 7, pp. 182–84, 293–94.
124. For the Mujahadeen's own publications on their connection with Taleghani, see *Taleghani dar Feyziyeh (Taleghani in the Feyziyeh Seminary)* and *Taleghani dar Daneshgah va Husseiniyeh (Taleghani in University and the Husseiniyeh)*, both published in Tehran in 1979. The Mujahadeen also published three volumes of Taleghani's speeches and Friday prayers immediately after the revolution, entitled *Majmu'eh Gaftar-e Pedar Taleghani*, vols 1–3 *(Collected Speeches of Father Taleghani)*.
125. Davani, *Nehzat-e Rouhaniyon-e Iran*, vol. 8, p. 283.
126. These declarations have been documented in volumes 7 and 8 of Davani's

book. In volume 7, see pp. 138–40, 213–17 and 217–19; in volume 8, see pp. 167–69 and 169–71.
127. Taheri, *The Spirit of Allah*, p. 230.
128. Akhavi, *Religion and Politics in Contemporary Iran*, p. 101.
129. Quoted in Robert Graham, *Iran: The Illusion of Power* (New York: St. Martin's, 1980), p. 260.
130. Mehdi Bazargan, *Enqelab-e Iran dar Dow Harkat (The Iranian Revolution in Two Phases)* (Tehran: n.p., n.d.), p. 22.
131. *New Statesman*, 6 January 1978, p. 5.
132. R. Ben Jones, *The French Revolution* (London: Hodder & Stoughton, 1967), pp. 11–17.
133. Interview with Bakhtiar.
134. Taheri, *The Spirit of Allah*, p. 184
135. Ibid., pp. 184–185.
136. Pahlavi, *Answer to History*, p. 163.
137. Interview with Dr. Gholam Reza Afkhami.
138. Taheri, *The Spirit of Allah*, p. 202.
139. Ibid.
140. *Ittela'at*, 17 Day 2536/7 January 1978, p. 7.
141. Dariush Homayun, *Dirouz va Farda (Yesterday and Tomorrow)*, pp. 92–93.
142. All of the information in this section regarding the Council of Revolution was provided by Banisadr in the different interviews he granted to this writer from 1985 to 1987. Despite its overwhelming importance in directing the revolutionary movement, so far none of the available literature on the Iranian revolution discusses the Council's composition or its works in detail. Other members of the Council from whom information could be obtained have by now either passed away (Taleghani, Bahonar, Qotbzadeh, and Beheshti), or are inaccessible or unwilling to be interviewed (Musavi-Ardebili, Hashemi-Rafsenjani, and Bazargan). Despite the paucity of complete information regarding its operations and structure, the significance of the Council of Revolution and its role in the Iranian revolution makes it imperative to give as detailed an account of the Council as possible.
143. According to Banisadr, members of the Council included Taleghani (chairman), Beheshti, Hashemi-Rafsenjani, Bahonar, Mahdavi-Kani, Musavi Ardebili, and Mottahari, all of whom were clerics, in addition to Qotbzadeh, Banisadr, Sahhabi, Sheybani, Musavi, and General Masoudi. Musavi later left the Council; Bazargan was a late-comer; and at one point Moinfar and Peyman were also appointed by Khomeini to serve in the Council.
144. For a collection of declarations issued by the *ulema* during the revolution, see Davani, *Nehzat-e Rouhaniyon-e Iran*, vols. 7 and 8.

Chapter 4: Social change

1. For Parson's 'neo-evolutionary' theory of social change see his *Societies: Evolutionary and Comparative Perspectives* (Englewood Cliffs, NJ:

Prentice-Hall, 1966), and 'Evolutionary universals in society', in T. Parsons, ed., *Sociological Theory and Modern Society* (New York: Free Press, 1967).
2. A. L. Kroeber. 'Diffusionism', in Edwin R. A. Feligman and Alvin Johnson, eds, *The Encyclopedia of the Social Sciences III* (New York: Macmillan, 1937), p. 140.
3. Wilbert E. Moore, *Social Change* (Englewood Cliffs, NJ: Prentice-Hall, 1963), p. 86.
4. Kingsley Davis, *Human Society* (New York: Macmillan, 1950), p. 631.
5. William Ogburn, *Social Change with Respect to Culture and Original Nature* (New York: Viking Press, 1950), p. 200.
6. Ibid., pp. 200–201.
7. S. N. Eisenstadt. 'Breakdowns of modernization', *Economic Development and Cultural Change* 12, no. 4 (July 1964): 345–67.
8. Edward Shils, 'On the comparative study of the new states', in C. Geertz, ed., *Old Societies and New States* (New York: Free Press, 1963), pp. 2-7.
9. Ann Lambton, *The Persian Land Reform, 1962–1966* (Oxford: Clarendon Press, 1969), pp. 60–61.
10. Ibid., p. 63.
11. See Mohammad Reza Pahlavi, *Enghelab-e Sefeed (The White Revolution)* (Tehran n.p., n.d.), especially pp. 1–173 and 207–11 for an outline of the government's programme. This book cannot be used as an objective source for the analysis of the White Revolution.
12. Lambton, *Persian Land Reform*, pp. 103–6.
13. Ibid., p. 354.
14. Ann Lambton, 'Land reform and rural cooperative societies', in Ehsan Yar-Shater, ed., *Iran Faces the Seventies* (New York: Praeger, 1971), p. 41.
15. Ibid.
16. Ervand Abrahamian, *Iran Between Two Revolutions* (Princeton, NJ: Princeton University Press, 1982), p. 430.
17. Bank Markazi Iran, *Annual Reports and Balance Sheets*, 1966, 1972.
18. Iran, *Census Report*, 1976.
19. Iran, *Census Reports*, 1956, 1966.
20. 'Mohammed Riza Pahlavi', in Oriana Fallaci, *Interview with History* (New York: Liveright, 1976), p. 281.
21. Eliz Sanasarian, *The Women's Rights Movement in Iran* (New York: Praeger, 1982), pp. 83-85.
22. Ibid., p. 94.
23. Shahrough Akhavi, *Religion and Politics in Contemporary Iran* (Albany, NY: SUNY Press, 1980), p. 129.
24. Ibid., pp. 130-131.
25. Ibid., p. 141.
26. Iran, *Census Report*, 1976.
27. N. R. Keddie, 'The Iranian village before and after land reform', *Journal of Contemporary History* 3, no. 3 (1968): 74–75.
28. Lambton, *Persian Land Reform*, p. 365.
29. Keddie, 'The Iranian village before and after land reform', p. 76.
30. Quoted in ibid., p. 88.
31. Byron J. Good. 'The transformation of health care in modern Iranian

history', in N. Keddie and M. Bonine, eds, *Continuity and Change in Modern Iran* (Albany, NY: SUNY Press, 1981), p. 79.
32. For a detailed study of the effects of irrigation on two Iranian rural communities (Bizhan and Rahmat Abad), see Grace Goodell, *The Elementary Structures of Political Life: Rural Development in Pahlavi Iran* (Oxford: Oxford University Press, 1986).
33. OPEC, *Annual Statistical Bulletin*, 1973.
34. Bank Markazi Iran, *Annual Report and Balance Sheet*, various issues. All figures in this paragraph are from the same source in different years.
35. For a detailed macroeconomic study of the consequences of the 'oil boom', see Hushang Moghtader, 'The impact of increased oil revenue on Iran's economic development, 1973–76', in E. Kedouri and S. Haim, eds, *Towards a Modern Iran* (London: Frank Cass, 1980), pp. 241–62.
36. A. Gilbert and S. Guglar, *Cities, Poverty and Development: Urbanization in the Third World* (Oxford: Oxford University Press, 1982), p. 37.
37. See ibid, Chapters 4 and 5.
38. Ibid., p. 59.
39. A. Quinjano, 'The marginal pole of the economy and the marginalised labour force', *Economy and Society* 3 (1974): 393–428.
40. Fred Haliday, *Iran: Dictatorship and Development* (New York: Penguin, 1979), p. 183.
41. Gilbert and Guglar, *Cities, Poverty and Development*, p. 27.
42. Farhad Kazemi, *Poverty and Revolution in Iran: The Migrant Poor, Urban Marginality, and Politics*, p. 56.
43. Ibid., p. 51.
44. Gilbert and Guglar, *Cities, Poverty and Development*, pp. 67–68.
45. Ibid., pp. 32–33.
46. Manfred Halpern, *The Politics of Social Change in the Middle East and North Africa* (Princeton, NJ: Princeton University Press, 1963), pp. 51–53.
47. For industrialization/import substitution see Gilbert and Guglar, *Cities, Poverty and Development*, pp. 51–53.
48. Hossein Bashiriyeh, *The State and Revolution in Iran* (London: Croom Helm, 1989), pp. 39–40.
49. See above, Chapter 4.
50. Mary-Jo DelVecchio Good, 'The changing status and composition of an Iranian provincial elite', in N. Keddie and M. Bonine, eds, *Continuity and Change in Modern Iran*, p. 230.
51. Abrahamian, *Iran Between Two Revolutions*, p. 519.
52. For an account of some of the strikes, see Abrahamian, *Iran Between Two Revolutions*, p. 512.
53. Bazaari merchants in Tehran had closed the bazaar on all previous occasions of political turmoil, dating back to the Tobacco Protests of 1891–1892 and the Constitutional Revolution of 1905–1911.
54. The leftist inclinations of Abadan's oil workers go back to the early 1950s, especially the oil nationalization movement of 1951–53. See Abrahamian, *Iran Between Two Revolutions*, pp. 359–65.
55. For a detailed and documented account of Bazargan's dealings with the

Abadan refinery workers, see Mehdi Bazargan, *Enghelab-e Iran dar Dow Harkat (The Iranian Revolution in Two Phases)*, pp. 66–68.

Chapter 5: Revolutionary mass mobilization

1. See Chapter 4.
2. Fred Halliday, *Iran: Dictatorship and Development* (New York: Penguin Books, 1979, pp. 174–75.
3. Ibid., p. 182.
4. For a discussion of trade unions in Iran, see ibid., pp. 197–206, and Habib Ladjevardi, *Labor Unions and Autocracy in Iran* (Syracuse, NY: Syracuse University Press, 1985).
5. See above, Chapter 3.
6. Robert Graham, *Iran: The Illusion of Power* (New York: St. Martin's Press, 1980), p. 225.
7. Amir Taheri, *The Spirit of Allah: Khomeini and the Iranian Revolution* (London: Hutchinson, 1985), p. 231.
8. G. Hossein Razi, 'Democratic-authoritarian attitudes and social background in a non-western society: a study of the Iranian elite', *Comparative Politics* 14, no. 1 (October 1981), p. 60. See also Marvin Zonis, *The Political Elite of Iran* (Princeton, NJ: Princeton University Press, 1971), Chapter 8.
9. Gavin Humbly, 'Attitudes and aspirations of the contemporary Iranian intellectual', *Royal Central Asian Journal* 51, no. 57 (April 1964): 135–36.
10. See Hamid Algar, 'The oppositional role of the *ulema* in twentieth century Iran', N.R. Keddie, ed., *Scholars, Saints, and Sufis* (Berkeley, CA: University of California Press, 1972).
11. See ibid., pp. 231–55.
12. Hamid Algar, *The Roots of the Islamic Revolution* (London: The Open Press, 1983), p. 11.
13. Shahrough Akhavi, *Religion and Politics in Contemporary Iran* (Albany, NY: SUNY Press, 1980), p. 159.
14. Farhad Kazemi, *Poverty and Revolution in Iran: The Migrant Poor, Urban Marginality, and Politics* (New York: New York University Press, 1980), p. 56.
15. Rouhollah Khomeini, *Touzih al-Masa'l (Explanation of Problems)* (Qom: n.p., n.d.).
16. Statement issued by Ayatollah Khomeini, Paris, 2 November 1978.
17. Ayatollah Khomeini, press conference, Paris, 9 November 1978.
18. Interview with Banisadr.

Chapter 6: Conclusion

1. Crane Brinton, *The Anatomy of Revolution* (New York: Vintage Books, 1965).
2. James A. Bill, *The plasticity of informal politics: the case of Iran'*, *Middle East Journal* 27, no. 2 (1973): 135.
3. Ibid.

Bibliography

Books and articles

Abrahamian, Ervand (1968) 'The crowd in Iranian politics 1905–1953', *Past and Present* 41: 184–210.
—— (1970) 'Communism and communalism in Iran: the Tudeh and the Firqih-e Dimukrat-e Azarbayjan', *International Journal of Middle East Studies* 1, no. 4: 291–316.
—— (1980) 'Structural causes of the Iranian revolution', *Merip Reports* 87 (May): 21–26.
—— (1982) 'Ali Shariai: the ideologue of the Iranian revolution', *Merip Reports* 102 (January): 25–28.
—— (1982) *Iran Between Two Revolutions* (Princeton, NJ: Princeton University Press).
Afkhami, Gholam R. (1985) *The Iranian Revolution: Thanatos on a National Scale*, Washington, D.C.: Middle East Institute.
Afrasiab, Bahman (1985) *Iran va Tarikh: Az Kudeta to Enghelab* (Iran and History: From the *Coup* to the Revolution), Tehran: Zarrin, 1364/1985.
Afshar, Haleh, ed. (1985) *Iran: A Revolution in Turmoil*, London: Macmillan.
Agah Publishing (1983) *Eelat va Ashayer* (Clans and Tribes), Tehran: Agah Publishing, 1362/1983.
Ahmadzadeh, Masoud (1979) *Mobareze-e Mossalahaneh, Ham Estratezhy Ham Taktik* (Armed Struggle, Both a Strategy and a Tactic), Tehran: Sazman-e Cherikha-ye Fedai-ye Khalq-e Iran, 1358/1979.
Ajami, Fouad (1986) *The Vanished Imam*, Ithaca, NY: Cornell University Press.
—— (1988) 'A history writ in oil', *New York Times Book Review*, 8 May, p. 3.
Akhavi, Shahrough (1980) *Religion and Politics in Contemporary Iran*, Albany, NY: SUNY Press.
Albert, David, ed. (1980) *Tell the American People: Perspectives on the Iranian Revolution*, Philadelphia, PA: Movement for a New Society.
Alden, John (1954) *The American Revolution 1775–1789*, New York: Harper & Row.
Al-e Ahmad, Jalal (1962) *Gharbzadegi* (Westoxication), Tehran: Ravvaq, 1341/1962.
—— (1978) *Dar Khedmat va Khianat-e Roushanfekran*, Vols 1–2 (On the Service and the Disservice of Intellectuals), Tehran: Khawrazmi,

1357/1978.
—— *Iranian Society*, Michael Hillmann, trans., Lexington, KY: Mazda.
Al-e Ahmad, Shams (1987) 'Jalal . . . Jalal!', *Keyhan*, 25 Shahrivar 1366/16 September 1987, pp. 16–17.
Algar, Hamid (1983) *The Roots of the Islamic Revolution*, London: The Open Press.
Amirsadeghi, H. and Ferrier, R.W. (1977) *Twentieth Century Iran*, London: Heinmann.
Amnesty International (1977, 1978) *Annual Report*, London.
Amuzegar, Jahangir (1977) *Iran: An Economic Profile*, Washington, D.C.: Middle East Institute.
Amuzegar, J. and Fekrat, M.A. (1971) *Iran: Economic Development Under Dualistic Conditions*, Chicago: University of Chicago Press.
Arendt, Hannah (1965) *On Revolution*, New York: Penguin.
Arfa, Hassan (1964) *Under Five Shahs*, London: John Murray.
Arjomand, Said Amir (1986) 'Iran's Islamic revolution in comparative perspective', *World Politics* 38, no. 3 (April): 383–413.
—— ed. (1984) *From Nationalism to Revolutionary Islam*, Albany, NY: SUNY Press.
Aronson, Elliot (1984) *The Social Animal*, New York: Freeman & Co.
Avery, Peter (1965) *Modern Iran*, London: Ernest Benn.
—— (1978) 'Iran: a culture challenged', Part 1, *Contemporary Review* 223, no. 1354 (November): 243–49.
—— (1978) Iran: a culture challenged', Part 2, *Contemporary Review* 223, no. 1355 (December): 298–303.
Aya, Rod (1979) 'Theories of revolution reconsidered: contrasting models of collective violence', *Theory and Society* 8 (1979): 39–99.
Azari, Farah, ed. (1983) *Women of Iran: The Conflict with Fundamentalist Islam*, London: Ithaca Press.
Bakhtiar, Shapour (n.d.) *See-o Haft Rouz Pas az See-o Haft Sal* (Thirty-Seven Days After Thirty-Seven Years), Paris: n. p.
—— (1982) *Yekrangi* (Honesty), Paris: n. p.
Baldwin, George (1973) 'Foreign-educated Iranians', *Middle East Journal* 17, no. 3 (Summer): 264–78.
Balta, Paul and Rulleau, Claudine (1979) *L'Iran Insurge*, Paris.
Banachen, R. E. Valdes (1972) *Cuba in Revolution*, New York: Anchor Books.
Banani, Amin (1961) *The Modernization of Iran 1921–1941*, Stanford, CA: Stanford University Press.
Banisadr, Abolhassan, (n.d.) *Eqtesad-e Tauhidi* (*Tauhidi* Economics), Paris: n.p.
—— (1971) *Bayaniye-he Joumhuri-ye Islami* (Manifesto of the Islamic Republic), Paris: n.p.
—— (1976) *Kish-e Shakhsiyat* (Cult of Personality), Paris: n.p.
—— (1977) *Naft va Solteh* (Petroleum and Sovereignty), Paris: n.p.
—— (1978) *Movazeneh-ha* (Equilibriums), Paris: n. p.
—— (1978) *Osul-e Payeh va Zavabet-e Hokumat-e Islami* (The Main Principles and Guidelines of Islamic Government), Tehran: n.p., 1357/1978.

—— (1980) *Sad Maghaleh az Abolhassan Banisadr* (A Hundred Articles From Abolhassan Banisadr), Tehran: Payam-e Azadi, 1358/1980.
—— (1981) *Kyhanat beh Omid* (Betrayal of faith), Paris: n.p.
Bashiriyeh, Hossein (1984) *The State and Revolution in Iran*, London: Croom Helm.
Batutu, Hanna (1981) 'Iraq's underground Shi'ite movement: characteristics, causes, and prospects', *Middle East Journal* 35 (Autumn): 578–94.
Bayne, E. A. (1968) *Persian Kingship in Transition*, New York: American University Field Staff.
Bazargan, Mehdi (n.d.) *Be'sat va Ideolozhi* (Mission and Ideology), Tehran: n.p.
—— (n.d.) *Sazegari-ye Iran-i* (The Iranians' Constitution), Tehran: n.p.
—— (n.d.) *Serr-e Aqab Oftadeghi-ye Mellat-e Mosalman* (The Secret of the Moslems' Backwardness), Tehran: n.p.
—— (n.d.) *Zarre-ye bi Enteha* (The Infinite Particle), Tehran: n.p.
Benard, Cheryl (1980) 'Islam and women: some reflections on the experience of Iran', *Journal of South Asian and Middle Eastern Studies* 4, no. 2 (Winter): 10–26.
Bharier, Julian (1972) 'The growth of towns and villages in Iran, 1900–66', *Middle Eastern Studies* 8, no. 1 (January): 51–61.
Bill, James (1963) 'The social and economic foundations of power in contemporary Iran', *Middle East Journal* 17: 400–18.
—— (1970) 'Modernization and reform from above: the case of Iran', *Journal of Politics* 32, no. 1 19–40.
—— (1972) *The Politics of Iran: Groups, Classes and Modernization*, Columbus, OH: Merrill.
—— (1973) 'The plasticity of informal politics: the case of Iran', *Middle East Journal* 22: 131–51.
—— (1988) *The Eagle and the Lion*, New Haven, CT: Yale University Press.
Binder, Leonard (1962) *Iran: Political Development in a Changing Society*, Berkeley, CA: University of California Press.
—— (1962) 'The cabinet of Iran: a case study in institutional adaptation', *Middle East Journal* 16, no. 1: 29–47.
Blackey, R. and Paynton, C. (1976) *Revolutions and the Revolutionary Idea*, Cambridge, MA: Schenkman.
Bonine, Michael and Keddie, Nikki, eds. (1981) *Continuity and Change in Modern Iran*, Albany, NY: SUNY Press.
Brammer, Lawrence (1964) 'Problems of Iranian university students', *Middle East Journal* 18, no. 4: 443–50.
Brinton, Crane (1938) *The Anatomy of Revolution*, New York: Prentice-Hall.
Brzezinski, Zbignew (1985) *Power and Principle*, New York: Farrar, Straus, & Giroux.
Buci-Glucksmann, C. (1980) *Gramsci and the State*, David Fernback, trans., London: Lawrence & Wishart.
Calder, N. (1982) 'Accommodation and revolution in Shi'ite jurisprudence: Khomeini and the classical tradition', *Middle East Studies* 18 (1982): 3–22.
Carey, J.P.C. (1976) 'Iranian agriculture and its development', *International Journal of Middle East Studies* 7, no. 3 (July): 359–82.
Carter, Jimmy (1982) *Keeping Faith*, London: Collins.

Charques, Richard (1965) *The Twilight of Imperial Russia*, Oxford: Oxford University Press.
Cooley, Charles (1962) *Social Organization*, New York: Schocken Books.
Cottam, Richard (1967) *Competitive Interference and Twentieth Century Diplomacy*, Pittsburgh, PA: University of Pittsburgh Press.
—— (1979) *Nationalism in Iran*, Pittsburgh, PA: University of Pittsburgh Press.
Craig, David (1978) 'The impact of land reform on an Iranian village', *Middle East Journal* 32, no. 2: 141–54.
Dahrendorf, Ralf (1970) 'Integration and values versus coercion and interests: two faces of society', in W. Richard Scott, ed., *Social Processes and Social Structures*, New York: Holt, Rinehart, & Winston.
'Daneshjuyan-e Mosalman-e Peyro-eh Khatt-Imam' (n.d.) (Moslem Students Following the Imam's Path), *Asnad-e Laneh-e Jasusi* 20 (Documents of the Spy Nest), Tehran: n.p.
Dastgheyb, Abdolhossein (1983) *Akhlaq-e Islami* (Islamic Ethics), Tehran: Mehrab, 1362/1983.
Davani, Ali (n.d.) *Nehzat-e Rouhaniyun-e Iran*, vols 1–10 (The Struggle of the Iranian Clergy), Tehran: Bonyad-e Imam Reza.
Davies, James (1962) 'Toward a theory of revolution', *American Sociological Review* 27, no. 1: 5–19.
Davis, Kingsly (1950) *Human society*, New York: Macmillan.
Dix, Robert (1983) 'The varieties of revolution', *Comparative Politics* 15, no. 3 (April): 281–94.
Djamilzadeh, M. (1951) 'Social and economic structure of Iran', *International Labour Review* 53: 23–40.
Dunn, John (1972) *Modern Revolutions*, Cambridge: Cambridge University Press.
—— (1983) *Rethinking Modern Political Theory*, Cambridge: Cambridge University Press.
Eisenstadt, S. N. (1964) 'Breakdowns of modernization', *Economic Development and Cultural Change* 12, no. 4 (July): 354–67.
—— (1978) *Revolution and the Transformation of Societies*, London: Collier Macmillan.
Eliash, Joseph (1979) 'Misconceptions regarding the judicial status of the Iranian "Ulema"', *International Journal of Middle East Studies* 10: 9–25.
Ellul, Jacques (1973) *Propaganda: The Formation of Men's Attitudes*, K. Kellen & J. Lerner, trans., New York: Vintage Books.
Elwell-Sutton, L. P. (1949) 'Political parties in Iran: 1941–1943,' *Middle East Journal* 3: 45–62.
Enayat, Hamid (1982) *Modern Islamic Political Thought*, New York: Macmillan.
Erikson, Eric (1958) *Young Man Luther: A Study in Psychoanalysis and History*, New York: W. W. Norton & Co.
Eskandari, Mansour (1984) *Mas'aleh-e Arzi, Jonbesh-e Dehghanan va Siyasat-e Ma* (The Land Issue, the Peasants' Struggle, and Our Policy), Tehran: Sazman-e Cherik-haye Fedai-ye Khalq-e Iran, 1363/1984.
Esposito, John, ed. (1980) *Islam and Development: Religion and Sociopolitical Change*, Syracuse, NY: Syracuse University Press.

Esposito, J. and Donohue, J., eds (1982) *Islam in Transition: Moslem Perspectives*, Oxford: Oxford University Press.
Fallaci, Oriana (1976) *Interview with History*, New York: Liveright.
Farmanfarmaiyan, Setareh (1970) *Piramoun-e Rouspi-gari dar Shahr-e Tehran* (Concerning Prostitution in the City of Tehran), Tehran: Amuzeshgah-e Ali-yeh Khadamat-e Ejtemaii, 1349/1970.
Farr, James (1982) 'Historical concepts in political science: case of "revolution"', *American Journal of Political Science* 26, no. 4 (November): 688–708.
Fatemi, Khosrow (1982) 'Leadership by mistrust: the Shah's modus operandi', *Middle East Journal* 36, no. 1 (Winter): 5–21.
Fedaiyan (n.d.) *Tarikhche-ye Sazman-e Cherik-haye Fedai-ye Khalq-e Iran* (A History of the Iranian People's Fedaiin Guerrillas), Tehran.
—— (1981) *Zan va Mubarezeh* (Women and Struggle), Tehran, 1360/1981.
Fernea, E. W. and Bezirgan, Q., eds (1978) *Middle Eastern Moslem Women Speak*, Austin, TX: University of Texas Press.
Firoozi, Ferydoon (1974) 'The Iranian budget: 1964–1970', *International Journal of Middle East Studies* 5, no. 3 (June): 328–43.
Fischer, Michael (1980) *Iran: From Religious Dispute to Revolution*, Cambridge, MA: Harvard University Press.
Fitzpatrick, Sheila (1982) *The Russian Revolution 1917–1932*, Oxford: Oxford University Press.
Floor, Willem M. (1980) 'The revolutionary character of the Iranian *ulema*: wishful thinking or reality?', *International Journal of Middle East Studies* 12 (1980): 501–24.
Forbis, William (1981) *Fall of the Peacock Throne: The Story of Iran*, New York: McGraw-Hill.
Freeman, Michael (1972) 'Review article: theories of revolution', *British Journal of Political Science* 2: 339–59.
Furlong, R. D. M. (1973) 'Iran – a power to be reckoned with', *International Defense Review* 6, no. 6 (December): 719–29.
Gable, Richard (1959) 'Culture and administration in Iran', *Middle East Journal* 13, no. 4: 407–21.
Garrod, Oliver (1946) 'The Qashgai tribes of Fars', *Royal Central Asian Journal* 33: 239–306.
Gastil, Reymond (1973) 'Middle class impediments to Iranian modernization', *Public Opinion Quarterly* 22: 325–29.
Gellner, Ernest (1985) 'A pendulum swing theory of Islam', in Ronald Robertson, ed., *Sociology of Religion*, Middlesex: Penguin, pp. 127–38.
Geschwender, J. (1968) 'Explanations in the theory of social movements and revolutions', *Social Forces* 42: 127–35.
Gharebaghi, Abbas (n.d.) *Haqayeq dar-bare-ye Bohran-e Iran* (Facts about Iran's Crisis), Paris: Soheil.
Gilbert, A. and Guglar, J. (1982) *Cities, Poverty, and Development: Urbanization in the Third World*, Oxford: Oxford University Press.
Golabian, Hossein (1977) *An Analysis of Underdeveloped Rural and Nomadic Areas of Iran*, Stockholm: Royal Institute of Technology.
Goldthrope, J.E. (1984) *The Sociology of the Third World*, Cambridge: Cambridge University Press.

Goodell, Grace (1986) *The Elementary Structure of Political Life: Rural Development in Pahlavi Iran*, Oxford: Oxford University Press.
Gottschalk, Louis (1944) 'Causes of revolution', *American Journal of Sociology* 50, no. 1: 1–8.
Graham, Robert (1980) *Iran: The Illusion of Power*, New York: St. Martin's Press.
Green, Jerrold (1980) 'Pseudoparticipation and countermobilization: roots of the Iranian revolution', *Iranian Studies* 18: 31–53.
—— (1982) *Revolution in Iran: The Politics of Countermobilization*, New York: Praeger.
—— (1984) 'Countermobilization as a revolutionary form', *Comparative Politics* 16, no. 2 (January): 153–69.
Greene, Thomas (1974) *Comparative Revolutionary Movements*, Englewood Cliffs, NJ: Prentice-Hall.
Gurr, Ted Robert (1970) *Why Men Rebel?* Princeton, NJ: Princeton University Press.
Gusfield, Joseph R. (1970) *Protest, Reform, and Revolt*, New York: John Wiley.
Hairi, A. (1977) *Shi'ism and Constitutionalism in Iran*, London: E. J. Brill, Leiden.
Haliday, Fred (1979) *Iran: Dictatorship and Development* New York: Penguin.
Halpern, Manfred (1963) *The Politics of Social Change in the Middle East and North Africa*, Princeton, NJ: Princeton University Press.
Hambly, Gavin (1964) 'Attitudes and aspirations of the contemporary Iranian intellectual', *Royal Central Asian Journal* 51 no. 57 (April): 127–40.
Heikal, Mohamed (1981) *Iran: The Untold Story*, New York: Pantheon Books.
Hickman, William F. (1982) *Ravaged and Reborn: The Iranian Army, 1982*, Washington, D.C.: Brookings Institute.
Hoffer, Eric (1951) *The True Believer*, New York: Harper & Row.
Homayoun, Dariush (1981) *Dirouz va Farda* (Yesterday and Tomorrow), United States: n. p.
—— (1984) *Negah az Biroun* (Looking from Outside), United States: Iran va Jahan.
Hooglund, Eric (1982) *Land and Revolution in Iran 1960–1980*, Austin, TX: University of Texas Press.
Hooglund, Mary E. (1982) 'Traditional Iranian women: how they cope?', *Middle East Journal* 36, no. 4, (Autumn): 483–501.
Hoveyda, Fereydoun (1980) *The Fall of the Shah*, New York: Wyndham Books.
Huntington, Samuel (1968) *Political Order in Changing Societies*, New Haven, CT: Yale University Press.
Irfani, Suroosh (1983) *Iran's Islamic Revolution: Popular Liberation or Religious Dictatorship?* London: Zed.
Jacobs, Norman (1966) *The Sociology of Development: Iran as an Asian Case Study*, New York: Fredrick Praeger.
Jansen, G. H. (1979) *Militant Islam*, New York: Harper & Row.
Javadi, Ali Asghar (1978) *Bohran-e Arzesh-ha.* (The Crisis of Values),

Tehran: Ravvaq, 1357/1978.
Jazani, Bizhan (1980) *Capitalism and Revolution in Iran*, Iran Cmt., trans., London: Zed.
Johnson, Chalmers (1982) *Revolutionary Change*, London: Longman.
Jones, R. Ben (1967) *The French Revolution*, London: Hodder & Stoughton.
Kambakhsh, Abolhassan (1972) *Nazari beh Jonbesh-e Karegari va Komonisti dar Iran* (An Account of the Workers' Communist Movement in Iran), Stassfurt, Germany: Hezb-e Tudeh.
Kapuscinski, Ryszard (1985) *Shah of Shahs*, W. R. Brand and K. Morczkowska-Brand, trans., London: Harcourt Brace Jovanovich.
Kasravi, Ahmad (1956) *Bahaigari* (Baha'ism), Tehran: Mard-e Emruz, 1335/1956.
—— n.d. *Shiagari* (Shi'ism), Tehran: Mard-e Emruz.
Katouzian, Homa (1981) *Political Economy of Modern Iran 1926–1979*, New York: New York University Press.
Kazemi, Farhad (1980) *Poverty and Revolution in Iran: The Migrant Poor, Urban Marginality, and Politics*, New York: New York University Press.
Keddie, Nikki (1968) 'The Iranian village before and after land reform', *Journal of Contemporary History* 3, no. 3: 69–91.
—— (1971) 'The Iranian power structure and social change', *International Journal of Middle East Studies* 2: 3–20.
——, ed. (1972) *Scholars, Saints, and Sufis: Muslim Religious Institutions Since 1500*, Berkeley, CA: University of California Press.
—— (1980) *Iran: Religion, Politics and Society*, London: Frank Cass.
—— (1981) *Roots of Revolution*, New Have, CT: Yale University Press.
——, ed. (1983) *Religion and Politics in Iran: Shi'ism from Quietism to Revolution*, New Haven, CT: Yale University Press.
Kedouri, Elie and Haim, Sylvia G., eds (1980) *Towards a Modern Iran*, London: Frank Cass.
Khomeini, Rohollah (n.d.) *Touzih al-Masa'el* (Explanation of Problems), Qom: Elmiyyeh.
—— (1941) *Kashf al-Asrar* (Discovery of Secrets), Qom: n.p., 1320/1941.
—— (1971) *Velayat-e Faqih* (Islamic Government), Najaf: n. p., 1350/1971.
—— (1973) *Khomeini va Jonbesh* (Khomeini and the Movement), Tehran: Davazdahom-e Moharram, 1352/1973.
Kianouri, Nurreddin (1981) *Hezb-e Tudeh Iran va Doctor Mohammad Mussadiq* (The Tudeh Party of Iran and Dr. Mohammad Mussadiq), Tehran: Hezb-e Tudeh, 1359/1981.
Kimmel, Michael S. and Himmelstein, Jerome L. (1981) 'Review essay: states and revolutions: the limits of Skocpol's structural model', *American Journal of Scoiology* 86, no. 5: 1145–54.
Kochan, Lionel (1966) *Russia in Revolution*, London: Granada.
Kramnick, Issac (1972) 'Reflections on revolution: definition and explanation in recent scholarship', *History and Theory* 11, no. 1: 22–63.
Kroeber, A. L. (1937) 'Diffusionism', in E. R. A. Seligam and Alvin Johnson, eds, *The Encyclopaedia of the Social Sciences*, vol. 3, New York: Macmillan.
Ladjevardi, Habib (1985) *Labor Unions and Autocracy in Iran*, Syracuse, NY: Syracuse University Press.

Laing, Margaret (1964) *The Shah*, London: Sidgwick & Jackson.
Lambton, Ann (1953) *Landlord and Peasant in Persia: A Study of Land Tenure and Land Revenue Administration*, Oxford: Oxford University Press.
—— (1977) 'A reconsideration of the position of the *marja' taqlid* and the religious institution', *Studia Islamica* 20: 115-35.
—— (1969) *The Persian Land Reform 1962-1966*, Oxford: Clarendon Press.
Le Bon, Gustav (1913) *The Psychology of Revolution*, London: T. Fisher Unwin.
—— (1952) *The Crowd*, London: Ernest Benn.
Ledeen, M. and Lewis, W. (1981) *Debacle: The American Failure in Iran*, New York: Alfred Knopf.
Lenczowski, George (1968) *Russia and the West in Iran: 1918-1948*, New York: Grunwood.
Lerena, Mario L. (1978) *The Unsuspected Revolution: The Birth and Rise of Castroism*, Ithaca, NY: Cornell University Press.
Litwak, Robert (1984) *Detente and the Nixon Doctrine: American Foreign Policy and the Pursuit of Stability*, Cambridge: Cambridge University Press.
Loeb, Lawrence D. (1976) 'Dhimmi status and Jewish roles in Iranian society', *Ethnic Groups* 1: 89-105.
Looney, Robert (1982) *Economic Origins of the Iranian Revolution*, New York: Pergamon Press.
McAlister, John (1969) *Vietnam: The Origins of Revolution*, New York: Alfred Knopf.
McQuail, Denis (1972) *Sociology of Mass communication*, Middlesex: Penguin.
—— (1984) *Communication*, London: Longman.
Maravall, J.M. (1976) 'Subjective conditions and revolutionary change: some remarks', *British Journal of Sociology* 27, no. 1 (March): 21-34.
Matthews, Herbert (1975) *Revolution in Cuba*, New York: C. Scribner's Sons.
Mehraban, Rasoul (1981) *Barresi-ye Mokhtasar-e Ahzab-e Bourgeoisie Melli-ye Iran dar Moghabeleh ba Jonbesh-e Karegari va Enqelabi-ye Iran* (A Brief Review of Iran's National Bourgeois Parties versus Iran's Workers and Revolutionary Parties), Tehran: Peyk, 1359/1981.
Midlarsky, Manus I. (1982) 'Scarcity and Inequality: prologue to the onset of mass revolution', *Journal of Conflict Resolution* 26, no. 1 (March): 3-38.
Miller, William G. (1969) 'The Dowreh and Iranian politics', *Middle East Journal* 23, no. 2 (Spring): 159-67.
Milward, W. G., ed. (1973) *Social and Cultural Selections from Contemporary Persia*, New York: Caravan Books.
Mohammadi-Nejad, Hassan (1977) 'The Iranian parliamentary elections of 1975', *International Journal of Middle East Studies* 8: 103-16.
Moore, Barrington (1966) *Social Origins of Dictatorship and Democracy*, New York: Penguin.
—— (1979) *Injustice, The Social Bases of Obedience and Revolt*, London: Macmillan.
Moore, Wilbert E. (1963) *Social Change*, Englewood Cliffs, NJ: Prentice-Hall.
Mortimer, Edward (1982) *Faith and Power: The Politics of Islam*, New York:

Random House.
Mottahari, Morteza (n.d.) *A'dl-e Elahi* (Divine Justice), n. p.
—— (n.d.) *Ashnayee ba Ulum-e Islami* (Familiarity with Islamic Sciences), Qom: Sadra.
—— (n.d.) *Ensan va Sarnevesht* (Mankind and Destiny), Qom: Sadra.
—— (n.d.) *Maqqadameh-i bar Jahanbini-ye Islami* (An Introduction to Islamic World View), n. p.
—— (n.d.) *Shenakht* (Discovery), Mashhad: Ommat.
—— (1978) *Elal-e Garayesh beh Maddighari* (Causes of Attraction to Materialism), Tehran: n. p., 1357/1978.
Mottahedeh, Roy (1985) *The Mantle of the Prophet: Religion and Politics in Iran*, New York: Pantheon, 1985.
Mujahadeen (n.d.) *Ettelai'ye-he Mavaze-ye Sazman-e Mujahadeen-e Khalq-e Iran dar Barabar-Jaryan-e Aportunist-ha-ye [Enharafi] Jap-nama* (Manifesto of the Stands of the People's Mujahadeen Organization of Iran Against the [Deviating] Leftist-Posing Opportunists' Affair), Tehran.
—— (n.d.) *Falsafe-ye Imam Zaman* (Philosophy of the Hidden Imam), Tehran.
—— (n.d.) *Varshekasteghi-ye Tarikhi-ye Dark-e Khorde Bourgeoisie az Islam* (The Historical Bankruptcy of the Petty Bourgeoisie's Understanding of Islam), Tehran.
—— (1975) *Dynamism-e Qoran* (The Koran's Dynamism), Tehran.
—— (1980) *Sharh-e Ta'sis va Tarikhche-ye Vaqaye-eh Sazman-e Mujahadeen-e Khalq-e Iran az Sal-e 1344 to Sal-e 1350.* (Explanation of the Establishment and the History of the Events of the People's Mujahadeen Organization of Iran from the year 1965 to 1971), Tehran, 1358/1980.
—— (1981) *Talil-e Jonbesh-e Khalq-e Ghahreman-e Tabriz* (Analysis of the Heroic Struggle of the People of Tabriz), Tehran, 1359/1981.
Mujahadeen (Communist Faction) (1975) *Bayaniye-he I'lam-e Mavaze'e Ideolozhik* (Manifesto of Ideological Stands), Tehran: n. p., 1353/1975.
Namvar, Rahim (1983) *Shahidan-e Tudeh-ii* (Tudeh's Martyrs), Tehran: Hezb-e Tudeh, 1361/1983.
Neshat, Guity, ed. (1983) *Women and Revolution in Iran*, Boulder, CO: Westview Press.
Neumann, Sigmund (1965) *Permanent Revolution*, New York: Praeger.
Nordskog, John Eric (1960) *Social Change*, New York: McGraw-Hill.
O'Connor, Edward, ed. (1978)a *Charismatic Renewal*, London: SPCK.
Ogburn, William (1950) *Social Change with Respect to Culture and Original Nature*, New York: Viking Press.
——(1964) *On Cultural and Social Change*, Chicago: University of Chicago Press.
O'Gorman, Ned, ed. (1969) *Prophetic Voices: Ideas and Words on Revolution*, New York: Random House.
Pahlavi, Ashraf (1980) *Faces in a Mirror: Memoirs from Exile*, Englewood Cliffs, NJ: Prentice-Hall.
Pahlavi, Mohammad Reza (n.d.) *Enghelab-e Sefid* (The White Revolution), Tehran: n.p.
—— (1960) *Mission for My Country*, London: Hutchinson.

—— (1980) *Answer to History*, New York: Stein & Day.
Pahlavi, Sorraya (n.d.) *Khaterat-e Sorraya* (Sorraya's Memoirs), Musa Habibi, trans., Tehran: n.p.
Park, Robert (1967) *On Social Control and Collective Behavior*, Chicago: University of Chicago Press.
Parsons, Anthony (1984) *The Pride and the Fall: Iran 1974–1979*, London: Jonathan Cape.
Parsons, Talcott (1951) *The Social System*, New York: The Free Press.
—— (1961) 'Some considerations on the theory of social change', *Rural Sociology* 26, no. 3: 219–39.
—— (1966) *Societies: Comparative and Evolutionary Perspectives*, Englewood Cliffs, NJ: Prentice-Hall.
—— (1967) *Sociological Theory and Modern Society*, New York: Free Press.
Paydarfar, Ali A. (1967) 'Modernization process and demographic changes', *Sociological Review* 15, no. 2: 141–53.
Pfaff, Richard (1963) 'Disengagement from traditionalism in Turkey and Iran', *Western Political Quarterly* 16, no. 1: 79–98.
Radji, Parviz C. (1983) *In the Service of the Peacock Throne: The Diaries of the Shah's Last Ambassador to London*, London: Hamish Hamilton.
Rajaee, Farhang (1983) *Islamic Values and World Views*, New York: University Press of America.
Rajavi, Masoud (1980) *Tabyeen-e Jahan*, vols. 1–15 (World View), Tehran: Mujahadeen, 1358/1980.
Ramazani, R. K. (1962) 'Modernization and social research in Iran', *The American Behavioral Scientist* 5, no. 6: 17–20.
—— (1975) *Iran's Foreign Policy, 1941–1973: A Study of Foreign Policy in Modernizing Nations*, Charlottesville, VA: University of Virginia Press.
Razi, Gholam H. (1968) 'The press and poitical institutions in Iran: a content analysis of Ettela'at and Keyhan', *Middle East Journal* 22: 463–74.
—— (1981) 'Democratic-authoritarian attitudes and social background in a non-western society: a study of Iranian elite', *Comparative Politics* 14, no. 1 (October): 53–74.
Rejai, M. and Phillips, K. (1979) *Leaders of Revolutions*, London: Sage.
Richards, Vernon (1972) *Lessons of the Spanish Revolution (1936–1939)*, London: Freedom Press.
Rieff, R., ed. (1970) *On Intellectuals*, New York: Anchor Books.
Robertson, Ronald, ed. (1985) *Sociology of Religion*, New York: Penguin.
Roosevelt, Kermit (1979) *Countercoup: The Struggle for Control of Iran*, New York: McGraw-Hill.
Rose, Jerry D. (1982) *Outbreaks: The Sociology of Collective Behavior*, New York: Free Press.
Rubin, Barry (1980) *Paved with Good Intentions: The American Experience and Iran*, Oxford: Oxford University Press.
Sadr, Hamid (1982) *Dar Ayene-yeh See-o Haft Rooz* (In the Mirror of Thirty-Seven Days), London: Nehzat-e Mughavemat-e Melli.
Saikal, Amin (1980) *The Rise and the Fall of the Shah*, Princeton, NJ: Princeton University Press.
Salert, Barbara (1976) *Revolution and Revolutionaries*, New York: Elsevier.
Salvemin, Gaetano (1963) *The French Revolution 1788–1792*, I. M. Rawson,

trans., London: Jonathan Cape.
Sanasarian, Eliz (1982) *The Women's Rights Movement in Iran*, New York: Praeger.
Savory, Roger (1972) 'The principle of homeostasis considered in relation to political events in Iran in the 1960s', *International Journal of Middle East Studies* 3: 282–302.
Schiffer, Irvine (1973) *Charisma*, Toronto: University of Toronto Press.
Schram, Stuart R. (1972) *The Political Thought of Mao Tse Tung*, New York: Praeger.
Shariati, Ali (n.d.) *Ali Tanha Ast* (All is Lonely), Tehran: n. p.
—— (n.d.) *Az Koja Aghaz Konim?* (Where Do We Begin From?), Tehran: n. p.
—— (n.d.) *Bazgasht Beh Khish* (Return to the Self), Tehran: n. p.
—— (n.d.) *Estekhraj va Tasfiye-h Manabe' e Farhangi* (The Exploitation and Purification of Cultural Resources), Tehran: n. p.
—— (n.d.) *Ideolozhi* (Ideology), Tehran: n. p.
—— (n.d.) *Islamshenasi*, vols. 1–6. (Islamology), Tehran: n. p.
—— (n.d.) *Mazhab Alayhe Mazhab* (Religion versus Religion), Tehran: n.p.
—— (1979) *On the Sociology of Islam*, Hamid Algar, trans., Berkeley, CA: Mizan Press.
—— (1983) *Hoboot dar Kavir* (Descenting in Desert), Tehran: Taqvim, 1362/1983.
Shils, Edward (1963) 'On the comparative study of new states', in C. Geertz, ed., *Old Societies and New States*, New York: Free Press.
Sick, Gary (1985) *All Fall Down: America's Tragic Experience with Iran*, New York: Random Books.
—— (1986) 'United States decision making during Iran crisis', *World Affairs Journal* 1, no. 1 (Winter): 33–37.
Skocpol, Theda (1979) *States and Social Revolutions*, Cambridge: Cambridge University Press.
—— (1982) 'Rentier states and Shi'a Islam in the Iranian revolution', *Theory and Society* 11, no. 3 (May): 265–83.
—— (1982) 'Review article: what makes peasants revolutionary?', *Comparative Politics* 14, no. 3 (April): 351–75.
Smelser, Neil J. (1963) *Theory of Collective Behavior*, New York: Free Press.
Smith, Jane, ed. (1980) *Women in Contemporary Moslem Societies*, London: Associated University Press.
Sorokin, Pitrim (1967) *The Sociology of Revolution*, New York: Howard Festing.
Sreedhar, M. (1979) 'The role of the armed forces in the Iranian revolution', *IDSA Journal* 12: 121–42.
Stemple, John D. (1981) *Inside the Iranian Revolution*, Bloomingdale, IN: Indiana University Press.
Stone, L. (1966) 'Theories of revolution', *World Politics* 18: 159–76.
Strasser, H. and Randall, S. (1981) *An Introduction to Theories of Social Change*, London: Routledge & Kegan Paul.
Sullivan, William (1981) *Mission to Iran*, New York: W. W. Norton.
Tabari, Azar (1982) 'The enigma of the veiled Iranian women', *Merip Reports* (February): 22–27.

Taheri, Amir (1985) *The Spirit of Allah: Khomeini and the Iranian Revolution*, London: Hutchinson.
Taleghani, Mahmoud (n.d.) *Islam va Malekiyyat* (Islam and Ownership), Tehran: n. p.
Tilly, Charles (1978) *From Mobilization to Revolution*, London: Addison-Wesley.
Tulsiran (1981) *The History of the Communist Movement in Iran*, Bhopal, India: Grafix.
Upton, John (1960) *The History of Modern Iran: An Interpretation*, Cambridge, MA: Harvard University Press.
Vance, Cyrus (1983) *Hard Choices: Critical Years in America's Foreign Policy*, New York: Simon & Schuster.
Weber, Max (1968) *On Charisma and Institution Building*, Chicago: Chicago University Press.
Westwood, Andrew E. (1965) 'Politics of mistrust in Iran', *Annals of the American Academy of Political and Social Sciences* 538 (March): 123–35.
Wienbaum, M. (1977) 'Agricultural policy and development politics in Iran', *Middle East Journal* 31: 434–50.
Woodside, Alexander (1976) *Community and Revolution in Modern Vietnam*, Boston, MA: Houghton Mifflin.
Yar-Shater, Ehsan, ed. (1971) *Iran Faces the Seventies*, New York: Praeger.
Yazdi, Ebrahim (1984) *Akharin Talash-ha dar Akharin Rouz-ha* (Last Attempts in the Last Days), Tehran: Qalam, 1363/1984.
Yoder, Dale (1926) 'Current definitions of revolution', *American Journal of Scoiology* 32, no. 3(November): 433–41.
Zabih, Sepehr (1966) *The Communist Movement in Iran*, Berkeley, CA: University of California Press.
—— (1982) *The Mossadegh Era*, Chicago: Lake View Press.
Zelder, Beatrice (1981) 'The Ayatollah Khomeini and his concept of an Islamic republic', *International Philosophical Quarterly* 21 (March): 83–98.
Zonis, Marvin (1968) 'Political elite and political cynicism in Iran', *Comparative Political Studies* 1, no. 3: 351–91.
—— (1971) *The Political Elite of Iran*, Princeton, NJ: Princeton University Press.
—— (1983) 'Iran: a theory of revolution from accounts of revolution', *World Politics* 35, no. 4 (July): 586–606.
Zorogin, Perez (1973) 'Theories of revolution in contemporary historiography', *Political Science Quarterly* 88, no. 1 (March): 23–52.

Official publications

Bank Markazi Iran (1966, 1972, 1977–78) *Annual Report and Balance Sheet*.
—— *The National Income of Iran: 1335–1350 (1956–1971)*.
Iran Census Bureau (1956, 1966, 1976) *Census Report*.
—— (1976) *Statistical Yearbook*.
OPEC (1973) *Annual Statistical Bulletin*.

Plan and Budget Organization (Iran) *The Fifth Economic Plan: 1352–1356 (1973–1978)*.

Unpublished sources

Correspondence
Brzezinski, Zbigniew, 9 November 1987.

Interviews (excluding confidential interviews)

Afkhami, Gholam Reza (Deputy Interior Minister, 1976–1978), Washington, D.C., 10 January 1986.
Amini, Ali (Prime Minister, 1961–1962), Paris, 16 December 1985.
Ardalan, Admiral Abolfath (Deputy Commander of Iranian Navy, 1977–1979), Washington, D. C., 11 January 1986.
Bakhtiar, Shapour (member of National Front, 1951–1979; Prime Minister, January-February 1979), Paris, 23 October 1985.
Banisadr, Abolhassan (member of Council of Revolution, 1978–1979; President of Iran, 1980–1981), Paris, 30 October 1985, 1 November 1985, 6 May 1986.
Borumand, Abdolrahman (member of National Front, 1951–1979; Executive Director of National Resistance Movement, 1979–date), Paris, 26 October 1985.
Homayoun, Dariush (Minister of Information, 1976–1978), Washington, D. C., 9 January 1986.
Sullivan, William (U.S. Ambassador to Iran, 1977–1979), Cuernavaca, Mexico, 2 November 1987.

Theses and dissertations

Alidoost-Khaybari, Yadollah (1981) 'Religious revolutionaries: an analysis of the revolutionary groups' victory in the Iranian revolution', Ph.D dissertation, University of Michigan.
Ashraf, Ahmad (1971) 'Iran: imperialism, class, and modernization from above', Ph.D dissertation, New School for Social Research.
Ferdows, Adele Kazemi (1967) 'Religion and nationalism in Iran: Fedaiyani Islam', Ph.D dissertation, Indiana Unversity.
Firoozi, Fereydoon (1966) 'The United States economic aid to Iran 1950–1960', Ph.D dissertation, Dropsie University.
Ghavamshahidi, Zohreh (1986) 'Dissidence and conformity in Iranian politics: political culture and Islamic revolution', Ph.D dissertation, University of Oklahoma.
Groves, Ralph George (1982) 'The evolution and development of radical parties in the context of Shi'ite Iran', MA thesis, California State University, Northridge.
Sreberny-Mohammadi, Annabella (1985) 'The power of communication: communication and the Iranian revolution', Ph.D dissertation, Columbia University.

Index

Abadan, demonstrations in 34
Ahmadzadeh, Masoud 64
air force mutiny 49–50
Al-e Ahmad, Jalal 66–7, 68–72, 97, 98, 113, 114
Al-Fatah organization 61
Ali's Shi'ism versus Safavid Shi'ism (Shariati) 67
Amini, Dr Ali 39, 40
Amnesty International 132
Amuzegar, Jamshid 19, 27–9, 32–3, 34–5, 127
Anglo-Iranian Oil Company (AIOC) 58, 59
Ansari, Hooshang 20
Arani, Taqi 53
armed forces 14, 15, 17, 25–6, 30; and Bakhtiar government 45, 47–50; military government (1978) 36–8, 39, 43, 46; and Mussadiq government 58–9; (overthrown by *coup* 16, 25, 30, 55, 57, 68, 121); planned *coup* 41–9 *passim*; and Shah 17, 18, 24, 26, 33, 35–6, 49; (loyalty to 39–40, 45, 46, 47, 49, 58–9, 90–1); and social change 111, 112, 114; and Tudeh Party 55
Arsanjani, Dr Hassan 98, 99
Ashraf, Princess 18, 58
Ashura demonstration (1978) 38–9
Assembly of Experts 85
Azhari, General Gholam Reza 37–8, 39, 43, 46

Bakhtar-e Emroz (journal) 59
Bakhtiar, Dr Shapour 42, 87, 88, 114; as prime minister 33, 38, 40, 45–50, 88
Ball, George 43, 44
Bani-Ahmad, Ahmad 88
Banisadr, Abolhassan 62, 66–7, 75, 77, 86, 88, 133; in France with Khomeini 35, 90, 91, 92, 133; as President 24
Baqai, Mozzafar 57
Bazaari merchants 6, 116–17, 118, 119, 121–2, 124; and Council of Revolution 91; and political parties 22, 57, 59; and social change 111, 112–13, 128
Bazargan, Mehdi 39, 66–7, 72–3, 91, 128; and Liberation Movement 42, 59, 84, 85; and oil refinery strike 46, 117; as prime minister 49, 50, 60
Beheshti, Ayatollah Mohammad 42, 80, 85, 86, 93
'Black Friday' (7 September 1978) 36, 38
Blumenthal, Mike 43
Borujerdi, Grand Ayatollah 79, 84, 85
bourgeoisie *see* middle classes
Britain 15, 25, 30, 52, 53, 133; ambassadorship to 18; and oil industry 57, 58; and revolution 43, 46
Brown, Harold 41, 42, 47

169

Index

Brzezinski, Zbigniew 41, 42, 44, 46, 47, 48
Budget Plan Organization 18
bureaucracy 14, 16, 17, 23–5, 30, 56, 115; reforms of 32–3, 34–5; and SAVAK 27; and social change 111, 112, 122; strikes 47
Bryd, Robert 43

cabinet government 19, 20, 28, 30, 36, 37
Carter, Jimmy 5–6, 15, 29, 31–2, 40–5, 47–9, 89; reforms induced by 32–6
Chinese revolution 5, 12
CIA (Central Intelligence Agency) (United States) 42, 43; and 1953 coup 16, 25, 59, 68
civil service *see* bureaucracy
class, social 3, 4, 6, 7–8, 10–12, 74; *see also* middle classes; upper classes; working classes
clergy *see* ulema
cold war 16, 30–1, 59
Confederation of Iranian Students (CIS) 60
Considering Leadership and Clericalism (Bahsi Darbare-ye Marjaiyat va Rouhaniyat) (Monthly Review Society) 78
Constitutional Revolution (1906) 15, 53, 125; 1906 Constitution 23, 45, 87
corruption: in government 24–5, 28, 37, 122, 123; of opposition 28; of Pahlavi Foundation 35
Council of Revolution (Shora-ye Enqelab) 49, 85, 91
coup(s), military: Mussadiq overthrown (1953) 16, 25, 30, 57, 58, 59, 68; (and Bazaaris 121; and Tudeh Party 55); Pahlavis take power (1921) 15; planned, to follow collapse of regime 41–9 *passim*; possible, during revolution 39–40
Cuban revolution 12

Cult of Personality, The (Banisadr) 75

Dashti, Ali 67
Dastgheyb, Abdolhossein 80
Davies, James 2, 3, 6, 8
Democratic Youth Club 54
Department of Religious Propagandists (Muravvejin-e Din) 101
Discovery of Secrets, The (Kashf al-Asrar) (Khomeini) 79, 80–1

Eisenhower, Dwight D. 30
Equilibrium (Banisadr) 75
Eskandari, Iraj 56
Eternal Guard 25, 48

Family Protection Acts (1975) 101
Farah, Empress 18, 35, 40
Fedaiyan (Organization of Iranian People's Fedaiyan Guerrillas) 63–4, 81, 87, 120, 133–4; and SAVAK 27, 64
Ford, Gerald 41
Forouhar, Dariush 57, 87
France: Khomeini's exile in 35, 40, 83–4, 85–6, 89, 90–3, 130; revolution in 5, 9
Freedom Movement *see* Liberation Movement
Freemasonry 36

gendarmerie 25, 26
Gharabaghi, General 26, 35
Golpaygani, Mohammed Reza 80
Green, Jerrold 4–5, 6, 8
guerrilla organizations 42, 52, 60–5, 87, 119; assassinations by 63, 81; following the revolution 133–4; popularity of 57, 62, 64, 120; and SAVAK 27, 61, 62, 64, 86; threat posed by 34, 132; and *ulema* 84, 85
Gurr, Ted 2–3, 6, 8

Haig, General Alexander 48

170

Hakim, Ayatollah 81
Hanifnezhad, Mohammad 60, 84
Hedayat, Sadiq 67
High Council of Economics 18, 19
History of Thirty Years of Politics (Tarikh-e See Saleh-ye Siyasi) (Jazani) 64
Hoveida, Amir Abbas: arrested 37; as Court Minister 27–8; as prime minister 16, 17, 18, 19, 23, 27, 87; and Rastakhiz Party 20, 21
How Does Armed Struggle Become Mass Strike? (Cheguneh Mobarezeh-ye Mossalahaneh Tudeh-ii Mishavad?) (Jazani) 64
Huntingdon, Samuel 4, 6, 7–8, 20
Huyser, General Robert 47–9

Imam Hossein's Movement (Nehzat-e Hosseini) (Mujahadeen book) 61
immigrants *see* rural immigrants
inefficiency 24–5, 27, 28–9, 115
inflation 22, 28, 33, 105
intellectuals 32, 65–7, 79, 126, 129, 132; with Khomeini in exile 91, 92–3; political activity of 33, 41, 52, 87–8, 119, 122, 123; and Rastakhiz Party 22, 32; recruited by regime 24; and social change 111, 112, 113–14; threat posed by 34, 132; *see also individuals*
Iran Party (Hezb-e Iran) 57
Iranian Nation's Party (Hezb-e Melli-ye Iran) 57, 59
Iranian Peace Committee 54
Iranian Society for the Defence of Freedom and Human Rights 86–7, 88, 123
Iranian Writers' Association 66, 87, 88, 123
Iraq: expulsion of Khomeini 35, 89–90, 130, 132; war with Iran 10
Isfahan, demonstrations in 34
Islam *see* religion
Islam and Ownership (Islam va Malekiyyat) (Taleghani) 84
Islamic Government (Velayat-e Faqih) (Khomeini) 79, 81–2, 133
Islamic Students' Society (ISS) (Anjoman-e Daneshjoyan-e Islami) 60, 90
Islamology (shariati) 67
Jazani, Bizhan 64
Johnson, Chalmers 1–2, 3, 5, 8

Kashani, Ayatollah 57, 58
Kasravi, Ahmad 67, 81
Kennedy, John F. 30
Khoi, Ayatollah Abulqassem 80, 81
Khomeini, Ahmad 92
Khomeini, Mostafa 89, 90
Khomeini, Ayatollah Ruhollah 78–80, 81–2, 88–94, 117, 124, 128–30; and Azhari government 38; exile in France 35, 40, 83–4, 85–6, 89, 90–3, 130; (and Bakhtiar government 47; funding by Bazaaris 121; and Sanjabi premiership 40); expulsion from Iraq 35, 89–90, 130, 132; and Islamic Students' Society 60, 90; return to Iran 47, 49, 130, 133–4; and rural immigrants 109; and Shah 34, 35, 89–90, 92, 130; and United States 44
Khonsari, Ahmad 80
Khosrowdad, General 48
Kianouri, Dr Nurredin 56
Korea, South 9

labour force *see* working classes
Land Reform Programme (1962) 20, 51, 97–8, 99–100, 103–4, 106, 119; opposition to 59, 61, 64
Lebanon 61
Liberation Movement (Nehzat-e Azadi) 42, 59–60, 84, 85
Lights from the Koran (Partow-vi az Koran) (Taleghani) 84
Literacy Corps (Seph-e Danesh) 98, 104

Main Guidelines and Principles of Islamic Government (Banisadr) 67, 75, 77, 133

171

Index

Majlis 15–16, 20, 23, 29, 30, 33, 35
Maleki, Khalil 54, 57, 69
Manifesto of the Islamic Republic (Banisadr) 67, 75, 77
Mao Tse-tung 12
Mar'ashi-Nujafi, Shahab al-Din 80
Marcos, Ferdinand 9
Mardum (journal) 54
Marx, Karl 95
Marxist-Leninist Organization of Tufan (Sazman-e Marxist Leninist-ye Tufan) 55–6
Mashhad, demonstrations in 34
middle classes 111–14; and political activity 4, 7–8, 116, 118, 122–3, 126–8, 132; (and Mujahadeen 62; and political parties 6, 21, 22, 56, 112); and social change 96, 99, 101–2, 112–14, 127–8
military *see* armed forces
Mohsen, Saeid 60
Montazeri, Ayatollah 80, 84–5, 86, 93
Monthly Religious Society (Anjoman-e Mahan-e Dini) 78, 79; *Monthly Lectures (Guftar-e Mah)* 78
Mottahari, Ayatollah Morteza 78, 80, 85
Mujahadeen (People's Mujahadeen Organization of Iran) 42, 60–2, 64, 84, 85, 120; and SAVAK 27, 61, 62, 64
Musavi-Khoiniha, Hojjatal-Islam 92
Mussadiq, Dr Mohammed 53, 54–5, 56, 58–9, 69, 73, 84; overthrown in 1953 *coup* 16, 25, 30, 57, 58, 59, 68; (and Bazaaris 121; and Tudeh Party 55)

National Action Committee 54
National Front (Jebhe-ye Melli) 40, 53, 56–60, 69, 84, 112; reactivation of 87; United States and 42; *see also* Mussadiq
national police (Shahrbani) 25, 26
National Resistance Movement (Nehzat-e Muqavemat-e Melli) 59

National Security Council (horaye Amniyate Melli) 26, 36
'Nights of Poetry' meetings 66, 87
Nixon, Richard M. 29, 30–1, 41, 131–2
Officers' Organization (Sazman-e Afsaran) 55
Ogburn, William 96
oil: cartels, and Westernization 70; industry 110; (nationalization 54, 55, 57, 58, 59, 125; strikes 38, 39, 46, 48, 117, 121); prices 5, 13, 132; (and social change 97, 104–5, 115, 116, 127)
On the Service and the Disservice of Intellectuals (Al-e Ahmad) 70–1
One Thousand Year Old Secrets (Asrar-e Hezar Saleh) 81
Organization of Iranian People's Fedaiyan Guerrillas (Sazman-e Cherik-ha-ye Fedai-ye Khalq-e Iran) *see* Fedaiyan
Oveisi, General 26, 46

Pahlavi, Shah Mohammed Reza 14–19, 29–30; and armed forces 17, 18, 24, 26, 33, 35–6, 49; (loyalty of 39–40, 45, 46, 47, 49, 58–9, 90–1; military government (1978) 37, 135–7); assassination attempt 54; and bureaucracy 24–5; and communist opposition 31, 34; image abroad 15, 41, 43, 60; and Khomeini 34, 35, 89–90, 92, 130; creates Rastakhiz Party 17, 19–21, 22–3; and SAVAK 27, 33; and United States 9, 15, 29, 30–1, 131–2; reforms induced by 32, 33, 34–6); unpopularity of 40, 51–2; and Western values 99, 115, 116, 127; and White Revolution 97, 98, 99, 100
Pahlavi, Shah Reza 14–15, 53, 79, 81, 99, 100, 115
Pahlavi, Crown Prince Reza 40
Pahlavi Foundation 35, 36
parliament *see* Majlis
Parsons, Sir Anthony 43, 45

Parsons, Talcott 95
Party of the Iranian Masses (Hezbe Tudeh-e Iran) *see* Tudeh Party
People's Mujahadeen Organization of Iran (Sazman-e Mujahadeen Khalq-e Iran) *see* Mujahadeen
Petrole et Violence (Banisadr & Vielle) 75
Peykar (Sazman-e Peykar dar Rah-e Azadi-ye Tabaqe-ye Kargar) 62
Philippines 9
Point Four Program 104
police forces 25, 26, 70
price control campaign (1976) 22, 121
professional classes *see* middle classes
propaganda 7, 10–11, 120, 123–6, 128

Qajar dynasty 15
Qom, demonstrations in 22, 34, 78, 81, 83, 124
Qotbzadeh, 35, 60, 90, 92

Radmanesh, Dr Reza 56
Rastakhiz Party 6, 16, 17, 19–23, 30, 121
religion: as revolutionary ideology 66–77 *passim*, 117, 125–6, 132–3; (and Mujahadeen 61–2); and traditional values 97, 99, 100–2, 109, 112–14, 127–8, 129; *see also* ulema
Religious Corps (Sepah-e Din) 101
Religious Endowments Organization (Sazman-e Owqaf) 28, 100, 101
Return to the Self (Shariati) 67
Revolutionary Tudeh Party 55
Riahi, General 99–100
rural immigrants 28, 96, 104, 106–11, 115–16; and agricultural conditions 102–4; and political activity 6, 108–11; 118, 122, 126–8, 132

Sadiqi, Gholam Reza 40
Sanjabi, Dr Karim 40, 59, 87

SAVAK (State Intelligence and Security Organization) 17, 26, 27, 30, 132; arrest of director 37; calls for abolition of 33, 47, 70, 87; and opposition groups 27, 56, 61, 62, 63, 64, 86; (and Mostafa Khomeini's death 89, 90; and Shariati's death 74)
Schlesinger, James 42, 47
Second National Front (Jebhe-ye Melli-ye Dovvum) 59
Second World War 15, 53, 69
Senate (Sena) 23
Shah of Iran *see* Pahlavi
Shahrbani (national police) 25, 26
Shariati, Ali 62, 66–7, 73–5, 86, 113, 114, 128; death of 74, 88
Shariatmadari, Ayatollah Kazem 35, 80, 83–4, 86, 93
Sharif-Emami, Ja'far 19, 35–7, 43, 56, 85
Shi'ism 11, 67–8, 71–2, 125–6; and Mujahadeen 62; Safavid Shi'ism 74–5, 76; *see also* ulema
shi'ism: The Religion of Protest (Shariati) 67
Shiraz, demonstrations in 34
Siyasat (journal) 54
Skocpol, Theda 5, 6, 7, 8, 9
Society of Iranian Socialists (Jame'e-ye Sosiyalist-haye Iran) 59
Society of Islamic Combatants (Jame'e-ye Mujahadeen-e Islam) 57, 58
Soltanpour, Saeed 87
South Africa 9
Soviet Union 15, 30, 42, 53, 54, 133; revolution in 5, 11; spies in Iran 27; and Tudeh Party 52, 54, 69; *see also* cold war
strikes 39, 116–17, 120, 121; by oil workers 38, 39, 46, 48, 117, 121; by public employees 39, 47
Sullivan, William 41–9 *passim*

Tabriz, demonstrations in 34, 83
Taleghani, Ayatollah Mahmoud 80, 84, 85, 86, 93

Index

Tas'ua demonstration (1978) 38–9
Tauhidi Economics (Banisadr) 67, 75, 77
tauhidi society 62, 74, 75, 77
Tehrani, Jalal 47
Third Force (Khatte Sevvom) 57
Third Force (Niru-ye Sevvam) 69
Third National Front (Jebhe-ye Melli-ye Sevvom) 59–60
Tilly, Charles 3–4, 6
Toilers' party (Hezb-e Zahmatkeshan) 57
trade unions 56, 120
Tudeh Party 52–6, 58, 60, 69, 112, 120, 133–4
Tufan 55–6
Turner, Admiral Stansfield 42

ulema 34–5, 52, 76–86, 93–4, 118, 119, 132; following the revolution 130, 133–4; popular support for 10, 11, 13, 102, 121–6 *passim*, 128; and Rastakhiz Party 22; and the state 14, 100, 101, 125–6; and White Revolution 16, 89; *see also individuals*
unemployment 6, 28, 33, 106, 110, 115, 127; and demonstrations 121, 122
United States: Iranian opposition groups in 60; opposition to 55, 68, 70, 75, 130, 133; relations with Iran 5–6, 9, 13, 29, 30–2, 40–5, 131–2; (and Bakhtiar government 45–6, 47–9; economic aid 16, 31, 32; overthrow of Mussadiq 16, 25, 30, 55, 59, 68; reforms induced by 32–6)
upper classes 99, 114–15, 116, 118, 128

Valian, Dr 100
Vance, Cyrus 41, 42
Vielle, Paul 75
Vietnamese revolution 11

Westoxication (Al-e Ahmad) 67, 69–70, 71, 72, 97, 113
White Revolution 16, 51, 89, 90, 97–100, 101, 125; *see also* Land Reform Programme
Women's Organization of Iran (Sazman-e Zanan-e Iran) 100
working classes 56, 104–11, 115–16, 118, 119–21, 132; *see also* rural immigrants
Writers' Association, Iranian 66, 87, 88, 123

Yazdi, Dr Ibrahim 60, 90, 92

Zahedi, Ardeshir 42

For Product Safety Concerns and Information please contact our EU
representative GPSR@taylorandfrancis.com
Taylor & Francis Verlag GmbH, Kaufingerstraße 24, 80331 München, Germany

www.ingramcontent.com/pod-product-compliance
Lightning Source LLC
Chambersburg PA
CBHW052125300426
44116CB00010B/1785